W9-BZP-711

MAKING MY PITCH

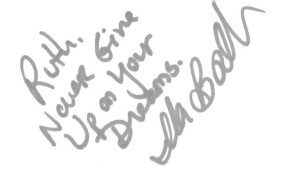

Ruth,
Never Give
Up on Your
Dreams.
Ila Borders

MAKING MY PITCH

A WOMAN'S BASEBALL ODYSSEY

Ila Jane Borders with *Jean Hastings Ardell*

Foreword by *Mike Veeck*

University of Nebraska Press | Lincoln & London

© 2017 by Ila Jane Borders and Jean Hastings Ardell
All rights reserved. Manufactured in the
United States of America. ∞

Library of Congress Cataloging-in-Publication Data
Names: Borders, Ila Jane, 1975– author. |
Ardell, Jean Hastings, 1943– co-author.
Title: Making my pitch: a woman's baseball
odyssey / Ila Jane Borders with Jean Hastings
Ardell; foreword by Mike Veeck.
Description: Lincoln: University of Nebraska
Press, [2017] | Includes bibliographical references.
Identifiers: LCCN 2016029037 (print)
LCCN 2016035649 (ebook)
ISBN 9780803285309 (cloth: alk. paper)
ISBN 9781496200204 (epub)
ISBN 9781496200211 (mobi)
ISBN 9781496200228 (pdf)
Subjects: LCSH: Borders, Ila Jane, 1975– |
Women baseball players—United States—
Biography. | Pitchers (Baseball)—
United States—Biography.
Classification: LCC GV865.B675 A3 2017 (print) |
LCC GV865.B675 (ebook) |
DDC 796.357092 [B]—dc23
LC record available at
https://lccn.loc.gov/2016029037

Designed and set in Minion Pro by L. Auten.

Delores Ann Carter
June 22, 1930–April 14, 1980

This book is for you, Grandma. I grew up to become a
baseball player and, later, a firefighter and paramedic.
I couldn't save you on that awful day in 1980, but I
have learned how to save myself, and others.

Contents

Illustrations

Foreword | Mike Veeck

AUTUMN 1999. Riding through Washington, DC, in the back of a cab in the middle of the night, I felt my eyes beginning to close. All of a sudden the Corcoran Gallery of Art came into view. Photographer Annie Leibovitz had a show there. On the facade of the building was a twenty-foot image of Ila Borders at the top of her windup.

"Stop! Stop the cab," I yelled at the hack. "That's Ila. Stop right here."

The cabbie was frightened. "You owe me thirty-five bucks," he said.

"Keep the meter running," I said. "Just stop. I have to get out."

I had been looking for a ballplayer like Ila Borders for much of my life. I joined my father, Bill Veeck Jr., who then owned the Chicago White Sox, as the club's director of promotions in 1976. I remember our hosting a softball game and picnic for the front office staff. During the game, a woman who worked in the accounting department launched a triple off the left-field wall. Dad and I immediately looked at one another with the same thought: Somewhere out there, in Keokuk, Iowa, perhaps, was a woman with the talent to play professional baseball.

If only we could find her.

Twenty years later I did.

In the spring of 1997 I was running the St. Paul Saints of the independent Northern League, when our pitching coach, Barry Moss, called. Barry also scouted for us in Southern California. He wanted me to know that he had found a young woman who was, he said, "the real thing, competitive and talented." Her name was Ila Borders. Should we give her a tryout? If she made the team, she would be the first woman to play men's professional baseball since the 1950s, when Mamie "Peanut" Johnson, Connie Morgan, and Marcenia "Toni" Stone played in the Negro Leagues, most notably with the Indianapolis Clowns. With a smile and a glance heavenward, where my father now dwells, I picked up the phone.

Ila flew into town on May 14 and came straight to my office. In my most avuncular manner, I said, "Let's take a walk around the parking lot." That was the only place we could get away from our cramped quarters in the front offices of Midway Stadium.

"Ila," I began, "we are about to embark on a great adventure. It will be fun. It will be all that we both could hope for. But it'll have its moments." I struggled to find the appropriate words. "You will be castigated, ridiculed, and called 'a promotion,' even though the Saints are already sold out for the season."

I had been raised to think of women as equals but knew it would take a strong woman in every sense of the word to play professional baseball. Breaking the color barrier in Major League Baseball is considered one of the defining moments in American history. I had never forgotten the stories Dad told me about his signing of Larry Doby in 1947 and the indignities the young center fielder had suffered as the American League's first black player. Perhaps it wasn't going to be the same scope for Ila, but the heckling, the name-calling, and the sexist comments that would come her way meant that she needed to be mentally and emotionally stronger than nearly anyone else who was going to set foot on the field that season.

Very quietly, very kindly, Ila responded. "Mr. Veeck, I know exactly what we're in for. I have been cursed, spat upon, beaned, and hit with all manner of missiles. I'm not afraid. I know what we're up against. Do you?"

She said it so softly, I wasn't quite certain I had heard her right. I laughed—what else could I do?—and said, "I guess this walk wasn't really necessary."

She waited; I whimpered. I had grown up one of nine children in a household with four opinionated sisters—one a child psychologist, one a writer, another an artist—and I was asking whether Ila could hold her own? Hey, women have survived us men for ages.

Eventually Ila smiled and said, "I just want to play ball, Mr. Veeck. Thank you for giving me the opportunity."

When Ila made the team out of camp, the reception she got from young girls—not just in the Twin Cities but around the country—was unlike anything I'd ever seen. Here was this woman who had a goal, something no female had ever done, and despite all the doors that had been slammed in her face prior to her time in St. Paul, she never gave up. What Ila did for girls all over this country was create a tremendous connection. That the St. Paul crowd gave her a standing ovation time after time is something I will long remember. She was the embodiment of strength and courage. People said I exploited her—there's no question about that—but as I have pointed out, she exploited me, too, because no one was standing in line behind me. Yet to me she was a ballplayer first and then a woman, and I think she responded to that.

At the time of her signing, I recall that my daughter, Rebecca (before retinitis pigmentosa robbed her of her sight), would flip through the newspapers, especially the sports section.

"What are you looking for," I asked her.

"I'm looking for Ila," she said matter-of-factly.

Rebecca was looking for the picture of Ila in uniform with her ponytail—and goodness knows my daughter was extremely upset with me when I traded Ila a few weeks into the season. After all, Rebecca was only six years old, too young to understand that St. Paul had become a media circus with Ila in the center ring, or that the Saints were in the pennant race, while Duluth was not. So I thought Ila would get more playing time in up there. But she wasn't just a role model for young girls everywhere. She was the ideal role model for anyone who has ever had a dream but took the easy way out and didn't see it through.

Not Ila. She had developed a sort of polyester finish: the hard stuff just rolled off her back. She had almost flawless mechanics, some of the purest I'd ever seen. Yet I recall that she could have a problem with her fastball. It wasn't her out pitch. I thought she needed to find one of the Niekro brothers and learn the knuckleball, or track down Gaylord Perry and learn the spitball. She just needed a variety of pitches to go along with her willful determination. And the guys she reached, she taught beautifully.

MAY 31, 1997. Ila Borders . . . first appearance . . . Sioux Falls, South Dakota. Sitting on my porch in St. Paul, staring at my radio.

"What do you think, Libby?" I asked my wife.

"I think it's great . . . and exciting," she responded.

"Now pitching, Ila Borders," is what I heard in the background on the radio broadcast. I could hear that everyone in the stands stood to cheer this courageous young person. It seemed like the whole world was cheering, and most were. However, Ila got roughed up that day.

She kept on pitching.

Ila Borders. St. Paul . . . camera crews everywhere. Leno. Letterman. *The Today Show*. She turned them all down. She just wanted to pitch. We didn't need her to sell tickets. I just wanted her to pitch.

And she did. For four seasons she not only played professional men's baseball but also did it with dignity and class.

Somebody was paying attention. *Women in Baseball* is one of the most visited exhibits in Cooperstown's National Baseball Hall of Fame and Museum. Over the years, Ila's memorabilia—her cap, jersey, and baseball from her days at Southern California College; the uniform she wore in her debut with the St. Paul Saints; an autographed baseball, the lineup card, and a ticket from the game that was her first win for the Duluth-Superior Dukes against the Sioux Falls Canaries—have been displayed at the museum.

I think that speaks well for having a woman play in the majors. I think it's going to happen. I think it should happen. Women are a source of new talent. This book is an extraordinary addition to baseball history. It should be read not just by young women who dream of playing hardball and by women fans but also by the men who run the game.

I've always been an Ila Borders fan and suspect that I always will be.

Acknowledgments

Jackie Robinson had Branch Rickey to thank for opening his way into the game. Throughout my years in baseball, there have been many Branch Rickeys. No matter how many people said no, there was always one guy who stepped up and said yes at an important point: first, my father, who thought it perfectly fine and good that I wanted to play baseball; my coaches in Little League; coach Rolland Esslinger, whose steady encouragement at Whittier Christian Junior High School meant so much; coaches Tom Caffrey and Steve Randall at Whittier Christian High School; coach Charlie Phillips, who signed me to a baseball scholarship—and with it, a college education—at Southern California College (now Vanguard University); and Coach Jim Pigott of Whittier College, who made me feel welcome on and off the field during my last year of college baseball.

I am grateful to scout Barry Moss for recommending me to the St. Paul Saints and for teaching me more about pitching technique than some players learn in their entire careers; to Marty Scott, my manager at the Saints, who put me on the roster in 1997; to Mike Veeck, the owner of the Saints and my ultimate Branch Rickey, who took a chance and signed me to the professional baseball contract I had dreamed of; and to Al Gallagher, my manager at the Madison BlackWolf, whose encouragement restored my confidence.

I also am grateful to photographer Annie Leibovitz, who demonstrated abiding graciousness and kindness at a time when I dearly needed them; to Connie Rudolph and Dave Glick for their friendship; and to Annie Huidekoper for her help with all manner of details from my weeks with the St. Paul Saints.

Ila Jane Borders

The number of people who gave invaluable assistance and encouragement in the making of this book would likely fill the Grandstand Theater at the National Baseball Hall of Fame and Museum. Matt Rothenberg, Tim Wiles, and the staff of the museum's Giamatti Research Center, including Mary Bellew, Michael Fink, Sue MacKay, and John O'Dell, offered essential archival support. Jim Gates, Bill Simons, and the annual Cooperstown Symposium on Baseball and American Culture gave support, fresh ideas, and so much more.

To Bill Kirwin, the founder of the NINE Spring Training Conference, who liked the idea for this book early on, and the Gang of NINE, as the board of directors is known—Larry Gerlach, Steve Gietschier, Lee Lowenfish, Roberta Newman, Anna Newton, Geri Strecker, and Trey Strecker—thank you for reminding us that baseball comes to us fresh each spring and that it is best enjoyed in the company of fellow believers. I also thank the men and women of the Society for American Baseball Research; David Kemp, for Northern League data; the Pettigrew Archives, Sioux Falls, South Dakota; Josh Buchholz, the general manager of the Fargo-Moorhead RedHawks; and the athletic department and archivist-librarian Pam Crenshaw of Vanguard University.

Gratitude is due the baseball historians who helped along the way: Adi Angel, Perry Barber, David Block, Richard Crepeau, Lee Lowenfish, Dorothy Jane Mills, Bill Ressler, Willie Steele, and John Thorn. Gratitude also goes to the virtual village of writers who offered counsel and friendship along the way: the Allegores Writers Circle (Mark Davis, Dave Ferrell, Sandy Giedeman, Micaela Myers, and Sue Parman); Ron Carlson of the Program in Writing at the University of California at

Irvine, who articulates so skillfully the value of telling the story well; Gordon McAlpine; Richard Simon; David Smith; and Marcia Sterling. Due a special note of thanks are friends who were particularly generous with their insights during the writing of this book: Sharon and George Gmelch, Bonnie and Arnold Hano, and Marjorie Coverley Luesebrink.

Our literary agent, Rob Wilson, was everything you'd hope to find in one: enthusiastic about the story, persevering in finding the right publishing house, and sensible about authorial digressions. It was a pleasure to work with Rob Taylor, Courtney Ochsner, Sabrina Stellrecht, copy editor Wayne Larsen, and the staff of the University of Nebraska Press. A special thank you to Teri Rider, whose diligence on the images is deeply appreciated.

When I attended Ila's first college game in February 1994, I knew that I wanted to follow her baseball story all the way through. The support from my husband, Dan Ardell, and my family for a book that would require more than twenty years to see completion has meant everything.

Jean Hastings Ardell

Note to the Reader

In the preface to her book *Koufax*, Jane Leavy writes, "You don't need to know everything to write the truth. You just need to know enough."

This is a memoir, so it is a book that relies on my memories of what happened on and off the field over the years that I played baseball. In the Game Day sections, I have reconstructed the inning-by-inning events, particularly the pitches I made, from those memories to the best of my ability. These memories were sometimes corrected by the game notes provided by the front office of the Fargo-Moorhead RedHawks. I also checked the statistics provided by Baseball Reference, the National Baseball Hall of Fame and Library, and individual clubs. I have also checked with family members, friends, coaches, and others in baseball whose lives touched mine, so as to provide the reader with an accurate account.

MAKING MY PITCH

PROLOGUE

JULY 30, 1998. I'm in the back of the bus, heading down the highway that goes from Winnipeg, Manitoba, to Fargo, North Dakota. This afternoon I'm the starting pitcher for the Duluth-Superior Dukes against the Fargo-Moorhead RedHawks. Last week I finally got my first win as a professional baseball player. I was in the zone that day, throwing six scoreless innings, giving up three hits and two walks, with two strikeouts against the Sioux Falls Canaries. So they tell me, because everything from that game is a blur. But my record is even now at 1-1, I'm pitching well, and I can feel the confidence of my manager, George Mitterwald. Today I'll start against the first-place team. If I do well again, maybe no one will say last week's win was luck, that I'm a novelty.

Though "novelty" is one of the nicer words used to describe the women who have fought to play professional baseball. Take Lizzie Arlington, who pitched in the minor leagues in 1898. The headlines were all about what a "sensation" she was, this "most famous lady pitcher in the world." After that, no woman played a season of pro ball until the early 1950s, when Mamie "Peanut" Johnson pitched and Connie Morgan and Toni Stone competed in the Negro Leagues. The word on these women, though, is that they were signed only to boost sagging gate receipts as the Negro Leagues faded into history once Jackie Robinson had integrated major league baseball in 1947. So no matter where I've played, from Little League on, people have been on my case. I still try to win them over, to change their minds about what a woman can do—not just in baseball but also even in life. Trying to win everyone over, though, has been a losing game. What matters most to me now is that my teammates respect me. And, hey, now I have a win on my record.

It's a blistering summer day, but inside the bus it's nice and cool. It's true what you hear about bus rides in the backwaters of baseball. In the Northern League, the rides can be up to fourteen hours long. We cross the Canadian border to play in Winnipeg and Thunder Bay, Ontario; we travel west to Fargo; southeast to Schaumburg, Illinois, and Madison, Wisconsin, and southwest to Sioux City, Iowa, and Sioux Falls, South Dakota. To pass the time I journal, read, listen to music, or watch a movie—*Tin Cup* and *Bull Durham* are usually the only ones on the bus, and I bet I've watched them a dozen times.

We all try to rest, but for me it's hard to fall asleep next to a teammate, never knowing if I might drool and provide a photo op for him to post in the locker room. Usually I stretch out in the aisle or on the floor between the seats, despite the empty beer cans that roll around on the floor. Then I wake up smelling like beer and sweat. Well, that is baseball in the Northern League.

I jam my headphones into both ears and throw a towel over my face, trying to ignore the guy next to me, who is watching porn on his laptop and seems to be enjoying it very much. The guys across from us are in a farting contest—how many can you belt out in sixty seconds? I tune my radio to a sports talk show and suddenly hear Doug Simunic, the RedHawks' manager, talking trash about "the woman pitcher." He is going off about how he will put his pitchers in the outfield, or only play his second string, or maybe just forfeit the game if I play. It turns out he's complained to the commissioner of the Northern League about me.

"There comes a time when you have to stop and take a look at the big picture," Simunic told a reporter for the *Winnipeg Free Press*. "But I guess the league thinks she's a good idea."

The league, it turns out, does think I am a good idea. According to the *Free Press*, the league commissioner, Miles Wolff, had responded to Simunic's complaints by sending a memo to all the clubs "reminding them of a league rule to field their best squads and compete at the highest level possible."

Listeners call in. It sounds like the entire town has gone ballistic over me pitching. Some say that I'm bringing down the game by playing men's baseball, the idea being if a woman can compete in a man's sport, it must not be much of a game. One caller gets bleeped, but a few say, "Give her a chance."

A chance is all I've ever wanted. Growing up, I read every book I could find about misfits like me who found the way past survival to success. Last season, just after I made the St. Paul Saints, Neal Karlen, who was writing *Slouching toward Fargo*, a book about the ball club, gave me Jackie Robinson's biography. "Read it," Neal said, "because I think this is the only thing that is going to give you advice and courage for what you're about to go through."

I read it in a day. I remember my surprise that Robinson felt the same emotions I was feeling—that sense of being cowardly, because you can't fight back against the naysayers. Back then, his skin, to Organized Baseball, was unacceptably black; my skin was white, though shaped around the less-than-acceptable form of a female. I wished I could have talked to Robinson about his experiences as the man who desegregated the modern game. He had to be so strong. I just wish I were as tough on the inside as I show on the outside. It's hard to hear people I've never met say they hate me—and all because I'm a woman who pitches in the Northern League. Playing in this men's independent league—it's outside Organized Baseball—is like skipping rookie ball and going straight to Class A ball. We have former Triple-A players trying to get their careers back on track, unsigned high draft picks like J. D. Drew who want to prove they are worth a bigger contract, ex–major leaguers like Jack Morris and Darryl Strawberry who want one last chance, and misfits like me. Call us the outback of pro ball.

But castoffs and misfits play well in the media. Who doesn't like a come-from-behind, against-all-odds story? So Mike Wallace's television crew from *60 Minutes* is on the way to Fargo to film the game. Wallace is doing a piece on me—and how many people ever get to experience that? I should feel grateful but can't get past the nerves. Like there isn't already enough stress in a league like this, because if you don't perform, or even if you do, you can be let go at any time. Now, courtesy of *60 Minutes*, I'll be on a national stage. Mike has turned out to be one of the kindest interviewers I've faced, but I know that the message in his story will be that I'm a sensation, a novelty. I'm also worried about the lumps I just found on the back of my neck, which I haven't told anyone about except God. And I worry about what the people of Fargo will do when our bus pulls into town. I remind myself that God approves of me, and that's all that matters, but right now He feels far away. The stress is the worst it's ever been. I'm twenty-three years old and wonder how in the heck I came to be on this bus filled with two dozen randy guys.

When our bus arrives at the parking lot of Newman Outdoor Field, fans and reporters surround it. "Good luck, Shorty," says one of the veterans. "Glad I am not you."

Then my best friend on the team and last summer's boyfriend, Dave Glick, puts his hand on my shoulder, and says, "We're all behind you, Ila. No matter what."

I grab hold of his words. I'll play them in my head all through the game.

"We're behind you." I first heard those words from Dad. That's what he has always said. He meant it, too, except when he couldn't or wouldn't or didn't back me up. But baseball's a game of failure, of errors large or small, and I learned early that having backup is a sometime thing. I learned it from my father, who was also my mentor, coach, agent, and nemesis.

As we exit the bus, people are yelling, "Go back home—we don't want you."

One man waves a sign: "Go back to the kitchen, Ila."

Can't you show more imagination? I want to say, though I don't. This is the same stuff that umpire Pam Postema heard in the minor leagues a few years back—"stick to doing the dishes." One day Postema arrived at home plate, and there was a frying pan. No wonder she called her memoir *You've Got to Have Balls to Make It in This League.*

Other fans reach to shake my hand or push baseballs at me, asking for an autograph, or they pull at my clothes. In the parking lot, people are already tailgating, and a few drunks are spraying beer all over. Some of my teammates form a human wedge around me as we move through the crowd. It feels good that they think to do this without my asking. Even though I have my teammates' support, I still feel alone in this quest. If I mess up I'll be letting down the cause of women everywhere. There's always a host of ghostly expectations out on the mound with me.

Shuffling along inside the wedge toward the locker room, I notice the RedHawks out on the field, taking batting practice. I see their manager, Doug Simunic, glaring at me.

Suddenly a cameraman appears from behind me: "Hello, Ila. We're from *60 Minutes*. Where can we set up?"

What I want right now is to be left alone. It's game day, and like every starting pitcher, I want my game face on. Where can I hide? I flee into the stands and find a women's restroom. So here I am, sitting in my uniform on the toilet with my feet up, so no one knows I'm here. Head down, I whisper a prayer. "Lord, give me the strength to do my best, to be focused, and let me reap what I have been working so hard for. Please be with me."

I want this win so bad. When we beat the Sioux Falls Canaries last week, we were at our home ballpark. Now I'm on the road facing the best team in the Northern League. Unlike the Canaries, the RedHawks have been bad-mouthing me. I want to shut Simunic and all the other critics up. So the inner Ila emerges—a controlled, competitive rage comes alive. I charge toward the bullpen like a soldier ready for battle. I've been criticized for the stone face I show when I pitch. Some have said, "You're a girl; smile."

Well, screw that. I'm an athlete here to win. Now get the hell out of my face. Would you tell a guy to smile? Growing up, I heard all about Don Drysdale, the Los Angeles Dodgers' star right-hander of the 1950s and 1960s. I was crazy about Drysdale, who everyone said was the nicest guy around—except for the days he pitched. Then, nobody went near him. Did anyone tell Drysdale to smile? So hell no—no smile. I've been fighting for this since I was ten years old.

1

BEGINNINGS
Little League

GAME DAY: FIRST INNING. Warming up in the bullpen, I look out at Newman Outdoor Field. Good, everyone on the RedHawks is at his normal position—no pitchers in the outfield, as their manager, Doug Simunic, had threatened. But the lineup card shows that Darryl Motley isn't playing. This is the guy who said on the radio he would not play against me. Motley, who used to play in the majors, is on a six-game hitting streak, and I wish he were in. I want to compete against the best they have.

I'm glad to be pitching against the RedHawks' number one starter, Blaise Isley, tied for most wins in the league. The game is sold out, and the stands are filled with five thousand fans in home-team red T-shirts. It's pennant night, so the fans are waving RedHawks flags. Newman Field reminds me of the diamond in the movie *Field of Dreams*, as if it emerged in some magical way out of the North Dakota prairie. Actually it's on the edge of the campus of North Dakota State University and is a beautiful new brick ballpark: the ironwork and seats are painted forest green, and the field kind of sits up instead of being sunk down. Unlike Midway Stadium in St. Paul last year, Newman is more of a pitcher's ballpark, because it has lots of foul ground and the prevailing winds don't turn fly balls into home runs, so I feel free to pitch the way I want to. Funny, the dimensions are the same as those of Yankee Stadium—a tribute to a Fargo native named Roger Maris, who broke Babe Ruth's home run record in 1961.

By the time I finish throwing, the sweat is dripping off me. And then comes the announcement, "Ladies and gentlemen, please stand and remove your hats for the singing of our national anthem."

I take off my cap, which I vainly hate to do because when I sweat my hair turns pouffy, wipe the salt from my eyes, stand tall, and place the cap over my heart. I can feel my heartbeat through my jersey. As the music begins, the words fill my heart and send a thrill throughout my body. I love this moment. "Land of the free and the home of the brave." The words remind me that this is where I belong, on the field. After the closing notes I head for the dugout, where everything begins to blur. Players and coaches are moving around me but in slow motion. Fans are yelling and pointing at me, smiling, waving, but I just hear my breathing. They are talking to me, their lips are moving, but I don't really hear them, focused as I am on the game.

The Dukes score a run in the top of the first, thanks to an RBI double by Big Papa, also known as Anthony Lewis, one of my biggest supporters. With the third out, I get ready to run to the mound when Dave Glick grabs my arm. He knows that's the only way to get my attention when I'm about to pitch. He looks me in the eye and says, "You've got this, Ila."

I grin at him and think to myself, *Just do what you did last week when you notched that win.* As I jog to the mound, the crowd erupts with cheers and boos. I see the lips of my catcher, Javier Rodriguez, move as he calls my name, but the noise from the stands is so loud that I can't hear his voice. Great to hear the love, but it's the boos that will drive me now. I grab the ball from behind the mound, rubbing it to get the last bit of gloss off and get the feel of the ball. I take my place on the rubber. The mound feels right, and I feel comfortable. Mounds are subject to regulation, but there are nuances. From mound to mound, the rubber doesn't always sit in the exact same place; in Fargo the dirt has more clay in it and feels more stable. After my eighth warmup pitch, I bend low as Javier throws the ball to second, who underhands it to Luis Brito, our shortstop, who throws it back to me. Luis points his mitt at me, as if to say, "Let's go." I scrape the dirt off my cleats on the edge of the rubber, take a deep breath, and push it out.

The RedHawks are intimidating, not just because they're in first place but because they're so damned big. They're also damned good: three of the first four hitters I'll face are batting more than .350 against us. All we have for big is our first baseman, Ozzie Canseco, six feet two inches tall, 220 pounds—and he's not even playing today because he's serving a three-game suspension from last night's game against the Winnipeg Goldeyes. That's because umpires don't like to be spit on. It's true that Ozzie has a temper, but despite his machismo he's always been respectful toward me and goes out of his way to offer tips.

Everyone on the RedHawks seems as big as Ozzie. No surprise, then, that they are a fastball hitting team. So I'll have to pitch backwards—get ahead with off-speed pitches for strikes, place the two-seam fastball on the outside corner of the plate running away, and spot the four-seamer high and tight to keep them from sitting on the outside pitches. I plan to hit the corners, frustrate them with junk, put a lot of movement on the ball, and put the ball in play. For that I need good defense behind me. Because I'm not a strikeout pitcher, the guys know they are going to be busy in the field.

"Song 2" by Blur is playing over the public address system. First up is shortstop Chad Akers, a right-handed batter with wheels. He's a first-pitch hitter, so I start him off with a screwball on the outside corner. He begins to move on it but decides to lay off. Strike one. To keep Akers honest and make my fastball look faster than it is, I throw the next pitch inside and straight. But it's high and tight. He takes it for ball one. Baseball's a game not just of inches but also of microseconds, and pitchers vary their speed to keep batters off balance. I figure he's a little anxious and looking for a fastball away. My next pitch is a slower screwball away. Akers bites and hits a slow nubber to third base. Briller is slow to get to the ball but fields it cleanly and fires to first. Too late. Akers's speed gets him an infield single. *Shit*, I say to myself. Off the field I don't cuss much, but when I pitch I am as foul-mouthed as they come. I grab the toss from Lewis, our first baseman, and think, *Don't panic, just throw a double play ball and keep this guy close.* As I wait for the next batter, I can feel the first base coach and Akers watching me. I don't have to look into the RedHawks dugout to feel Simunic staring my way. I'm aware that there are four people in the league who despise my presence: Hal Lanier, the manager of the Winnipeg Goldeyes; Ed Nottle, the manager of the Sioux City Explorers (who called me "that thing" in a radio interview last year); Larry See, who is playing out his minor league career with the Thunder Bay Whiskey Jacks; and Simunic, who likes to spit on the ground whenever he catches my eye.

As Steve Hine comes to the plate, Ozzie Osborne's "Crazy Train" plays. Always liked that song. Hine doesn't bother to look down to third for a sign but gets in the batter's box like he owns the plate. Maybe he does—he's hitting .385 against us this season. Last night, with two out in the bottom of the ninth, he hit a walk-off double to beat the Madison Black Wolf. Digging in, spraying lots of dirt around, making holes, Hine reminds me of a dog that just took a crap and now he's trying to cover it. I say to myself, *Fuck you, asshole, you are going down.*

Over at first I see to my surprise that Chad Akers hasn't taken much of a lead. So I slide step toward home and throw the ball hard—chin music. I don't want to hit Hine and give him first base, but I want to send a message: *You better fucking not dig in on me.* The fastball also gives my catcher a chance of throwing Akers out if he tries to steal second and, if it's a hit-and-run, doesn't give Hine much chance to get a solid piece of the ball. Hine returns the message with a glare. Ball one. I keep the same cadence on the next pitch but throw to first, not a great pick-off move but just to say, *I know you're there.* When I get the ball back, I hold it until Hine steps out of the box. Baseball is considered a slow game, but there is so much going on that most spectators don't see—trying to break the batter's rhythm and timing, get his legs heavy, and not letting a runner get a good jump.

At the plate, Hine hasn't dug in, and I know he'll be anxious. I slide step fast just after coming to a complete stop and throw one fine screwball. It's a bit faster than the others, and the bottom falls out of it, like it's a sinker, but it's also moving away. He swings and lofts a fly ball to right for the first out. The path he takes back to the dugout brings him right by the mound—maybe he's testing me to see if I'll talk crap to him. I do not.

Third baseman Johnny Knott is up. He's hitting .412 against us, but he's kept his mouth shut during the pregame hollering and shouting about me pitching. He comes across as quiet and all business. I'm still hoping for a ground ball, a quick double play, and getting out of the inning on the fewest pitches possible. I turn and point my glove to Brito at short, the message being, *If I get a comebacker, get ready for the throw.* Brito points back: *We're good.* Akins hasn't budged from first, and I concentrate on Knott, who strikes out on a screwball away. *Holy crap,* I think. *My stuff is really breaking today.* Two down.

Metallica's "Enter Sandman" blares as Marc Fink strolls to the plate. Well, he can afford to stroll—he's hitting .421 against us. At six feet three, 220 pounds, Fink is another of the RedHawks' power hitters, a lefty. He's a loudmouthed, in-your-face type of guy. With two out and the number four hitter up, Akers is likely to try to steal second. If he gets thrown out, no big deal because the RedHawks get to start off the next inning with Fink's power. And better yet, if Akers steals second, Fink has a chance to even the score with a base hit. I think about keeping Akers close and not giving anything good to Fink. I throw to first base twice in a row, both better pick-off moves but not my best. I hold the ball as long as I can before testing Fink with a straight change-up. He swings so hard I'm surprised the bat doesn't break when it hits the ball. He catches only a piece of the ball—if he had connected, it would have landed on the highway behind the stadium. Instead he skies a deep fly ball, and I turn and watch our center fielder glove it. Cool. So far, no drama. No runs, one hit, no errors, one left on base.

As we head for the dugout, the guys coming in behind me slap my back instead of my butt because people are looking, though I wouldn't care if they treated me just like any other player. They're saying, "Good job." I find a place far down the bench, put on my jacket, and focus on the game. Fans wonder why pitchers sit alone, unlike the position players, who interact on the bench. I have a bias about this: A hitter can go three-for-ten and be a success. But if a pitcher makes a costly mistake on two out of a hundred pitches, that can mean failure. To get a better edge, while I'm on the bench I analyze the batters for any clue to their weaknesses. When I'm pitching I am on the verge of insanity, taking the stress and converting it into energy and a laser focus. I've been honing these habits since age eleven in the Little League playoffs, but in truth I have been this way ever since I first played ball in my family's front yard. I look down at the splinter that's worked its way into my thigh through my uniform. It reminds me that you always have to watch your moves, a smart choice when your first diamond's second base was a lemon tree, with its thorny trunk.

1980, LA MIRADA, CALIFORNIA. BEGINNINGS. The first time I left home for baseball, I was about five years old. It was a short trip. When you walked into our front yard you saw that where other families had a garden, Dad had staked out a baseball diamond. First base was a tree with an old tire hanging from a branch, where we liked to swing when we weren't playing ball. Second base was the lemon tree; and another tree served as third. To be safe you had to grab the tree trunks and hold on (like the stakes used in the nineteenth-century game of town ball). But home plate was real—I don't know where Dad found it—with six-inch metal spikes that he hammered into the ground, like he meant it to stay there forever.

We lived in La Mirada, a hilly suburb southeast of Los Angeles that was paradise for kids' sports. All the kids in the neighborhood showed up to play ball in our yard. We'd play until it was dark, and sometimes the next morning you would see aluminum bats and leather mitts scattered on our grass, left out from yesterday's game. If we got hungry we grabbed an instant snack: the best tangerines you've ever tasted from one of the trees in our yard. In our family, we kids were not allowed to stay indoors unless it was raining—and hey, it hardly ever rains in Southern California.

Our porch was littered with empty Budweiser cans, usually crushed, as if Dad had squeezed out the last drop of brew. When he first courted Mom, he arrived to pick her up in a red Corvette. Dad sat there, waiting for her to come out of the house and jump in. This had concerned Mom's conservative parents, as she was a very naïve seventeen, and so they walked her out to the car. When they looked into the Corvette, I expect that they saw the stuff of a semipro ballplayer: gym bag, sweaty towels, faded baseball caps, and empty beer cans.

Dad was my first and best baseball coach. I think the idea to help me develop my skills began early: when I was an infant, he noticed that I was struggling to feed myself with a spoon—until I picked up the spoon with the other hand, my left hand. Dad said that he immediately thought, *Well, left-handed pitchers don't grow on trees.* After I broke a few windows batting on our front-yard diamond, he started taking me to Behringer Athletic Park to work on the fundamentals. Could not have cared less that I was a girl—he worked on my pitching and hitting and fielding as if I were headed to the major leagues. So it felt like a natural move from our front-yard field onto an organized team. I began playing Little Miss Softball at age six and did well. In my second season I was invited to play on an all-star traveling team. That meant weekend tournaments and playing year-round. Being on the field became my second home, but something was missing, and I knew what it was.

When I was eight years old, Dad took me to a ball game at Dodger Stadium. I saw one of the African American players—I want to say it was Dusty Baker, the Los Angeles Dodgers left fielder in 1983—go long, and it sparked something in me. That same summer I was tossing a baseball around in our front yard when I looked—I mean really looked—at the ball in my hand. It was smaller and harder than the one we used in girls' softball. Besides, pitching underhand, like we did in softball, had never felt quite right. I wanted to pitch overhand, like they did in the big leagues. At night I began to dream of playing in the major leagues. And so began my campaign with Dad to put me into baseball so I could pitch. Finally he said, "Okay. But if you're going to play with the boys, you are going to wear your hair long, so everyone knows you're a girl."

I will always be thankful that he was far ahead of his time in his attitudes toward girls on the diamond. The likely reason for his encouragement goes back to his childhood, given this story he liked to tell: When

Dad was in grade school he knew a girl named Judy Emmett. She was always his first pick when he was captain of the team, because Judy happened to be an unbelievably good baseball player. "She helped us to win ballgames. That's what it was all about," Dad said. "Winning the game."

So Dad saw nothing wrong with a girl playing baseball. And he didn't care what people thought about my playing ball; he just supported my love for the game. Mom felt the same. When I was ten years old, she and I went down to the La Mirada Little League sign-ups at Behringer Park, where we joined a line of about fifty people. A lady came up to us and said, "This is the baseball line. Softball sign-ups are at Los Coyotes Park."

Mom smiled. "I know," she said. "I'm here to sign my daughter up for baseball."

You should have seen this woman's face. It was like she found a roach in her soup. Then she caught herself, gave a fake smile, and said, "Okay, well, if you come back tomorrow at this time, the line will not be as long."

Mom, being sweet but naïve, said, "Okay, we'll come back tomorrow when you open. Thank you."

That night I slept with my mitt under my pillow. But when we showed up at the park the following day, no one was there. Finally we ran into the vice president of the league, who told us that the last day for sign-ups was yesterday. We explained what happened. He was very sorry, but all the teams were filled. I would have to go on a waiting list. Even though I was young, I knew what they had done. I was pissed, and so was Dad. He said he would fix it. He could be a bulldog when he had a mission.

Uh-oh, I thought. *What's he going to do?* Dad grew up in the era when, if you had a problem, you duked it out. But after a week went by without a call from the league, he said to me, "Get your stuff. You're going for a tryout today."

I grabbed my bat, mitt, and cap and was ready to go in three minutes. Dad hated to wait, and no way was I going to make him mad today. We went down to the field where the minor A division Twins were practicing.

While the players fielded grounders, took batting practice, and ran the bases, he reasoned with the coach, "Hey, I know you guys have an opening, and my child is next on the waiting list. Can she try out for you?"

The coach said, "She?" A couple of other girls were already playing in La Mirada Little League this season, and Dad recalls the coach saying, "Aw, no. Not another one." This despite the fact that Little League had been open to girls since 1974, the year before I was born.

"Yep," Dad replied. "Let my daughter take some cuts and pitch for you, and if you're not blown away by what she can do, then we'll walk away."

"Okay," came the answer. "Let's see this."

Dad looked at me. "You're up. Take some hacks and throw the ball like you do. Go for it."

I stepped up to the plate, got five pitches, and nailed all of them. After that I pitched and struck out four kids in a row. Right then and there the coach signed me to his team, and I learned my first lesson in how to succeed in baseball: persevere in the face of those who would deny me the chance to play; then be so good that they could not say no. Dad put it this way: "Don't push your way in, win your way in."

In my first Little League at bat, I blasted the ball off the center-field fence and, with my long hair flying, steamed into second. Dad remembers that one of the major division coaches on the sidelines wondered aloud who the hippie was that hit that double.

I pitched and played first base and shortstop the whole season. And yeah, I made a lot of trips to first base on pitches that found me rather than the strike zone. What I didn't know how to protect myself against was the opposition in the stands. Little League parents, especially the moms, absolutely hated to see me strike out their sons, and they didn't hold back their feelings. The Twins finished the season by winning the La Mirada Little League minor division title. The upper division (the majors), which usually had only eleven- and twelve-year olds, still had two games left. The White Sox of that division called and asked me—aged ten-and-a-half—to move up to their team. Their next game was against the undefeated first-place Pirates. In my first at bat I faced the MVP of the division, a big twelve-year-old right-hander. His first pitch was a fastball to my head. No way was he going to let a girl get a hit off him, so he plunked me. Nowadays parents go nuts when something like this happens, but back then all Dad said was, "Take your base."

He knew the kid meant to hit me but saw it as a lesson I would have to learn. As I ran to first, I thought, *I'm gonna remember that kid.*

In my next at bat, same pitcher—smack. I nailed his first pitch, an outside fastball, down the right-field line. I ran my ass off and got a triple. The guys in our dugout were going nuts, jumping up and down and shaking the chain-link fence. The pitcher slammed his mitt down on the mound. We beat the Pirates that day, and on the way home, Dad gave me a few more pearls of advice: "Never let them see that they got to you," he told me. And don't ever retaliate by hitting a batter in the head. Hit 'em in the ribs, where they have no protection."

He was half-kidding, I think. But his message was clear: if you're going to play hardball with the boys, you better learn how to take the knocks and know how to fight back. He knew from his time playing semipro baseball what it would take for me to survive in the game.

I am surprised Dad wasn't a drill sergeant in the military, because he raised me like a soldier. When I was ten, he taught how to shoot a BB gun. Our town was still pretty rural back then, and it became a family tradition to sit out by the pool at dusk and shoot BBs at the rats that walked on the power line that led to our roof.

As with baseball, order and neatness were preparation for the game of life. No TV unless it was Friday night and *Dallas* or Los Angeles Lakers basketball was on. It wasn't until I was ten that I was allowed to watch baseball on TV. I couldn't play ball until the chores were done. Dad was big on chores. From the age of five on, my Saturday morning chores involved mowing the front lawn, side lawn, and backyard, sweeping the carport, picking up after our German shepherd, Timber, and raking the leaves on our half-acre lot. I had two hours to get everything done, and he timed me. At our house it often felt like we lived on military time.

Dad's discipline was harsh. As a child, he had been beaten with a belt, so that's all he knew. So I was either hit, though never on my throwing arm, or had dog poop shoved into my face if I was not done in time, had not done it right, or had broken something around the house. As a kid I couldn't put words to why he acted this way. It would take me years to understand what alcohol can do to a person. To this day Dad feels horrible about his treatment and has asked my forgiveness many times. Eventually I was able to forgive, though I still struggle to not expect others to give 110 percent all the time. I am even thankful for the discipline I learned, but growing up, never knowing when Dad would flip his angry switch, life could be tough.

Looking back I can see why Dad might have been short on patience. He loved playing baseball—besides pitching he possessed a good bat and good speed. During their courtship, Mom remembers driving with him throughout Southern California and as far north as Visalia, in the San Joaquin Valley, to his Sunday afternoon games. But he was coming off an arm injury, and the next year he was married with a brand-new baby, me. He was twenty years old. He never complained about giving up any dreams he had of continuing in baseball for family life, but I wonder. By the time he was twenty-six, he was the father of three. My sister, Leah, was born when I was five; my brother, Phillip, arrived when I was six.

Another reason for Dad's harsh discipline came, I think, from his religion. He had been raised Southern Baptist in the "spare the rod, spoil the child" tradition. On Sundays he took me to Calvary Baptist Church in Bellflower, where he had attended services as a child. I did not attend Sunday school there; it was just Dad and me, sitting in the pew together. Week after week I heard the hellfire and brimstone sermons. I learned early on that Dad valued outward appearances, which I've come to believe is a common quality among people with a fundamentalist faith. In public Dad was downright charismatic. If I was mowing the yard when a neighbor stopped by, he'd grab the lawnmower and hold it, as if he were doing the work. After the neighbor left, I was back on the job. This ticked me off because I felt that he wasn't being truthful to who he really was. Meanwhile, Mom stayed home with my brother and sister. She had been raised Roman Catholic and lived her faith in a quiet way that I admired, though she never preached. Her open-door policy with the neighborhood kids drew them to her whenever they had a problem. She was safe to be with.

I dearly wanted to be a credit to God, but the God of my childhood Southern Baptist church seemed like an angry Old Testament one, bent on punishment. Even when we sang the old hymn "Amazing Grace" the words did not seem to apply to me. I knew I could never measure up. In kindergarten I first sensed that I was different when I developed a serious crush on my female teacher. I also sensed that this sort of feeling was unacceptable at Calvary Baptist Church. So I always tried to stay close to the kindlier Jesus, though for many years it would be the game of baseball that was my god.

Dad's temper played out on the field. He was always supportive of my playing, though in the hard-nosed way he knew. Every Saturday and Sunday he took me out to Behringer Park to practice. Mom often went along to shag balls in the outfield. We'd start at eight o'clock in the morning and play for hours. In the movie about the All-American Girls Professional Baseball League of the 1940s and '50s, *A League of Their Own*, there's a classic scene where the manager, played by Tom Hanks, yells at a player who has made an error. When she breaks into tears, he gets mad. "No crying," he yells in her face. "No crying! Everyone knows—there's no crying in baseball!"

That could have been Dad. He was big on keeping my head in the game. "Never let 'em see you sweat," he liked to say. "If someone hits a home run off you, Show No Emotion. If one of your teammates drops a fly ball, Show No Emotion. Later in the game, he could be the one who saves your sorry ass."

So for me there definitely was no crying in baseball—though there definitely was swearing in baseball. Despite our faithful attendance at Calvary Baptist Church, Dad cussed, and I cussed, and it seemed a normal way to let go of the emotions that streamed through me during a game.

By age eleven I had become obsessed with hitting more home runs. In my first season of Little League, I had hit a couple, but they hadn't cleared the fence—so to me they did not really count. I kept begging Dad to pitch batting practice so I could perfect a mighty home run swing. One afternoon we went to Behringer Park. After what seemed like hours into it, I had no success. I kept making the same mistakes—late on my swing and late getting my hands through. Despite the batting glove on my left hand, both hands began to blister. On one swing, the ball hit my left hand—I was too tired to get the bat around on an inside pitch. I broke down and cried. Dad yelled, "Get back in the box."

When I said I couldn't, he replied, "We're not going home until you stop crying. Now step in the batter's box and take another swing."

I did but once again couldn't get the bat around on an inside pitch, and the ball hit my hand again. My knuckles were swelling and bloody. Something turned inside me, something I had never felt before. I stepped into the box in a rage without tears, determined to hit the ball right back at him. I wanted to hurt him. I hit a line drive off his foot. It did not faze him—or me. On the next pitch I wanted to hit the ball right at his head. I swung as hard as I could, and, for the first time, hit the ball out of the park. Suddenly the rage turned to joy. In the years to come, there would be plenty of injustices to rage about, and I would remember that afternoon when I learned to channel and control my emotions on the field. Bloody hands and all, I hit for fifteen more minutes, now belting the ball deep. I felt invincible, like I could do anything. Afterward Dad shook my hand and, for the first time, as far as I could remember, gave me a hug. "Ila, that's what makes a winner," he said. "Someone who never gives up, works hard, and is determined. Congrats, you did it."

For me, the joy I found in the game would always be mixed with pain. But in that moment at Behringer Park, I knew what it took to excel in baseball and would take that energy into my next two years in Little League. Dad was a great coach. He knew he would not always be there to cover me as I went deeper into baseball, and over the next few years, he would test me to get me ready to deal with the adversity as well as the glare of attention coming my way.

"It's up to you," he told me. "But if you want to be successful you have to start working out twice as hard and twice as long as the guys. The injury to his pitching arm years ago had prompted him to research conditioning—exercises, elastic bands to build strength. He believed in being proactive. "For starters," he told me, "to keep your arm healthy do your exercises three times a day, and run."

My dream of making it to the major leagues did not waver, but I was beginning to understand the obstacles Dad talked about. For the most part, the guys I played ball with were fine with me. I could get guys out, so they wanted me on their team. At age eleven, I learned to hit the curve ball, a skill that is the great divider between players who continue in the game and those who fall away. "Read the seams," Dad would say. "Keep your head still and watch the seams as the ball approaches the plate, to see which way it's gonna go. Read the seams."

In this way I lost my fear of getting hit by the ball.

To keep my bat in the lineup, my coaches played me at short and first base when I was not pitching. Opposing pitchers, though, still sometimes threw at me—not exactly up to the youth baseball code, but that's how it was. As the teams got used to me, though, the opposition began to fade. Yet I still heard the catcalls from the stands. It was the Little League mothers and fathers who were the angriest. During a game, a Little League mother said to Mom: "How can you let your daughter play a boy's sport?"

Dad recalls a Little League father confronting him: "What are we supposed to do, put dresses on our boys and send them to school?"

As the jeers continued—and because she had two young kids at home—Mom stopped going to my games. Sometimes I felt like I was out there on my own, trying to perform while I shook off the insults being thrown at me. I knew it was hard for Dad to not clobber the critics. One day I saw him fume while a parent screamed at us as we left the field. Dad didn't blow up, he just kept walking to the car. I asked why he didn't say anything back and shut the guy up, and he repeated his mantra about winning: "Some people will never understand or accept your dream, no matter what you do. So don't give them any reason to stop you. Stay out of trouble, turn the other cheek, and just perform. People want to be with winners. So win."

In my first full season of Little League, I showed that I was there to stay. Few home runs are hit in the majors, and the elite players usually hit the few balls that do go over the fences. Players can win the home run title with just a couple. I hit my first one, a solo shot over the centerfield fence, as Dad watched. Rounding second, I caught his eye and waved. I hit one more that season, but one of my teammates on the White Sox,

Stephen Pereira, won the home run title with three. That year I was named to the all-star team.

We went on a roll, rallying against Metropolitan of Norwalk to win 11–6, beating the same team again 2–1. Pitching against Eastside of Norwalk, I threw a one-hitter, with eleven strikeouts and five walks. My friend Mike Moschetti's two-run homer was the only score of the game. The next day Mike matched my one-hitter for another 2–0 win. In the third round of the tournament I had a no-hitter going for four and two-thirds innings before giving up a hit. I drove in the only two runs we scored with an RBI single and a home run. We'd made it to the semifinals but were losing 4–2 until we rallied with four runs in the third inning and four more runs in the fourth. We played Metropolitan again for the tournament championship and won a nail-biter, 2–1. For the first time in ten years, the La Mirada major division all-stars had won the district 29 tournament. If it's possible to be high on baseball, I was. We went on to the Big League sectional tournament in Long Beach to compete for the western division district 3 championship. But our ride ended there.

My record should have convinced any remaining critics that I was for real. After all, they couldn't argue with my stats, but some coaches' and parents' thinking was stuck in the past. I was able to compete in Little League because of the girls and their parents who fought for their right to play in the 1950s and '60s. Little League spent nearly $2 million defending lawsuits in fifteen states to keep girls out, which I will never understand. I am so gosh-darn grateful for those girls and for the New Jersey judge who ruled in 1974 that a girl from Hoboken, New Jersey, named Maria Pepe could play. By then, Maria was in high school, too old for Little League, but she and the others who would not take no for an answer made all the difference for those of us who followed. In response Little League immediately launched a division for softball, which has become the organization's de facto sport for girls.

In spite of the dramas that played out on my Little League diamonds— or maybe because of them—by age eleven I had grown into a confident daredevil. If there was a challenge I was all over it, ready to squash the idea that it could not be done. Borrowing the next-door boy's Honda

125 dirt bike and popping wheelies all the way up our driveway was a favorite stunt. These boys were older than me and could not do it, so of course I had to try. What made me successful was that I didn't even think about the pain of falling. Mom knew this about me, and it worried her terribly. I especially enjoyed riding my bike off the roof of our house and trying to land correctly on the Bermuda grass lawn or, even better, into the backyard pool, with an audience of Leah, Phillip, and the neighbor kids. One day, with only Leah watching, I rode my bike down the shake shingles of our roof as usual and lifted off. This time I overshot the grass and hit the asphalt. My chin went numb, and I could feel blood running down my chest. Leah started to scream, and I remember thinking, *Oh, no. Mom is going to freak out, and Dad is going to kill me.* My crying days were behind me, and I walked into the kitchen to show Mom the bad news. I remember her eyes opening wide, like she had seen a ghost. "Your bone is showing," she said, and we were off to the emergency room.

Fourteen stitches later, I faced Dad. To my surprise there was no beating that day; he just took away my bike. I am grateful that Mom did not put me on meds for hyperactivity, but I know that I drove her nuts with my energy and shrank her wallet by breaking our windows with baseballs. And always, I tried to fix things before Dad got home.

After my second year in Little League, I took Dad's advice and began my own daily workouts. He never had to wake me up in the morning on school days, because I was already out of bed, doing my arm exercises; after school I ran, then did my second round of arm exercises; and right before bed I did the last round. I also ran whenever I could—I actually loved it because my hero at the time was Madonna, who liked to run. I saw the increase in my strength, the feel of solid muscle.

If I was a local celebrity on the field, by fifth grade I was also becoming known as the local rebel. In school, I had often gotten into minor trouble—from hitting the tetherball too hard at recess to playing with unauthorized worms in class. Seeing someone pick on an underdog made me really angry, and I would jump in to defend the victim. If Mom had put a bumper sticker on her car it could have read, "My kid beat up the bully that was picking on your kids." I became known as the "good bully" of Dulles Elementary School.

I was also sneaking out of the house at night with my friend, Alyse Issac. I think that lots of people grow up with a friend like Alyse, who's always up for anything. When we met in second grade, we quickly saw we would be partners in mischief. At night, we'd meet up down the hill to play football with some older kids. We also liked to ride around town with a girl named Janine Lindemulder, a softball star at La Mirada High School, where I planned to go one day. Alyse's older brother had a crush on Janine—well, a lot of the boys did—and Alyse, who was into softball, really looked up to her.

On another night, I was riding around town in the back of a pickup truck crowded with older boys and girls when they started pairing off to make out. I was not afraid of a good fight, but this scared me badly. I had a crush on the sister of a guy I was playing with. All I wanted to do was be with her and kiss her. She liked hanging out with me, but when she fell for a guy named Kevin, my heart broke. And that's the way it went over the next few years: one crush after another would find a boyfriend, and my imaginary romance would be over. I tried everything in my power to make my feelings for girls go away. I prayed, and when that didn't work, I prayed harder. Growing up in the Southern Baptist church, I came to believe there was something terribly wrong with me, like there was an evil spirit lurking within. To keep it at bay, I accepted Christ into my heart and was baptized at age twelve. I was born again and awaited the transformation to "normal," but it didn't come. I continued to get crushes on girls, I continued to swear, and I continued to fight with other kids.

Looking back, I think fighting was the only way I could show my anger. At home Dad was the only one allowed to get angry, and on the diamond he had taught me to keep my emotions in check. With Leah, Phillip, and even Mom afraid to stand up to Dad, I appointed myself the defender of the family. I expanded that role by beating up on the neighborhood kids who teased others who couldn't or wouldn't fight back. As fifth grade wound down that spring, I had two fights: one with a girl who had been picking on another girl, the other with a boy named Jason who had been picking on one of my friends. For some reason, he had a Halloween mask with him, and I grabbed it and beat him with it. The good bully had gone too far. Parents of other kids showed up at our house. Conversations were held. I knew that my parents did not like the path I was on, sneaking out at night, running around with older kids, some of them troubled, and beating up on people. With Mom pregnant again, I felt guilty for causing her grief. My parents weren't the only ones worried. I worried about what was coming next—in our family and inside my own confused self as I approached puberty. Could I will myself to like boys? Would I still have a place in baseball when they grew taller and stronger than me?

Given my behavior, it should not have been a surprise when my parents told me that for sixth grade I would not be returning to Dulles Elementary School, where I had been confident of my place in kid society. I had never doubted that I was accepted for who I was—a loud, feisty, athletic girl with a big heart. Instead I spent sixth grade at the local Christian elementary school, where I knew no one. I went from being popular to not fitting in. I didn't even fit into my own body. I was developing breasts and took to wearing sweatshirts to hide them. I call it the lost year. The great bright spot came early in December, when my brother Randall was born. The afternoon Mom brought him home from the hospital, I sat with him in my arms. It was the beginning of a lifelong bond.

Baseball became my sanctuary from all that went on at home and at school. Dad showed me how to use our isometrics machine to strengthen my rotator cuff, which I think helped me avoid shoulder injuries later in my career. When Little League season began again, I threw myself into the games. Early one Saturday morning, Dad brought me down to Behringer Park. He put a baseball in my hand and showed me how to throw a one-fingered curve, a pitch that the Los Angeles Dodgers pitcher Don Sutton had taught him. He arranged my fingers on the ball, and said, "Throw it like a fastball. I don't care where it goes; just get used to the feel of throwing it."

What was great about this pitch is that it didn't add strain to my elbow because it's thrown like a fastball. Most kids my age couldn't do that yet, but I had really large hands, which helped me master it. It would prove to be a good pitch to master because I never did develop the elbow injuries that plagued other Little Leaguers who had started throwing the traditional curve at this age. At that time and place Little League had no rule against throwing curveballs or, for that matter, the number of pitches a player could throw in a game.

At age twelve, I had a golden season with the La Mirada White Sox, throwing two perfect games and three no-hitters. Sportscaster Rick Lozano of KABC's *Eyewitness News* showed up to film me pitching. What I remember most from that game is the sixth and final inning. I had struck out all fifteen batters I'd faced and was going to move heaven and earth to get the last three. I got the first guy, but the next batter came up and tried to bunt, just so he wouldn't strike out. His bunt went foul, and I remember my fury that he'd tried to avoid a strikeout. I threw the ball as hard as I could. Another K, or strikeout, and then the final one.

I was hearing sweet music from my coaches. My regular season coach, Patrick Van Horn, told a reporter, "You don't get many 12-year-olds who can throw the ball with the speed and consistency that she can. . . . Last summer she was clocked in the 68 mph range. . . . Even for a 12-year-old boy that is unheard of."

As the head of the sports program for the city of South Gate, Joe Moschetti had seen many athletes. So it meant a lot to me that as my all-star coach, Mr. Moschetti, liked my style. As he told my coauthor:

At twelve, her fundamentals were just so good. Nobody could touch her; she was dominant. She was one of the most competitive youngsters I've ever seen—and I ran a sports program for twenty years. I always felt that when Ila pitched, we were going to win. . . . This girl could hit the ball farther than most boys, including one home run that I figure went close to 300 feet. She was by far in the best shape of anyone on the team. I used to see her running in the park—this was before regular practice—and I didn't see the other guys or my son, Mike, doing that, and he was a pretty good athlete. I think she knew she was going to have to try harder to play ball. I think she knew what she was up against, much like Jackie Robinson [did].

Yeah, Mike Moschetti was more than a "pretty good athlete"—the Oakland A's drafted him out of high school in the second round of the 1993 MLB June Amateur Draft, and he played three seasons of minor league ball.

Over the sixty innings I threw that season I gave up a total of ten walks while averaging about ten strikeouts per game. I ended the season with a 9-1 record and a 0.75 ERA. At the plate, I hit .500 and struck out six times in fifty-six at bats. The home runs so dear to my heart had started coming, too: I led the league with eight.

I was named to the La Mirada major division all-stars, and we made it to the western division district 3 championship game, one step farther than last year. I poured everything I had into that game, going the maximum innings allowed. I struck out seventeen, giving up two hits and two walks. At the plate I doubled and scored on Mike Moschetti's double, and I repeated the feat in the ninth. I got three of the team's eleven hits and figured in both runs scored. But in the thirteenth inning, we lost 4-2. Our season was over, yet I knew I had again proven myself. The city of La Mirada awarded me a certificate of appreciation. Many of the critics in the stands had quieted down. Dad had been right: I had to win my way into acceptance. Then I read that my hometown newspaper, the *La Mirada Lamplighter*, questioned how much longer I could play. And I learned that the father of one of my Little League teammates told Dad, "Soon as Ila becomes a teenager and puts on lipstick, she won't make it."

So it would come down to this. Would my baseball dreams be defined by lipstick?

2

LIPSTICK ADOLESCENCE

GAME DAY: SECOND INNING. Ever since I started playing ball, I've jogged to my position on the field and back to the dugout. I can't stand the laziness of walking there. Coaches call this "hustle" and love it, but for me it's also a sign of my impatience to get on with the game. After the Dukes go down fast in the top of the second inning—two strikeouts sandwiched around Rodriguez's ground out—I hustle out to the mound.

Catcher Chris Coste, a homegrown boy from Fargo, is up. Right now Chris ranks ninth in the league in batting average: .333. He's also third on the RedHawks in slugging percentage: .507. With those numbers he can afford to talk trash, but he hasn't. He didn't do it on the pregame radio show and hasn't been part of the stare-downs from the dugout. (This is the same Chris Coste who will go on to the Philadelphia Phillies World Series championship team of 2008.)

Coste likes fastballs and hits for power; he'll likely be swinging the bat. I start him off with a screwball. He swings: strike one. After Javier throws the ball back, I keep it in my mitt. Dad taught me that the less a batter sees of the ball the better. He considered this a psychological advantage for the pitcher, as a batter is always looking to pick up the ball early. The longer I hide the ball before my release, the faster it makes the pitch look. I figure to keep throwing the screwball until Coste proves he can hit it. It helps that I can go after him a bit more because no one is on base and we have a one-run lead. I know a one-run lead isn't likely to get me a win against this team, but there's no use in pitching around him. Given how the entire Fargo lineup is hitting, they should all be walked.

I peer in at Javier, like we're pondering what to throw, then offer up another screwball. A little slower and lower this time. Coste swings again: strike two. Javier holds onto the ball and comes to the mound. He tells me that the bottom of my screwgie is falling out—that's a good thing. "Hey, trust me," he says. "I'll block it if you throw in the dirt. I think we keep throwing this until he hits it. What do you think?"

I place the mitt over my mouth and say, "Yeah, that's what I was thinking. Just mix it up and let me shake you off a couple of times."

"Got it," he says, and runs back behind home. As agreed I shake Javier off twice, then hold the ball for a moment while I send up a quick prayer. *Dear God, Please help me strike this fucker out.* I deliver another screwgie, and Coste swings and misses.

"Strike three," the umpire yells and jerks his thumb up.

Holy crap, two innings and two strikeouts—and I am not a strikeout pitcher.

Coste takes it like a grown-up. He walks back to the dugout and doesn't say a word. So far the RedHawks have been very professional, if you discount the glares coming my way from manager Simunic.

By now you would think the jitters have settled down, but the vein in my neck is still pulsating. So far, though, the adrenaline is working for me. Usually a pitcher catches a break in the lineup at some point but not now, with Forry Wells up to bat. Wells is hitting .368 against the Dukes. He's another guy with speed. The guys with wheels always make me more nervous than the home run hitters. I stand on the rubber waiting for him to get set. He has one foot in the batter's box, but the other one is still out. I think, *Step in, you stupid fuck.* I throw a four-seam fastball inside to back him off the plate. Ball one. Wells really likes to get his hands extended, so I need to work inside and, when I throw away, to keep it down more than usual. Next pitch is a screwball outside; he swings and misses.

Soon as I get the ball back I step on the rubber, as if to say, *Let's go, I am ready.*

But Wells is outside the box again, stalling. A voice from the stands yells, "Step in the box. You afraid of her?"

It's the same old fear that goes back to Little League—a guy of any age doesn't want to look bad hitting against a woman. I throw Wells a cut fastball and he bites at it, sending a fly ball to right for an easy out. I didn't think he'd swing at that pitch. It isn't the greatest, but today I have a little more zip in my fastball. The fastest I have been clocked is eighty miles per hour in Canada and my last year in college with the Whittier Poets. I have never been a hard thrower, because you have to throw a lot faster than that to be effective. So I need to stay out of what they call batting practice range, eighty to eighty-four miles per hour. If I threw that speed all the time, I would be easy to hit; but by slowing it down to seventy-five miles per hour and mixing up the speed, it becomes more difficult for professional hitters. So when I throw the ball at seventy-eight and move it around, it looks like ninety. I throw my next pitch as hard as I can. I've been throwing seventy-five miles per hour for the majority of this game, according to Fargo's radar gun, but that pitch read eighty. Wells swings and flies out to right. Sweet. Two outs and nobody on.

As Ruben Santana walks to the plate, I check where my outfielders are playing him. So far they have been playing deep. I figure if I can get through the lineup once without many base runners, I can go six or more innings. Then Roberto Giron, our closer, can come in, and he is usually lights out. I look in for Javier's sign, and on the first pitch Santana hits a shallow fly ball to center. Like I always do, I turn around to make sure he catches it. "Fuck, yeah," I say, and jog toward my favorite spot on the bench. No runs, no hits, no errors, no one left on base.

The chatter in the stands has changed. From "Go home—you don't belong here" to "Please sign my ball." Fans send their balls into the dugout and ask my teammates to hand them to me for an autograph. And after I've thrown two scoreless innings, the guys on the bench are leaving me alone. They know I'm in a groove and don't want to mess it up. They're also staying put in the dugout. Usually they perch near the fence, so they can get a good view of the girls in the stands. One of the guys' biggest perks in pro ball is finding women to sleep with. It's funny—baseball's such an orderly game, the way the diamond lays out, the fundamentals pure and clear—and then there's the other side of it, the unruliness of the guys' hunt for sex. When this subject comes up, writers love to quote Casey Stengel, the New York Yankees manager of the 1950s, who said, "Being with a woman all night never hurt no professional baseball player. It's staying up all night looking for a woman that does him in."

From what I've seen, the players don't have to look very hard. The women are so available. It's a game for both sides, and they act like teenagers about it. It's not limited to baseball, though—lots of people seem to act like kids about sex. Like Dad, whose midlife crisis collided with my teenage years, when I was crushed with guilt over what I saw as my abnormal attraction to girls.

1987, LA MIRADA, CALIFORNIA. A LIPSTICK ADOLESCENCE. I wasn't aware of it then, but looking back I can see what a rocky path I was on at age thirteen: a born-again, closeted gay girl in a Christian school who lived to play baseball. I had only to look at two other La Mirada girls to see how simple my life could have been. For one there was Janine Lindemulder, my old friend Alyse's role model, who had just graduated from La Mirada High School. Janine was blonde and beautiful, and the sort of natural athlete who makes the game she plays look easy. A few years later, as I watched Ken Griffey Jr.'s effortless grace, he reminded me of Janine's style in softball. All the boys were crazy about her, but she was very much her own person, which caused a lot of girls to resent her and gossip about her, the only flaw I could see in her perfect life.

Then there was Jennie Finch, five years younger than I was. Her family lived nearby, and Dad took me to their home sometimes to develop arm strength on the machine that Jennie's father had invented. Like Dad, Mr. Finch devoted himself to his daughter's sport, in her case, softball. The family was devoutly Christian. Like Janine, Jennie was blonde and pretty. She tended to wear pink ribbons in her hair when she played ball. Sandwiched between Janine and Jennie was my baseball-loving self. At puberty my own silky hair had turned dark, curly, and unruly. I did not wear pink bows; I was immune to boys chasing me; the only place I fit in was on the baseball diamond—and the odds were not in my favor that I could continue with the game I loved best. No stats exist as to how many girls are strongly encouraged to leave baseball for softball when they reach puberty and start to wear lipstick. Instead you have to rely on the stories you hear. Whole books have been written about it: when Jennifer Ring, a professor of political science at the University of Nevada, Reno, saw what her daughter Lily went through to keep playing baseball past Little League, she began to collect her daughter's and other young women's stories and published *Stolen Bases: Why American Girls Don't Play Baseball* and, later, *A Game of Their Own*. "What happens," Ring asks in the latter book, "when a baseball-playing girl is made to understand that she should not feel at home where she has felt most at home her entire life?"

I was about to find out.

Whittier Christian Junior High School sits on a hill in the tree-shaded town of Whittier, which was settled by Quakers in the late 1800s. Calvary Baptist Church of Whittier founded the school. Chapel in the auditorium was mandatory. The campus is in a peaceful setting, but that didn't help my spirits on my first day of school. Mom had warned me how strict the school would be. I looked down at the plaid skirt the girls were required to wear—no more jeans and sweatshirts for me—and bit my lipstick-free mouth. *This is not me,* I thought. *This isn't happening.* But it was happening. Mom dropped me off with a hug and a cheery "Have a great day."

Some of the kids I used to beat up, like Jason of the Halloween mask incident in fifth grade, were my classmates again. When Jason and I first saw each other, we both sort of paused and then walked on by. Nothing said, no connection. Some of my rowdy old friends were here, too. To them, seeing me in a skirt was hilarious. Our skirts had to be long enough to cover the top part of the knees, or else you were sent to the office to be measured. If it was short by an inch, you were given a huge, flowery skirt that went down to your ankles. It was as ugly as a skirt could get, so most of the girls would not test the length rule. Rebel that I was, I sometimes rolled my waistband up to make the skirt length just a little too short. They always called me on it.

Why was having to wear a skirt such a big deal? I felt like my freedom to move freely had been taken away. During recess I felt uncomfortable playing in a skirt. It made me feel awkward and shy. I was also ashamed because I liked girls. And Dad was sending a strong message to me to look like a girl. One afternoon he was at the field, and as the players walked off, he pointed out that on the field in our uniforms we were a team. But away from the field, each player was an individual. And so was I.

"Be a girl," he advised me. "Off the field wear high heels. Look like a girl."

Add to this list of grievances and anxieties a serious case of acne. Dad told me that I didn't clean my face enough. He had me scrub my face with bar soap and then apply ice cubes to seal the pores from dirt. My skin began to scar, so Mom told me to wear foundation, but I hated the sticky feel of makeup on my skin. I obsessed over my hair, going through can after can of Aqua Net hair spray as I tried to blow-dry my bangs straight. There are no photographs of me during middle school—I ran from the camera, though that's probably just as well. I had really big hair. Adolescence may be the beginning of a whole new world, but it's also the end of so much. I often wished I could go back in time to the happy days of elementary school when I had self-confidence to burn.

I took to eating lunch alone by a tree or behind one of the school buildings. One day my math teacher, Janet Thomas, saw me. She didn't ask me to explain, just started inviting me to have lunch with her in her classroom. My grades began to improve—I was pulling A's in everything except English.

Salvation also came through sports. I played girls' basketball and helped the team win our school's first-ever league championship. We played hard, and in one game I was smacked in the mouth with the basketball. People rushed over because they thought I was bleeding, but the ball had just smeared my lipstick. Maybe wearing lipstick wasn't such a good idea. I was named MVP. The following year we went undefeated, and I was named co-MVP. I treasured Coach Susan Johnson's pride in our team's winning the sportsmanship award. At our end-of-the-season dinner, Coach Johnson mentioned something that I held dear—our team's closeness and the great fun we had together: "Remember . . . Ila's 'round the back' layup at the Globetrotter game? When backing up on the press, Denise [Huizing] and Ila fell over each other? The game where our goal for the quarter was to get the parents to quit laughing? Remember the things we learned about teamwork and friendship."

I also ran track, anchored the mile race, and set a school record in the shot put. For these competitions, of course, I didn't have to wear the dreaded plaid skirt. I felt more like myself in uniform. And sometimes, when Mrs. Thomas, Mrs. Johnson, and Coach Esslinger went golfing, I was invited in as the fourth. At a time when I sorely needed it, these three teachers offered me companionship and acceptance. As much as I enjoyed competing in track and field, basketball, and golf, these other sports could not take the place that baseball held in my heart. In different ways, they just contributed to the game I loved best: The shot put strengthened my throwing arm. Basketball and golf improved my hand-eye coordination, so important to hitting a baseball. And running cross-country built up my legs for pitching.

The weather was chilly and rainy that winter, as if spring and baseball would never come. Suddenly it was the end of February. Soon our lemon tree would be filled with fragrant white blossoms. It was time for baseball tryouts. Dad sat me down and explained that he was not going to plead with the coach to give me a chance to try out—it was up to me to take the next step and approach the coach, if I wanted to. *If I wanted to?* The Whittier Christian Crusaders were an awesome baseball team; they had gone undefeated the previous season. The next day I lasted until lunch before I approached the office of the baseball coach, Rolland Esslinger. *If playing baseball was going to be taken from me, you might as well kill me now*, I thought. When I walked into Coach Esslinger's office, I could barely whisper the words: "Coach, is it okay if I try out for the team?"

His response blew me away. With one of the biggest smiles I had ever seen, he said, "Sure." He had not even hesitated.

Wow.

Whittier Christian Junior High School had 240 kids, and fifty or so of the boys wanted to play baseball. When I showed up for the first day of tryouts, it felt like all eyes were staring at me. We were competing for the fifteen spots available on the team. Coach Esslinger began by telling us to form two lines and start warming up. No one wanted to take a chance and warm up with me. I could see the boys watching out of the corner of their eyes, wondering, *How does she throw?* But the familiar smell of the field's freshly cut grass calmed my nerves, and after my first throws landed in another guy's mitt with loud smacks, I overheard someone say, "Oh, my gosh. She can throw."

Next came batting practice. Trees beyond the field's chain-link shaded the traffic on Telegraph Road. It was 200 feet to the right-field fence and 250 feet to left. When my turn came, I saw the pines and sycamores as my target. It reminded me of my first Little League tryout. After I launched a few balls into the trees, the mood of the guys improved even more: I sensed I would be welcome if I made the team. After two days of tryouts and an intrasquad game, the roster was posted on the window outside the boys' locker room. I read the list and walked away with a big grin on my face. Big hair and all, I was on the team.

Coach Esslinger quickly called me to his office. I listened as he spoke about how it was going to be. To avoid embarrassment in the locker room, the team would dress ahead of time for away games. Other than that, I would be treated like anyone else on the team. "We'll try to do things to deemphasize your being a girl," he said. "You'll have to prove yourself by your performance and attitude. But I want to know about any problems you run into."

Rol Esslinger was the first person outside my family to go to bat for me. He was a religious guy with good morals, and I respected that. He was powerful—built solid, like a brick house—and athletic, and I felt that leadership came naturally to him. He was one of those coaches who instinctively knew how to get the best out of his players. He constantly encouraged me, pushing me at the same time. I wanted to do everything possible to play my best for him. After Dad, Coach Esslinger turned out to be the best coach I ever had.

My teammates never gave me any crud on the field, and I always got a friendly hello from them off the field, but that's as far as it went. They were popular on campus and hung out with the girls who liked them. But it wasn't quite so cool at a Christian school for a girl to be a jock in a perceived boys' game. I didn't fit in with the Goth group either and was too much of an athlete for the nerds. I was too different to fit in with the popular athletic girls. And I refused to try to conform just to fit in. While everyone else was figuring out this boy-girl stuff, I was dreaming of playing ball in the major leagues. Which is why I gravitated to my old friend, Alyse. Because she would do anything for a laugh, Alyse drew me out of my shyness—and was a nice counterbalance to the self-discipline and perfectionism that I practiced in baseball. Sometimes we let down too much. Alyse remembers thinking how cool we were: "We still liked to sneak out at night. Once we borrowed the Borders family car and practiced driving around the parking lot of a nearby school. I'm the type that says, 'Let's have fun—why not,' while Ila was always a little nervous about things."

My high times with Alyse also brought me into an odd triangle. Alyse had stayed in touch with her softball heroine, Janine Lindemulder, and some nights we rode around town in Janine's car, listening to elevator music on KOST 103.5 FM. Janine was graduating from high school, but she still liked to hang out with Alyse and advise her about boys and sex. (Janine seemed like a good source of information. In 1987 she had posed for *Penthouse*; for December she was named the magazine's Pet of the Month.) I'd sit in the backseat, with absolutely no interest in the boring music or the subject of heterosexual love. Sometimes they'd remember I was there and call out, "Hey, you still back there?"

Well, physically I was, though some nights, when I tired of their conversation about boys, I'd leave the car and walk home alone. In 1987 in La

Mirada, California, I was thirteen and had not a soul to talk with about finding my kind of love. Even if I had, could I have found the words to explain myself or frame a question? I doubt it.

To my surprise when baseball season started, the teams we played against did not hassle me, nor did the coaches. I didn't know that Coach Esslinger was taking the flak for playing me. As he later said:

> One coach called, extremely upset about having his team play against a girl, but I didn't see it that way. The nature of our school philosophy was built around how we treated one another. . . . Ila was mild-mannered and carried herself as she needed to, and that helped her do what she needed to do. . . . It was pretty much a shock to the boys because she was so good. When she didn't pitch, I played her at first. I batted her third because she was the best hitter on the team, with the ability to hit for power and for average. She was also strong on defense.

Coach Esslinger was all about the team. He allowed the media to focus not on me but only on our team as a whole. And our team was one fine story—we were all about keeping the winning streak alive. In our first game against Paramount Junior High School, it was close. In my first three at bats, I singled, doubled, and had two RBIs. The score was tied when I came to the plate again with a runner on base. I fell into my usual habit of pressing my batting helmet down as far as it would go, muttered, "Gotta get a hit," and looked to our third base coach for a sign—bunt, swing, or take the pitch? Our team had spent a lot of time learning the signs. Now the coach clapped his hands a couple of times, before pointing his index finger at me. No sign was on. I was on my own. I jammed my helmet down tighter, swung at the first pitch, and lined a single up the middle for the game-winning hit. The streak was alive.

Our second game was against our big rival, Brethren–La Mirada Christian Junior High School. The two schools are near one another, and we all tended to play up in front of the families and neighbors who showed up to watch. It meant a lot that Mom was in the stands, encouraging baby Randall to let out a yell for his big sister. I had arrived in seventh grade with a two-seamer fastball mph and an effectively loopy 11-5 curve ball. They proved to be enough. Over four innings I struck out seven and gave up one hit. I also went two-for-two at the plate, with three RBIs: The score: 14–0 for Whittier Christian.

The streak was still going when we faced Pasadena Christian School for the championship. I was the starting pitcher, and we had a pitchers' duel going until I left after the fourth inning, with seven strikeouts and two hits. Then we broke it open. I went four-for-five with six RBIs. We won the game 21–3, and with it the Christian School League Southern California championship. Infielder Anthony Morales and I shared the MVP award. I'd put the lie to the idea that once I started wearing lipstick, which was a sometime thing for me, I'd be unable to keep up with the boys on the diamond. My batting average was .571, and my ERA was 0.44, with thirty-seven strikeouts.

Rol Esslinger had been able to play me because the Christian School League of Southern California had no rule against a girl playing baseball. I was the first to do it, and with the numbers I put up, no one could argue that a girl was not up to the challenge. But after the season ended, the league raised the question, Did my presence on the diamond mean that girls should also play boys' football or basketball? Rol Esslinger was at the meeting. "There were never any faith-based issues raised over whether it was biblical for a girl to play baseball with or against boys," he recalled. "The discussion was heated, but when it came down to a league vote, it was agreed that baseball's a different game than softball, so a girl could play boys' baseball even when there was a girls' softball team. But that would be the only crossover sport. In the end the right decision was made, and it felt good to be on Ila's side."

I was glad that my season had helped open the door for other girls to play baseball in the league.

After the Crusaders' season ended, I kept on with baseball, playing PONY League and Senior League. With a full schedule of games, I often changed jerseys in the car as we traveled from game to game on the Southern California freeways. Dad and I kept the car radio blaring with hard rock music, from Led Zeppelin to Cinderella, which helped channel my nerves into energy. You could say we both just rocked out. Some of my teammates did not like riding with us because the music was so loud or, possibly, because they thought we were nuts—probably the latter. That summer I played up to six games a week, driving myself to build my strength and my skills. I sometimes ran short of energy and conserved it by holding back in a game, knowing that I had to be up for the next one. I became aware that I might not be invincible. No matter how well I pitched—or because I was pitching well—I still heard chants from the stands: "Go back to softball." Once, when I was pitching a good game in PONY League and notching lots of strikeouts, I came to bat and tripled. It was all too much. A crowd of screaming parents surged into the chain-link fence, and some of the fathers spilled onto the field. The umpire called a forfeit.

That was the year my brother Randall fell ill with spinal meningitis. My parents had me watch Leah and Phillip while they rushed Randall to Children's Hospital in Los Angeles. His temperature shot up to 106 degrees, and for forty-five minutes he went into seizures. The doctors didn't think he would survive, but he did. Dad's medical insurance didn't begin to cover Randall's large medical bills, and my parents fell deeply in debt. Dad had to sell his champagne Mercedes 300 SD and the red Porsche 924 that Mom drove. He replaced them with a 1985 Chevrolet orange truck with white side panels and a bench seat. Mom would drive Dad to work in it and then use it to drive all of us kids wherever we had to be.

Our cars were only the outer sign of our changing fortunes. For years Dad had run a lucrative auto painting and body shop business. Then the insurance industry changed its policies, making it much less profitable for shops like Dad's. To help out, Mom started A Child's Place, a Christian preschool in nearby La Habra. After Randall got sick, she had to hire a director to run it. She would stay home with Randall for three years, a time when she wasn't able to run her business properly. The preschool barely broke even. I learned to cook and look after my sister and brothers when Mom ran errands. By now she called me the "second Mom." I also tended to the household chores and repairs: fixing leaky toilets and pilot lights that went out and setting traps underneath the house for rats.

Our family had always enjoyed sitting together in front of the television as we watched baseball, including my favorite teams, the local Los Angeles Dodgers and the Kansas City Royals—me staring at Brett Saberhagen and George Brett and mentally analyzing various batters' swings. Now I saw how financial stress changed the climate of our home. Dad was often depressed. When he did lash out, much of the anger that used to come my way was directed at Mom, who couldn't defend herself. But I had learned to fight back, and some nights it came down to fighting him off with my fists. It was Mom's habit to serve as family peacemaker—and after all, she had the history on all of us. She knew that Dad had come from a difficult background. She had been told that when he was a boy, he was playing with the neighbor kids and took his shirt off when it got too warm. His parents had gone out and the neighbor who was watching him saw welts all over his back. He had been beaten. The neighbor called Child Services. Mom's own parents, Delores and Theron Carter, feared Dad's background would rear up and had opposed their marriage. They had not even attended the wedding. The estrangement lasted until I was three months old. After that, Mom said that Grandma had dedicated herself to using love to try to coach Dad into the goodness of life. She also used love to introduce me to the world. Grandma and I would climb trees, catch bugs—grasshoppers were her favorite—take tea, and garden. She taught me how to ride a bike. I would never put on a dress for Mom or Dad, but I did for Grandma. As Dad liked to tell Mom, "I think Grandma is raising Ila instead of us."

Which made what happened to Grandma when I was five such a loss for our whole family. My parents had just bought their first home in Whittier, and it came with a swimming pool. Growing up in Duluth, Minnesota, Grandma had never learned to swim; now she quickly took lessons. Every day we swam to our hearts' content. She would throw rings into the water, then both of us would dive for them, or we would race to see who could swim the length of the pool the fastest. She was forty-nine years old, but in the water she was like a little kid.

One day, Grandma and I were swimming laps when Mom called out to say that she had to run an errand. She would be right back.

"Okay," we said. "See you soon."

Grandma and I were on our tenth lap when we bumped up against each other. I came up laughing, but she sank to the bottom of the deep end. I thought she was joking. Sometimes we stayed under water to see how long we could hold our breath. But I saw no movement and suddenly realized this was no joke—she was drowning. I dove to the bottom and pulled at her with all of my might. Three times I tried to lift her but failed. Then I raced down our street, screaming for help.

A neighbor came back to the house with me, pulled my grandmother onto the diving board and started cardiopulmonary resuscitation. Just then the fire department showed up and took over. But somehow I knew that she was dead. I remember feeling responsible, weak, scared, and beyond sad. When Mom came home she fell apart. At the funeral, I stood by Grandma's casket. I told myself right then, *You will not be weak. You will be responsible and strong. And you will honor her by packing two lives into one.*

Grandma's death had brought the first traumatic change in our family. Mom turned from outgoing and fun-loving to shy, without self-confidence. Dad became the ruler of the house, a dictator. According to my parents, I grew stone-faced and stopped talking about my feelings and emotions. When Mom was pregnant with me, they had looked through a book of names and saw the name "Ida." But Dad, wanting something that seemed softer and more feminine, changed the consonant to "l." Later he was told that "Ila" means "island dweller." After Grandma's death, I think that in my heart I really did become a sort of island dweller.

One night Leah ran into my bedroom and said there was a man outside her window. I looked—she was right, and I ran into Mom and Dad's bedroom. I remember telling Dad there was a prowler, but he thought I was crazy, so I grabbed the hunting rifle, loaded it, and told Leah to call 911 if things went bad. I went out the back door and pointed the rifle at the intruder, who was in our carport. "I have a gun," I said. "Now get the fuck out of here."

He ran down our hill. For the rest of the night I stayed with Leah in her room, the rifle nearby. When Dad went outside the next morning, he found that some tools were missing. Despite all of Dad's bluster, I had become the defender of the family.

That summer something in our relationship turned sour. Dad still drove me to baseball games and coached, sharing everything he knew about the game, but he could also be downright cruel. I didn't understand his despair or that he was working his ass off for our family's financial survival. I did know that emotionally he just disappeared. He began an affair. What made me so mad about it was his lying. He had always said to save yourself for sex until marriage. And now this? Everyone in the family knew about the affair, though he denied it. This woman would sit in the living room and flirt with him; other nights Dad would come home late. We called her the Hot Pants Lady because her shorts barely covered her butt. How ironic that we lived on a street called Olive Branch Drive. There wasn't much peace at our house.

Eighth grade came, and everyone wondered whether our team could keep the streak going. I think the pressure brought the team closer. Coach Esslinger counseled balance. He told us the streak was important and that we should work hard to keep it alive, but we all knew it would someday end. "God doesn't expect us to win every game on the scoreboard," he said. "But I do believe that He wants us to do our best and play for His glory (not our own)."

Most of our wins that season were lopsided. I faced Bethany, giving up one hit with ten strikeouts. Against Paramount I threw a six-inning shutout, with another ten strikeouts. In addition to my two-seam fast-ball and curve, I was working on a change-up but had yet to perfect it. Batting third in the lineup, I had a great season at the plate. There was no cockiness about this—Coach Esslinger didn't allow that; I was thrilled that we'd added another win to the streak. When we faced Brethren in the playoffs, I went four-for-four with four RBIs. For the championship game against Pasadena I was the starting pitcher. I always felt that I get the edge by arriving at the field early, and Mom drove me over to Los Coyotes Field ahead of time. As I paced the outfield alone, shaking my arm to loosen it up, I could hear the rush of traffic on nearby Rosecrans Boulevard. Could we win one more game for a perfect season? I pitched shutout ball for six innings, striking out twelve. The score: Whittier 6, Pasadena 1. Coach Esslinger explained why I was named MVP:

> Ila was a key member of an excellent team, but she also taught the boys a great lesson about life. She showed them what hard work and determination could do. Also, she was not out to prove girls were better than boys. The lesson was: here was someone a little bit different—in this case, a girl—who was a worthy teammate. I think the boys grew up a lot.

I grew up, too. I knew where I belonged—on the diamond—and I prayed that wherever baseball took me I would be able to find an advocate like Rol Esslinger. I'm still listed in the school's top-ten record book: first in innings pitched (forty) and first in strikeouts (seventy); fourth in ERA (0.44); sixth in batting average (.613); eighth in total hits (nineteen); and ninth in doubles (five). The years as a Whittier Christian Junior High Crusader would be the time I truly felt part of a team.

After my junior high championship season, I took the summer off from PONY League and Senior League. The problem was the different distances from the mound to the plate. In Little League and junior high I had thrown from forty-six feet. Senior League and PONY League were fifty-four feet. It would have been a huge challenge to adapt, just as it is in changing from the aluminum bats used in college ball to the wooden bats in pro ball. My pitches had to get a tighter spin on the ball, which gives a quick last-minute break. And my release point had to shift with the new distances.

Instead I spent the summer before high school in a very different sort of baseball climate. Dad signed me up on his semipro adult men's team. He wanted me to understand what the adult baseball life was truly like—the men's culture of the locker room and the dugout. Would I want to continue? And could I adapt to pitching on a mound that was now sixty feet six inches from home? You had to be at least eighteen years old to play, so Dad fudged on my birth certificate. The manager knew I was underage but kept quiet about it. The games were played on Sunday mornings, which put an end to our church attendance. Dad rationalized this by arguing that I could reach a lot more people as a Christian ballplayer than by sitting in church. Mom saw it differently. "I was very much opposed," she recalled. "I even went to someone at the church about it. It was a tough one. I also worried about the exposure she'd get, being around adult ballplayers. It's hard to see your daughter go up against that."

But by now baseball was keeping me much too busy to make time for God, though I'd revert back when loneliness got the best of me. The first time I came into the dugout, the guys were kind of surprised to see me. One guy, a former minor leaguer, walked out. Another team picked him up, and the first time I faced him, he struck out. All that summer, Dad and I drove to games from San Bernardino to San Diego and in between. I quickly saw that my opponents were all better and stronger than I was. This was a first for me. I was not going to be able to overpower them, as I had in kids' baseball, but I could outsmart them. I learned to pitch with my brain that summer: to keep the ball low, to pitch inside, and watch for weaknesses. With a count of 3-and-2 or 1-and-2 on the batter and two outs, a runner on first base will usually break for second base. So I developed a neat pick-off move for that situation. I learned to change the rhythm of my motion, making it more difficult for batters to guess my pitches. I was also learning how to change the tempo of the game and slide step to the plate in my stretch. My teammates helped me out with tips on pitching, but they also treated me like just another ballplayer, as did our opponents. Going into second base, it wasn't *Excuse me* but *I'm gonna hurt you.* Nobody backed off because I was a girl.

Sometimes when Dad was on the mound, the manager would come out and say, "You're done. I'm bringing Ila in."

When he handed over the ball, Dad liked to say to me, "Give 'em hell."

He got a laugh out of this—"Hey, Ila, your Dad's outta gas. Close this thing out, will ya?"

Nobody else kidded about it, though. Our team was competitive and wanted to win ball games—and if I could get outs, then great. Sometimes the intensity boiled over. After a game in which I struck out an opposing player, I looked up to see the player's girlfriend coming at me, swearing. Suddenly I saw sunlight flash off something metal in her hand. It was a knife. As the woman broke into a run, I turned and fled. I'm hazy on what happened next. Somebody managed to stop her. Dad was there. An umpire or a security guard escorted us to the car, and we got out of there. During another game, I was sitting on the bench between innings when a fight between two players broke out. The violence scared me. Back on the mound for the next inning, I realized that in the long run, this summer was going to help me. I think when you're thrown into a situation over your head, there's only one way out. You have to rise above it. That summer brought out my determination. I started throwing harder. I also learned to look out for myself. Sometimes I'd be dropped off at a field at night, when it was dark. I learned to look over my shoulder; I'd check around before I went into the restroom. I figured this was how kids in New York City lived.

While I came out stronger physically and mentally, playing semipro baseball opened my eyes in other ways, too. Some of the men were disrespectful toward women. They'd be reading *Playboy* or *Hustler* and joking about it in the dugout. I was still pretty naïve, and here I was in an adult world. Sometimes I wondered what I was doing there. Dad understood and stayed close by. When asked why he encouraged me to play in the semipros at age fourteen, he liked to say, "I exposed her to the real world when she was not alone—and I think that made a difference. I was there to advise her when she felt uncomfortable. I told her, 'You can play with them on the same team, but you don't have to associate with them or be like them.'"

As the summer went on, my teenaged view toward life changed. One of my teammates was married with a child. His wife was pregnant again and having problems. I listened as he worried over his wife's health and the baby's. I had entered the adult world, with all of its complexities. Witnessing the fights and the swearing, encountering jealous and angry women, and listening to the men's concerns for their families changed me. I still lived in my fourteen-year-old body, but my sensibilities were more adult.

September loomed and with it high school. Would I fit in with the team at this level—would I even fit socially into the teenage world again? After empathizing with the player whose wife had miscarried and escaping a knife-wielding woman, how could I relate to my classmates' worries over what to wear to school or a bad test grade? Normally I would have attended La Mirada High School. That's where Janine Lindemulder had played. I had been surprised when Janine didn't continue her softball career—she was good enough to go to college on a scholarship. Instead, she turned to Hollywood. In 1988 she appeared as Janine Linde in an Italian-made film, *Moving Target*, followed by *Spring Break USA* and *Caged Fury*. La Mirada High School was also where Jennie Finch was headed to play softball. But not me.

In the 1980s, Title IX was murky about girls playing boys' baseball if there was a girls' softball team—it was the coach's call. Given its strong softball tradition, La Mirada High's coach told Dad that the baseball diamond was no place for a girl. No way was I going to play for him. Dad decided not to challenge the decision legally. He wanted me to understand that if someone did not want me out there, then go find the coach that does. His philosophy was, If you run into a roadblock, go around it.

Whittier Christian High School's head baseball coach was Tom Caffrey. His son-in-law, Steve Randall, had umpired a game I pitched and told Dad that he liked my ability and my attitude. Coach Randall, who coached frosh-soph baseball at Whittier Christian, was concerned about how I'd be accepted by the guys on the team. After he spoke with Rolland Esslinger, Coach Caffrey was willing to give me a fair shot, according to Dad. If I was good enough, I could play frosh-soph baseball.

The policies of a private Christian school such as Whittier, unlike those of a secular school, would continue the conservative values I was taught in middle school. I wouldn't go to dances here, but I would attend chapel every Wednesday. Yet this place was open to giving me a chance when the public school would not. This difference was curious. In the late 1980s the Religious Right was strong in Southern California, earnestly trying to restore women to their "proper" role as homemakers in American society. Was it even biblical for a girl to play with the guys? Coach Randall said that he didn't think the issue was an important one for the teachers and administrators at our school. And no one cited the Bible on me, though I held the impression that playing the game I loved was just not quite right. Nothing, God forbid, was said about gay girls. If there was a school rule about sexual conduct, I didn't know about it. All I remember is the message in chapel about saving yourself for marriage. But it was tough to overhear a conversation Dad had with the father of a softball star, who casually said that despite being recruited, his daughter would never attend a certain university because the coach was a lesbian. So I was to be a Whittier Christian High School Herald, though a closeted Herald.

Coach Randall explained that no matter how talented a ballplayer was, no freshman was allowed to go straight to varsity. I was to play freshman ball. The boys were bigger now than most of the girls, and I had to work harder than ever to keep up. I got up routinely at five in the morning to run and lift weights. That spring I tried out for the team: one girl in a crowd of seventy boys. I had added a four-seam fastball to my pitching repertoire as well as a not-so-loopy curve that I'd tightened to a 10-2 arc. And I kept dabbling with the change-up. Would these be enough? I'd also be pitching from the major league regulation distance to home plate: sixty feet six inches. Luckily I'd been doing that since age fourteen in the semipro league.

After freshman baseball ended, three players were bumped up to the junior varsity team. I was one of them. I pitched one game against Orange Lutheran High School. In the stands that day I noticed a stern-looking man watching my every pitch. I knew who he was—varsity coach Tom Caffrey. Was he pleased to see a girl pitcher out there? I couldn't tell from his expression whether he liked what he saw or not. Actually Coach Caffrey was thinking. It was one thing for me to play freshman ball—but varsity? It was 1990 and he had been coaching high school sports for thirty years. "I had to deal with some of my archaic attitudes," he told a sportswriter for the *Orange County Register*. "Coming from the old school of baseball, that [girls competing with boys] just doesn't happen."

We won the game, and that night Dad received a phone call. "We're going to the California Interscholastic Federation championships," Coach Caffrey told Dad. And he planned to bump two of the freshmen up to varsity. I was one of them. I played first base in the fourth and fifth innings and was on deck when the last out was made. But I had achieved something: my record was 5-1, with a 3.05 ERA and fifty-one strikeouts; and I got to play varsity baseball as a freshman.

At age fifteen I again played Senior League. Our team ended up going all the way to the PONY League regional playoffs, just one victory away from the USA Senior League championship. In the bottom of the ninth, we were up by one run, with two outs and the bases loaded, when I came in to pitch. I got the hitter to hit a lazy fly ball to center field. With the runners going, our center fielder, Chet Van Horn, camped out under it—so much time to think. The ball hit the tip of his glove, and he scrambled but failed to recover it before it hit the ground. Game over.

Even though I was disappointed, I went up to Chet, and said, "It's okay, we'll get them next time."

I could imagine how bad he felt. Chet's father was the head coach, and you could see the humiliation in his son's face. We never did get them next year—we aged out of Senior League—and I don't think Chet ever played baseball again.

If the diamond was open to me in high school, acceptance off the field was not so good. I had lost touch with most of my elementary school friends, who went on to La Mirada High School. The culture at Whittier Christian, however, wasn't very different: the guys were trying to be cool with their cars and seeing how many girls they could be with, while the girls were wearing makeup and sexy clothes, talking about the latest fashions, and dating guys. There was drinking and some drug use. Except for being a daredevil, I was a pretty straight kid. I never did try drugs, though I did drink alcohol. Alyse and I liked to camp out in our front yard with my neighbor Julie. Mom knew I was sneaking beer and wine coolers into the tent. She also knew that I was the kind of kid who, if told no, was going to do it, but if given the freedom to do it at home, wouldn't be so interested. She was right. The longer the leash, the better I behaved. And when it came to tobacco, Dad once had me smoke a whole cigar to warn me off it. It worked—I vomited. What I wanted from high school was to learn, play baseball, and get a scholarship to college. I was driven at that age and didn't want anything to get in my way. Sure, there were times when I wanted to go out and party, but I knew if I focused on baseball now, I could progress down the road. Besides, Dad would have thrown me out of the house—his threat whenever any of us kids got out of line.

Whittier Christian had a lot of kids from families with money. Our family was still struggling financially. Mom made sure our clothes were always clean, but our wardrobe was limited—I had a couple shirts and pants, and a pair of shoes. When my school called, it was not to talk about my grades or unexcused absences but to learn when the tuition check would arrive. To help out with the cost, I cleaned Mom's preschool at night. Unknown to my father I was traveling the three miles to school on an old motorbike that had been lying around the carport. I kept to the side streets while riding to school, so my classmates wouldn't see me and because I had no license to drive a motorbike. You might think this would be seen as cool, but my classmates' attitude seemed to be, "Look at her, she has no money, poor thing."

If one quality describes my life at this time, it was loneliness. Thank God for baseball, or I could have ended up somewhere bad. I had way too much energy, harbored no fear, and could not relate to anyone my own age. I wanted to be part of a group of friends to hang out with. That group became the team on the baseball diamond once again. Everything that was wrong in my life disappeared when I hit the field. No worries over being unpopular, liking girls instead of guys, or dealing with my family's drama—all I had to think about was what was going to get us a win. Away from the field, I took to wearing black, with Doc Marten–type boots. I went a little punk, with a pale face and my light-brown hair dyed dark. It sent the message that I wanted to be left alone, even though I really didn't.

As sophomore year began, Coach Caffrey seemed impressed that I had survived another summer of heated semipro competition, and he promoted me to the varsity team. I felt that he was pulling for me to do well. He worked me hard at first base, giving me lots of advice, almost as if I were his daughter. Hyper kid that I was, I kept to a daily routine that involved an eight- to ten-mile run and six light workouts with weights. My change-up had developed to the point where I could trust it, and when the season started, I was the number one pitcher.

I avoided the locker room, instead seeking out a nearby bathroom to change in. But that didn't mean I escaped the locker-room culture. Before the game we stretched on the field, and some of my teammates liked to test me by changing their jockstraps in front of me or throwing their cups nearby. They gave it up after a while, and I started to loosen up with them. After practice I sometimes took the position of catcher with some of our pitchers. I have good vision and could tell when their mechanics were off or when they were telegraphing their pitches. I started giving them pointers on putting spin and movement on the ball. Many coaches just say, "Get your hand on top of the ball," when that has nothing to do with it. Other pitchers on the team threw harder than I did, but they envied my control. So I also told them how I visualized my pitches when I was away from the field. One of our pitchers finally said, "God, I learn more from you than our coaches." I felt that too few players spent enough time on the mental aspect of the game—visualizing themselves being successful.

That season I had attention from one teammate that went beyond my pitching performance and coaching. When I'd eat alone outside, Jim would somehow find me and sit down. He was a nice guy, fit and kind of quiet, and I could tell he liked me. He introduced me to his friends. Other girls told me, "What a catch."

"Wow, he looks like Mel Gibson," Mom said.

Jim invited me to a couple of picnics on campus. One day we drove twenty miles down Beach Boulevard to Huntington Beach State Park. Other kids looked on while he flirted with me, but I had my eye on a girl. No matter how much I tried to like him, I couldn't get there. I'm sorry to admit that I dated Jim because it made me seem straight. Sometimes I looked around, hoping to find a girl interested in a romance with me, but the world at the time showed me no one. I decided I would rather be alone than a miserable phony.

Another reason for not wanting to get too close to Jim was my parents' arguments, which had spilled over from finances to just about everything. Sometimes when I got home from school, I'd stand at the door and listen for sounds of a fight. If it was quiet I knew it was safe to come in. Then I would jam into my room and hide. I couldn't imagine bringing a boyfriend into this mess. Jim kept calling, but I stopped returning his calls. I'm not proud I broke off our friendship that way—I just wish I could have been honest with him. About a year later I called to apologize, but he never called back.

My good luck with teachers who recognized I was a decent kid, just different, continued in high school. I spent a lot of time with them, getting academic help. Math and science were my strong subjects, English and languages not so much. "I stink at this," I complained to my English teacher. "I want to get better. Can you help me out?"

Over lunch, she worked closely with me. I admired her creativity and her kindness. Other teachers encouraged me to hang out in the science lab and the woodshop. I started to enjoy carpentry and learned how to use the tools. I was told I was good at it. While other kids sketched art, I was sketching houses. I brought home a report card that showed my GPA had risen to 3.5. I began to think I might be worthy of an academic scholarship to college.

Dad's response: "You're not giving enough time to baseball."

I came to believe that nothing would please him, and I sometimes avoided him, so he wouldn't bring me down. Meanwhile Coach Caffrey's decision to let me play varsity turned out to be a good one. He had scheduled me to be a spot reliever and a sometime starter. Developing a good sinker helped my effectiveness. By midseason, I had thrown a one-hitter and led the team in innings pitched. I was named Cal Hi Sports Athlete of the Week. I ended the season with a 5-2 record, a 2.07 ERA, and fifty-seven strikeouts. That summer I re-upped for a third season of semipro men's baseball.

For my junior year Steve Randall was now the head baseball coach. (Coach Caffrey still taught history but had retired from coaching.) Coach Randall had inherited only two returning players. Would we be able to stay competitive in the Olympic League this year? I was working on a circle change-up, which would successfully evolve into a screwball, and this new pitch added to my confidence. Any harassment I got was mostly from the girlfriends and parents of opposing players. After a game I'd go to my car and sometimes find flat tires that looked like they'd been cut with a knife. Our team's second baseman, Eric Willie, worked at a gas station and gave me a hand. Dad had trouble with the continuing catcalls from the spectators and began watching my games alone, standing near the right-field foul pole. "I had to get out of the stands," he said. "As a parent I had two choices: complain or step back. If I really tried to change those people it could end up in fist fights or hurt the chances for other girls to play baseball."

At school, the girls could be critical, too. Coach Randall thought their mixed reactions gave me the most trouble off the field. As he recalled, "Some really encouraged her while some thought, *What're you doing in a man's game? Or is it the publicity?* They questioned her motives—just as a lot of other coaches questioned my integrity. Was I playing her for the publicity? . . . We kept wondering when . . . the boys would overtake her in physical ability, but about junior year we realized she [had] the tools to make it."

After my years of semipro baseball, the doubts and criticism didn't faze me. It was the hitters I faced that tended to be fazed.

As our catcher, Brock Lumsford, observed to a reporter, "The hitters ask, 'Is that a chick out there?'

"I say, 'Yes, and you'd feel pretty dumb if she strikes you out.'"

Our left fielder, Chad Callahan, told a reporter that the "fear of striking out against a girl does work to [my] advantage. When they first see her, they say, 'Gosh, I can't strike out against a girl,' . . . It definitely has an effect."

I struck out a satisfying number of players that year and made the All-Olympic League first team. One day I was going to be late for practice. I blew my cover and, trailing my usual bag and mitt, rode my motorized dirt bike onto the field and parked by the dugout. My coach suggested that it wouldn't be a good idea to do that again—these bikes weren't legal to drive on the street. Dad also freaked out when someone told him about it. Time for a car, he decided. I got a 1976 turd-brown Toyota Corolla. The color embarrassed me, perhaps because I was sixteen.

By contrast, Mom was not ashamed to drive us kids all over town in her '85 Chevy truck. She was the coolest of moms. My brothers' and sister's friends always liked coming over because of her—they called her "Mom"—and our home often looked as messy as a frat house. When I forgot my mitt, which happened too often, she'd drive it over from the preschool. She was my comfort when things in baseball went bad. Though I never told her everything that went wrong, she somehow knew when things were tough and found a way to make me laugh or took me on a quick trip to the beach or the mall to get away. Much as I loved Mom, I was dying for a strong female role model. Madonna was someone I could look up to—a woman who did what she wanted, worked hard, stayed in killer shape, and made things happen. She inspired me not only to get into running, which I did whenever I wasn't working out or playing baseball, basketball, or golf, but also to stand up for myself. I played Madonna's music all the time.

Dad continued to mold me into a warrior. He taught me to change a tire on my car in ten minutes or less; change the oil; replace the fuses; sand, buff, and pinstripe a car; and jump-start the battery. I thank him for making me tough, handy, and independent. But his anger took its toll. To this day, someone can yell at me at the top of their lungs or try to humiliate me, and as the voice rises I tune them out. I was determined not to hate Dad—I wished him well—I just did not want to be angry like him.

The Heralds ended with a 4-11 record. Coach Randall said that my 3-4 win-loss record did not accurately reflect my performance, pointing out that in the four games I lost, the opposing team had scored three or fewer runs, and that I led the staff in strikeouts (thirty-nine), innings pitched (thirty-five and two-thirds), and complete games (four). My ERA was 3.25. He also appreciated that my fastball clocked at eighty-three to eighty-four miles per hour.

In the summer of 1992 the movie *A League of Their Own* came out. The director, Penny Marshall, had had trouble raising money for the film because Hollywood's financiers did not believe people would pay to see a story about women playing baseball in the 1940s. They were mistaken. The movie was one of the ten highest-grossing films of the year, and its popularity continues. You could say that the movie proved to have legs in an important way. When Leah and I went to see it, my first thought was, *Skirts? These women had to play in skirts?* Given my junior-high phobia about that piece of clothing, this aspect of the film was awful. But Dottie Hinson, the character played by Geena Davis, appealed to me. She was strong, the catcher who led the team. Yet she still had to fit that role of the all-American girl, the feminine wife of the husband away at war. I watched the story unfold, knowing I was never going to be that sort of person. I also envied the League's camaraderie, singing together a cappella as they traveled the Midwest from game to game. I'd had a taste of that closeness on the girls' basketball teams I'd played on and missed it.

As senior year began, I was still driving my brown Toyota Corolla but no longer worried much about my high school image. I was looking ahead to college. Steve Randall and Don Rounds coached varsity now, and I was the number one starter. In a telephone interview with my coauthor, Coach Randall recalled a tournament we played that year:

> The competition was tough, and opposing coaches did not want her to pitch. But she turned those guys upside down, pitching one of her best high school games. Sixth inning she got into trouble and loaded the bases. Then she struck out the side. We won, 5–3. And the way she walked off the mound, I knew then she was something special.

I finished the season with a 2.52 ERA and was named the team's MVP. Over four years of pitching at Whittier Christian, I had gone 16-7 over 147 innings, with a 2.31 ERA and 165 strikeouts.

When I was twelve years old a coach had asked Dad how far he thought I could go in baseball. Dad replied that it would be great if I could get a college scholarship.

"You've got to be kidding!" the coach said.

Dad always remembered that conversation. (We both knew I wouldn't be the first woman to play college baseball: in 1987 Susan Perabo played a game at second base for Webster College; two years later Julie Croteau played first base for St. Mary's College of Maryland.) During junior year, local community college coaches had started scouting me. During senior year, so did Jim Pigott, the head coach at Whittier College. Just as other students look for a good law school, business school, or medical school, I wanted a baseball scholarship at a Christian college where the players were seen by scouts in touch with organized baseball clubs. The school also had to be affordable. My parents had no money for college, which was not part of their thinking anyway. I would be the first person in our family to go to college.

Coach Rounds helped me organize my stats, told me how to write a letter, and suggested that I make a video. I showed him my drafts, and he edited them. I sent my package to twenty-five schools. Three colleges responded with "We want you": Bellevue University, a Christian school in Nebraska; Dordt College, in Iowa; and King University, in Tennessee, with ties to the Presbyterian Church. We heard from schools in California, too: Westmont College, a small Christian school in Santa Barbara; Cal Poly Pomona; Cal State Dominguez Hills; and nearby Cypress College, a two-year community college. Dad pushed me to stay in California so I could play baseball year-round, though I could've done that in the South, too.

On the night before Christmas Eve, I watched as a tall, handsome man walked up our driveway to the front door. My parents welcomed him into our living room, and we all sat down. He was Charlie Phillips, a crafty, rather than hard-throwing, left-hander who had played for the great coach Rod Dedeaux at the University of Southern California. After the Dodgers drafted him in 1976, Charlie spent the late 1970s in the minors. He was now the head baseball coach at Southern California College (scc), of the Golden State Conference, the National Association of Intercollegiate Athletics (naia), in Costa Mesa, about an hour's drive from our house. I had sent him a newspaper clipping from the *Orange County Register* about me. I didn't know that he had read it, had seen my high school stats, or had confided to his wife, Maiko, "I'm going to sign that kid someday. She's something special."

I fit Charlie's trio of requirements: interest in spirituality, good academics (a 3.3 GPA), and athletic talent. He told Dad he wanted to work on my mechanics and help me develop a split-fingered fastball. He wanted me to be a starting pitcher. Dad liked that during Charlie's four seasons at SCC nine players had signed with professional baseball clubs, among them the Blue Jays, the Cardinals, the Dodgers, and the Tigers, as well as a couple of independent league clubs. Charlie said that SCC was a great place to be seen by scouts. A big draw for me was that the SCC Vanguards also played division 1 teams of the National Collegiate Athletic Association (NCAA) like Cal Poly Pomona and that they had a preseason in the fall. To me, that meant plenty of baseball, plenty of time to improve. I saw in Charlie Phillips a good guy with baseball smarts. I saw my baseball savior.

Charlie explained that he had only seven scholarships to spread over twenty-one players. He offered a scholarship that would cover half of the $4,500 tuition, though not room and board. He told me what I could expect in the way of financial aid, schooling, and baseball. As we talked, I felt a huge burden lift. It seemed I had a place to go next September. It was far enough away from home that I could live on campus but close enough to home so I could keep in touch with Mom.

I asked about playing girls' basketball in college, too, a sport I enjoyed. But Charlie explained that it would be difficult to expect a baseball scholarship when I would have to miss most of the fall baseball pre-league games for basketball. My heart sank, because I truly wanted to play both. But with my main mission to play pro baseball, that settled it.

The letter of intent was on the table, and we read through it. Charlie could have vetoed the idea, but as he rose to leave he encouraged me to play girls' basketball during my last semester of high school. "Relax, live it up," he said. "Just don't get hurt."

When he left, he had my signed letter of intent.

Charlie had told us that he planned to tell his players about me before announcing it to the press. On February 4, 1993, I was getting ready to pitch when sportswriters from the *Los Angeles Times*, the *Orange County Register*, and the *Orange Coast Daily Pilot* crowded around me. Suddenly I was big news. One reporter asked whether I realized the impact my presence would have on the team. I hadn't thought much about it. I didn't know that when the news broke, some of Charlie's returning players told him how unhappy they were about the idea.

I took Charlie's advice and played one last season of girls' basketball. I was friends with Stephanie de la Corte, the team captain, and Denise Huizing, the co-captain. Both girls were motivated athletes, had boyfriends, and planned to excel in college. They did not seem to mind going out in my brown Toyota for ice cream after the games. I was excited to hang out with them. Denise was popular and told others to give me a chance, that I was fun and good-hearted. They did.

It helped that I had finally grown out of the awkward stage. My skin cleared up, my hair was soft, curly, and styled. I was getting pointers on how to dress. Guys started to notice and asked me out. I tried to be kind about saying no, using the line that I was saving myself for marriage. This seemed to make me even more appealing to them—though no one ever challenged me by asking how I expected to marry without first dating. I stopped sending "don't hang out with me" vibes and became more approachable. I was learning how to be a friend and to be smarter and not just punch my way through life. I read books on psychology, the power of positive thinking, and visualization. High school life greatly improved. Looking back, I could see how fearful I had been to reach out to others. Now I was learning that when I did communicate and didn't hide what was going on in my home life, I felt freer. Though I never told Denise I was gay.

At home things only got crazier. Dad and Hot Pants Lady were still together. Then a neighbor boy, who was a year older than my twelve-year-old brother Phillip, talked him into an adventure. They "borrowed" a Ford Thunderbird and drove it to San Francisco. Once there, they got scared and called the police with a story of being kidnapped. My parents got the call, and we all thought Dad would thrash Phillip. But by then Dad had mellowed somewhat—or just gotten tired—though he still held on to the threat of kicking us kids out of the house. We'd be living on the streets, he would warn. By senior year I didn't care anymore, because I had a place to go. When Dad's fights with Mom got too bad, I turned to Denise Huizing's family, who lived two blocks away. They took me in and gave me a safe place to sleep. I spent much of my senior year there. The only time I went back to my house was to see Mom and my sister and brothers. Denise's mom had grown up in a similar situation, and she understood. When I turned eighteen, she made me a birthday cake and we went out for ice cream. They were into academics and helped me study. They were Christians but not fundamentalists. I admired the kindness of their relationships and the way they showed their faith, rather than lecturing about it. Being with the Huizings gave me a self-confidence that carried into freshman year in college. Sometimes Denise and I went out and played basketball until midnight. We played at a Catholic school down the street that had lights. One night Coach Randall showed up and shot some hoops with us before saying, "Girls, you better go home—it's late."

In June 1993 Denise and I graduated from Whittier Christian High School. I had encouraged Denise to go for a basketball scholarship, and she wound up at Chapman College, just up the Costa Mesa Freeway from Southern California College. I graduated with honors and received the National Army Reserve Scholar/Athlete award. At our graduation ceremony at the Crystal Cathedral in Orange, I posed for the family photo, but to me it felt false, a pose to present the image of our perfect family. It was a relief to know I'd soon be getting away from the troubles at home. I spent the summer practicing my pitching skills. Dad worked with me on the screwball. He wanted me to be able to throw the ball in both directions. But he resisted teaching me the split-fingered fastball, which he said would take years to perfect until I would be able to throw it on a 3-2 count and know it was going exactly where I wanted it to go.

It's funny how adolescence goes. In a few short years my list of anxieties had shrunk. I had not just survived six years of boys' (as well as three summers of men's semipro) baseball but also had thrived in my chosen game. At age thirteen I had envied Janine Lindemulder and Jennie Finch for the easy path they chose in softball. But after Janine's mainstream film career faltered, she went a different way. In 1992 she starred in her first porn film, *Hidden Obsessions*. She would become well known in her new field, in part for her refusal to have on-screen sex with men, only women. Meanwhile Jennie Finch was developing into a well-known softball pitcher. In 1992 she led the California Cruisers to the twelve-and-under American Softball Association national championship. La Mirada High School was later delighted with her arrival on campus, where she went 50-12 with a 0.15 ERA during four years of varsity softball. It only got better: on scholarship at the University of Arizona, Jennie would lead the Wildcats to the 2001 NCAA championship and was named National Player of the Year. Playing for the USA softball team, she won Olympic gold in 2004 and silver in 2008. In 2011 she coauthored *Throw Like a Girl: How to Dream Big and Believe in Yourself*. The book's blurb says, "In a society that sends incredibly mixed identity messages, sports help preteen and teenage girls make the right choices. Athletic girls not only grow up to be healthier, they learn teamwork, gain self-confidence, and mature into society's leaders."

I think anything that helps a teenage girl gain self-confidence and discipline can shape them in a positive way and help keep them out of trouble. It can be playing a musical instrument, being on the debate team or student council, or playing sports. Playing baseball gave me strength of character: perseverance, determination, audacity, a good work ethic, and physical stamina. Yet I was also the odd one out because my dream was different from the norm. So often people—adults and friends—had said to me, "Take the easy road and play golf, softball, or basketball."

"Easy" in the sense it was considered normal for women to play these sports. Well, what about Babe Didrikson, the golfer? She was a renegade for her time—more of a renegade than I, at age eighteen, knew. Besides, I didn't want easy—why be afraid to step up and go after what you really want? And I wanted to play baseball. So I was called ugly, gay, and weird all through junior high and high school. Janine was called names, too, and some of the other girls on the softball team told her she would not amount to anything, and ultimately she took a different path. I made it through because I believed there was a God out there who loved me unconditionally. Jennie was the girl next door and fit the American girl profile. I was the opposite of that.

Looking back at Janine's and Jennie's and my paths, I have to wonder how responsible we are for our passions. Do we choose them, or do they somehow find us? Maybe we're only responsible for how we deal with our passions. For people like Jennie Finch, the choice is a comfortable fit that's acceptable within society's norms. I envy her that. For others, like Janine Lindemulder, the choice takes you down a whole other path. And for some people, like me, it's a continuing battle for the freedom to do what you love.

On my way out the door toward college, I knew that my decision to stick with baseball may have been difficult but was the right one for me. I was deeply grateful that my faith in God had kept me together through the uncertain times of the past few years. Now if I could just do something about being gay.

3

COLLEGE
Pitching through Adversity

GAME DAY: THIRD INNING. The Dukes have two outs in the top of the third when Luis Brito and Chris Schmitz both single. But Anthony Lewis flies out, and the score remains 1–0 when I take the mound. The number eight and nine hitters come up this inning, and I tell myself to go after them and keep the ball down. Keep them off the bases for when the big guys come up again. One batter at a time, one out at a time.

It's said that the difference between a pitcher's success in major league baseball versus that in the minors has less to do with talent than with consistency and keeping your team in the game, even when you don't have your best stuff. Every game day is different. Tonight is one of those times when I'm hitting my spots and my stuff is moving. Right now I'm so in tune with the ball in my hand that I can, in the instant before I release my pitch, add a last bit of pressure for even more spin. To sum it up, I feel great. So I step on the mound, peer in at Javier, and tell myself, *Throw the hell out of this ball, Ila.*

The first batter, center fielder David Francisco, has been hot lately— 11-for-24. He bounces a grounder to our shortstop, Luis Brito. But Luis bobbles it, and then, trying to make up for lost time, throws it away. *Oh, shit.* A pitcher's feelings about errors in the field behind him vary with the situation. Most pitchers will publicly say that it's no big deal, that it doesn't affect them, but sometimes it does. If the batter is a slow runner, no big deal; if he is a power hitter, no big deal; but the number eight hitter with wheels, with the top of the lineup coming up and a two-run lead over the first-place team—that is a big deal. I need to keep Francisco close and get a ground ball. I knew I had very few mistakes, if any, to make with Fargo. So this error was of the "Oh, shit," variety but not a national tragedy. The ground ball misplayed by Boston Red Sox first baseman Bill Buckner late in Game Six of the 1986 World Series, taking with it the team's chance at its first World Series championship since 1918—for Red Sox Nation, that was a national tragedy.

With a runner on first, I pitch out of my stretch, rather than a full windup. Francisco is fast, though not as disciplined a runner as others, and I know he's going to try to steal. Tim Fortugno's name flashes through my mind. During freshman year in college, Tim, then pitching for the Cincinnati Reds, taught me an effective pickoff move. Successfully picking off a runner takes the pressure off the catcher and lets the air right out of a potential rally. And it makes the pitcher feel terrific.

Bless you, Tim, I think, as I come to the balance point in my stretch. I step off the rubber and hurl the ball to first base. But Francisco's bolted for second. Plenty of time for the first baseman to throw to second— he'll be out by a mile. Anthony Lewis, who's filling in for the suspended Canseco, doesn't cover, and the throw plunks the runner in the back of the head. Luckily the ball doesn't roll far, and Francisco stays at second.

Fuck all over again. Light-hitting Cory Smith walks to the plate and looks to the third base coach for the sign—he's likely to call for a bunt to advance Francisco to third. I throw a fastball inside and it's a hit-and-run play action. Smith hits a grounder to shortstop for the out at first, but Francisco has indeed advanced to third. Okay, one out, and it's still 1–0.

Chad Akers come to the plate again—last time he had an infield single, so I think, *Keep it low for another ground ball and give my fielders a chance.* Our manager, George Mitterwald, calls time and comes out to the mound, along with our third baseman, Chris Briller, and shortstop, Brito. George tells Briller to stay close to third and remain even with the bag in case they try a suicide squeeze. Brito is to play his normal position and toward third. We need outs right now. We all nod seriously—we know we need outs—and return to our positions.

I deliver a screwball and Akers hits a grounder to shortstop. I hold my breath as Brito comes up firing to Anthony Lewis at first. His throw beats Akers—two outs now—but Brito forgets to check and hold Francisco at third. As Francisco digs for the plate, Anthony throws home. It's going to be close. Javier blocks the plate, and Francisco collides with him. The home plate umpire jerks his thumb up and yells, "You're out!" No runs, no hits, one error, no one left on base.

Holy shit, yes! Javier and I slap a high five. He is jacked, I am jacked: third out at home with the number two hitter coming up—a beautiful thing. The guys coming off the field go nuts, yelling, "Yeah, come on . . . Let's do this now . . . Ila needs some run support."

As I was finishing college and hoping for a call from Organized Baseball, Dad had told me the consensus was that it would create dissension or be a distraction among the other players if I went to spring training camp for a shot with an affiliated team. As you can see by *Moneyball*, the film about the Oakland A's general manager Billy Beane's fight to change player evaluation, baseball is not often a game open to change, though when it is, it's usually great—remember Jackie Robinson. Now, here I am, pitching for another win, and the guys are playing their asses off. It has kind of worked the reverse of how Organized Baseball thought it would go down. Here it seems the guys are playing even harder behind me. The problem was that the decision makers didn't know me; the players on the Dukes do. Day by day, they know I'm out to win, just like they are.

Returning to the bench, I stare out on the field, concentrate on controlling my breaths, and try to relax with positive thoughts: the Dukes are winners. I look around at my teammates and think how different this is from college, when some of my teammates hated the very idea of me being on the field.

SEPTEMBER 1993, COSTA MESA, CALIFORNIA. As soon as I stepped on the campus of Southern California College (SCC), I could smell the ocean—it was a ten-minute drive to Balboa Peninsula or Huntington Beach, and that meant surfing. The school's nine hundred students are screened from the rush of traffic on the nearby Costa Mesa Freeway by the tree-shaded campus. I headed directly to Vanguard Field, where I inhaled the scent of freshly cut grass and scuffed the rich red dirt of the infield. This field meant a fresh start, an escape from the teenaged angst of high school and the anxieties that continued to boil through our family. Just as I was getting ready to leave for college, my sister Leah, realizing that she would now be the point person for our father's discipline, had run away from home. Well, so had I, just in a different way.

This campus attracted me in other ways, too. I had grown up learning about the world through the books I read. Here, away from the distractions of life beyond the campus, I would be surrounded by knowledge. I looked forward to the challenge of digging deeper into the mysteries of this world and the people in it. I also appreciated that this college, with its ties to the Assemblies of God Church, was far from the secular world of beer and frat parties. Curfew was midnight; attendance was taken at the mandatory Wednesday afternoon chapel. The school objective was to foster in its students a "[Holy] Spirit-empowered life of Christ-centered leadership and service." That was my goal, too. I wanted to be a Christian role model for the baseball-playing girls behind me. True, there was that problem with liking women rather than men, but at this point in my life I was well practiced in telling God what I wanted Him to do and prayed regularly that He would set me straight. I put my faith in Philippians 4:13: "I can do all things through Christ who strengthens me."

It was encouraging to learn that scc was a member of the National Association of Intercollegiate Athletics (naia), an early leader in granting collegiate scholarships to women. Now I was the first woman to hold a baseball scholarship, though a partial one. The school was a member of the Golden State Athletic Conference, made up of Christian schools, whose code holds that "opponents are our guests," umpires' "honesty and integrity are never questioned," and "an outstanding play deserves a hand—regardless of who made it."

I had to wonder, though, whether these standards would survive the heat of a ball game. Pentecostal churches like the Assemblies of God preach that women must be subservient to men. I had been raised on hard-nosed Bible verses like I Timothy 2:12: "I do not permit a woman to teach or to have authority over a man." How would a school with these values support a woman playing hardball? After all, a pitcher carries much of the responsibility for how the game goes, though I feared that some would cite this verse no matter which position I played on the field. Besides, what if they found out that I was gay? *Pray harder,* I told myself.

I also hoped to make some friends. That wish began to come true on my introductory tour of the campus. As we approached the immaculately kept softball field, I saw some girls playing catch. It looked like a pickup game was about to start. "Let me grab my mitt from the car," I said to my guide. "I'd like to play." And I left the tour.

I took ground balls and fly balls, hit ground balls and fly balls, and fed balls into the pitching machine for batting practice. I took some swings. These girls were good—the softball team was favored to win the World Series of the NAIA that year. *At last,* I thought, *sports-minded girls like me, who want to have a good time playing ball, not just go out partying.* I hit it off with everyone. For the first time in my teenaged life I began to develop a circle of friends and, with it, experienced a happy dose of the carefree adolescence I had mostly missed. Because preseason baseball did not involve travel I had plenty of time to chill with the girls I had met. We would go together to the basketball and soccer games and to movies, or hang out in the dorm and play cards. One friend helped me develop better study skills and taught me how to use the computer. (In 1994, like many of the other students, I did not own a personal computer, but the dorm had two computers that everyone could use). She also got me a job where she worked. Sometimes we went over to her parents' place for a home-cooked meal. For spring semester I found two roommates to live with in the dorm that looked out to the baseball field.

Preseason baseball began the last week of September. I had come to college with a two-seam and a four-seam fastball, a curve, and an underdeveloped cut fastball. I knew I needed to develop new ways of getting batters out. Coach Phillips noticed my long fingers and showed me the split-finger, though I struggled with it—it is a pitch better suited to guys who throw ninety miles per hour or faster. Throwing the split-finger also bothered my elbow. Charlie differed from Dad in his philosophy on pitching, but I was there to pick up new skills. Charlie liked my split-finger pitch, but it never did work for me—whenever I threw it, they hit it. It would take a few years to find the out pitch that I needed for pro ball, the straight change screwball.

There was more to learn in other ways, too. During an early intersquad practice, I stood on the mound, peering in for the sign, even though I knew what I wanted to throw. I had felt good in the bullpen and was confident. Yet with every ball I threw, I was getting rocked; and the batters were laying off some really good pitches. Maybe I was tipping my pitches.

Finally our catcher, David Seeley, came out to the mound and said, "Had enough?"

"I don't know what I'm doing wrong," I complained. "I feel good, I'm hitting my spots, and I have good movement on the ball . . ."

"Stop shaking me off, and then see if they hit the ball."

"What?"

"I've been telling them what was coming every time," David explained from his lofty position as senior. "Now quit shaking me off, freshman, and they won't hit it anymore."

I was ticked. David had pulled a time-honored catcher's trick on an independent-thinking pitcher. (In Ron Shelton's film of 1988, *Bull Durham*, Crash Davis will pull it on the rookie Nuke LaLoosh.) But I had always thrown my own game and did not want to live and die by my catcher. If I was going to go down, I wanted it to be because of my mistakes, not his. Sometimes I had to throw backwards, like a knuckle-ball pitcher, because I threw only seventy-eight to eighty miles per hour. Not a lot of catchers got that—they tended to make the same calls for every pitcher. We had a pitcher named Rick Homutoff who threw ninety miles per hour. Of course, he should throw lots of fastballs. Whenever he threw change-ups, he got ripped. Plus, I did not trust David. He was a senior trying to make a point and was also friendly with some of the guys who were giving me a hard time. But for the rest of that game, I threw the pitches he wanted and did much better.

After practice was over, I said to David, "You know a lot of the hitters in the league, and I trust your judgment. But sometimes I just feel more comfortable throwing certain pitches at certain times, like using my curve on a 3-2 count, bases-loaded situation. I explained that I was there to win baseball games, get my degree, and make it to the pros. I knew he just wanted to get his degree and become a cop. That season we would go on to develop a better relationship, but whenever he thought he was not in control he tipped my pitches. Still, there were times when I stubbornly shook him off. Then he would come out to the mound, and I would say, "Have faith in me."

I held my own in the preseason games against local community colleges, giving up four runs and going 2-0 in eighteen innings. In December we played the alumni game. Pitcher Tim Fortugno of the Cincinnati Reds, the only scc alumnus to make it to the majors, was on the field. Most of my coaches had been right-handed, but Tim was a lefty. He worked patiently with me, showing the nuances of using my fingertips for spin. His greatest gift was in teaching me how to take advantage of my left-handedness to perfect a good pick-off move to first base. He wanted me to feel like if someone got on first, I still had a chance to get him out. So he taught me to know my running counts, know my runners: do they go on first movement, or do they wait a bit, stay close but inch forward slowly? He coached me on finding my balance point, making a good slide step, and understanding the importance of fast feet. Switching up the cadence was the most important, and close to that was not giving away to the runner any clues about where you were going until the last minute. I practiced these skills for fifteen or twenty minutes a day on the ball field. Even in my dorm room, I would have my roommates pretend they were base runners and test my pickoff move. I still have Fortugno's autographed photo: "To Ila, It's been a pleasure working with you! Remember, focus on the glove, throw in a downhill plane. Success will follow! Your friend, Tim . . . Phil. 4:13."

I liked the way Charlie Phillips handled our team. He was not hierarchical. On the field we called him "Coach Phillips," but off the field it was "Charlie." From the beginning of workouts, I had thought I was getting along pretty well with my teammates. I didn't know about the heated meetings he was holding with some of them, or that a few of the returning players had told Coach Phillips they would rather quit than play with a woman. Charlie said he warned them, "If you can't put up with this, you won't be here."

To which one senior reportedly replied, "Thank God I won't be here."

Another player said, "We'll beat her out, so it doesn't matter."

As for players who worried how I would affect the clubhouse chemistry, Charlie pointed out, "We don't have a clubhouse, so it doesn't matter. And Ila uses the equipment shed to change into her uniform."

During intrasquad games our pitchers sometimes threw inside to me, and I got hit a number of times. I also remember getting hit by pitches a number of times by our opponents in preseason games, but here's where Charlie's and my memories disagree. He maintains he used designated hitters during those games. I had hoped to play first base on days I didn't pitch, but although Charlie liked my swing and I had been competitive in a home run derby, he had little room for pitchers to play positions on days we didn't pitch—too many position players on scholarship to fill those spots. I was disappointed because I had always enjoyed coming to bat.

And then Coach Phillips announced that I would start the home opener. Traditionally this honor went to a veteran. Our ace, Jeff Beckley, was a junior and looking to go pro—no surprise that he expected to start. In my opinion he was also the biggest ass on the team. Jeff made a huge stink about me starting and rallied some of the other guys against me. I was just doing what I was told, but I could tell there were bad feelings about it. From what I could tell, Charlie did nothing to stop the plague from spreading. Charlie says that he knew Beckley resented the attention I was getting and discussed Beckley's attitude with him many times. I think that Charlie got caught up in the drama of a woman starting a college baseball game, though I was not the first—in 1990 Jodi Haller had started in two games for St. Vincent's College in Latrobe, Pennsylvania. But if I won, history would be made. Oh, I was going to win. My confidence in this was solid. The night before the game, I stood at the window of our dorm room. The diamond below was quiet and dark. I imagined myself on the mound the next day going the entire game for a win. Too excited to sleep, I stayed up most of the night playing cards.

FEBRUARY 15, 1994. The campus of SCC is a frenzied blur. Reporters and sportscasters from the *Sporting News*, *Sports Illustrated*, the *Los Angeles Times*, CNN, ESPN, WABC, WCBS, WNBC, Fox Sports, and a television crew from Tokyo, Japan, crowd the sidelines, their cameras focused on my every move. I stare past them, refusing to speak to the press until the game is over. My classmates mill around the sidelines in "Jammin' for Jesus" T-shirts and caps that read "In the Beginning God." The bleachers, where a couple dozen friends and family of the team usually sit, overflow with hundreds of spectators. A crew from the nearby Costa Mesa Fire Department is here, as are some of my professors, Tim Fortugno, and Alyse Isaac, my friend since second grade. Construction workers in the scaffolding of the new dorm building pause when I step onto the mound. As usual Dad paces alone down the right-field line, cigarette in hand. So they tell me. Right now I see only the field. I'll be pitching on pure adrenaline.

I take a deep breath, exhale, and stare at the first batter. If I face pressure, so do the Claremont-Mudd Stags—what if they cannot hit me? After Gabe Rosenthal flies out to center field, he angrily spikes his bat, which bounces up out of the dirt and hits his teammate in the on-deck circle. No damage done, though, except to Rosenthal's ego. The next few batters go down in order. So far so good; my focus is the best it has ever been.

Early on my teammates behind me are edgy—our third baseman, Brian Penner, makes an error. We are in a pitchers' duel and every out counts. Then, suddenly, in the bottom of the third, we break loose with eight runs.

"Hey," yells a classmate in the stands to the opposing Stags. "Maybe you should put a chick in there."

Pitching with a big lead in a game is like going out on the town with a bunch of cash in your jeans—you get to make choices. I keep a good rhythm going: mixing my pitches, changing speeds, and working the corners.

Top of the fourth, with two on and two out, Jake Schwarz becomes my first strikeout victim. Meanwhile, my teammates add insurance runs. I hear the crowd cheering, though at a distance. I'm in the zone, that blessed state of centeredness, a gift granted by whatever gods you believe are in charge of these things. For me that's Jesus, and right now I feel His presence all around me. I pray for strength, wisdom, and peace of mind, and feel His calming smile.

In the stands, I later learn, Alyse Isaac relaxes as she chats with a spectator, Jean Ardell, who years later will become my coauthor.

"This is what makes Ila happy," Alyse tells her, explaining that for me the game has always come first.

"Is Ila always this self-contained?"

"She's smarter than a lot of us," says Alyse. "She's always sensed when to be open and who she can trust."

A grandmotherly woman in a red hat nods. "She's a cool one, that Ila."

My teammates pick up the emotion in the stands. In the eighth a solo home run ruins the shutout, and I give up two walks. I throw thirty-two pitches before getting the third out of the inning.

Coach Phillips wants to pull me, get me a standing ovation and a graceful exit.

"How do you feel?" he asks. "Whaddya think, honestly?"

"I feel fine," I lie. I want a complete game, a clean finish. I want all twenty-seven outs.

"Tell you what," he says. "If you can get the first hitter, you can finish the game."

Bottom of the ninth, and the spectators hang on every pitch.

"Go girl! . . . Put it over, babe!"

I try: after a ground out to short for the first out, I turn to my sinker and get two more ground outs. With that our 12–1 victory goes into the record books: first complete college game pitched by a woman; first college game won by a woman.

When the game ends, it is like the mute button in my head has been released, and I become conscious of my place in this: 104 pitches; one run;

five hits; three walks; two strikeouts; 1.00 ERA. My teammates baptize me with ice water. Our catcher, David Seeley, looks pleased.

"We were on a really good page today," he tells a reporter. "She stuck with the pitches I called, except for maybe three times."

As I stand on second base and look out at the mass of reporters on the outfield grass, I see a bouquet of microphones thrust in my face. My future coauthor is in the crowd, and I like the questions she asks. Not the usual "What's a woman doing in a man's game?" Later she will tell me that she was never more aware of the impact of my playing men's baseball than when she stepped across the foul line to join the scrum of interviewers—as a woman she even felt a resistance in the air to crossing that line.

"I was confident, happy, in shape, superaggressive, and excited," I say to the assorted reporters. "It was weird. I could hardly hear anyone off the field—it was as if I had gone deaf and was in tune only with my head and body. All I saw was David signaling pitches and the infielders telling me who had what base."

The next morning sportswriter Mike Penner will declare in the *Los Angeles Times*, "Winning pitcher: Borders (1-0). That's what it will say in the box score, now and forever, a simple notation that will stand as one of the greater understatements of our time."

After winning that first game, I figured the novelty of my presence on the mound would fade. But that week Pat Guillen, our sports information director, fielded seventy-five to eighty interview requests. The athletic department's secretary took more than 160 phone calls. Jay Leno's *Tonight Show* called one morning. David Letterman's staff called in the afternoon. ESPN2 arrived on campus for a live interview. *Good Morning America* and KABC radio did phone interviews. Paramount Pictures called. It seemed like I was in the local papers every day. Headline writers had a good time with my last name, finding all sorts of ways to play with the idea of the gender border I was crossing. Richard Dunn, of the *Orange Coast Daily Pilot*, kept regular tabs on me in his sidebar "Border(s) lines."

The *Los Angeles Times* called the frenzy "Ila-mania."

Being on an athletic scholarship, I felt obligated to cooperate. I asked the athletic department to not schedule interviews during practice, but sometimes they did. I began missing meals and struggled with my studies. After giving up three hits and an unearned run in another win, it all caught up with me. I pitched seven innings against the University of California San Diego (UCSD), eighth-ranked in Division III of the NCAA. The team's players were a raucous, name-calling bunch. "Their players were very abusive," Pat Guillen told the *Orange County Register*. "They were calling Ila names and using profanities throughout the game."

But it had been no different at our NAIA games, despite its code of ethics. Charlie recalls the worst he heard was at Christ College (now Concordia), a Lutheran school in Irvine. "We had beaten them twice and their players were all over her: 'Didn't know a pussy could throw a ball. Whose cock did you suck to get the chance? Your boyfriend hates you for trying to be a man.' 'Cunt' was used a lot. This was a Christian school?"

In our game against UCSD I threw 109 pitches, giving up four earned runs and six hits in a 4–3 loss. Afterward Dad intervened and cut the number of interviews. His position to the press: "You saw her pitch Friday—no arm strength. She's worn out. If she doesn't get some rest, she's not going to be effective, and she'll be off the team. And if she doesn't get her grades, she'll be out of school. Then there'll be no story for anyone."

But the campus still buzzed. Charlie, my cool and supportive coach, seemed to be enjoying it all, though I didn't know at the time that he too was overwhelmed. He remembers walking onto campus the day after our 12–1 win and seeing the story all over the sports pages of the local newspapers. "Media-wise I was shocked," he said. "Later, with all the interviews, phone calls, et cetera . . . who would have thought?" He recalled listening to the radio one morning as he drove to school and was surprised to hear a local broadcaster named Charlie Tuna announce an interview with himself and me scheduled for 8 a.m. that day. We did the interview live on the school intercom so the rest of the students could hear. On the road, Charlie remembers arriving at the hotel and finding twenty requests for interviews: "I would call Ila and say, 'Pick one or two.' . . . We tried to cut down media stuff and limit things for her, both Pat Guillen, the SID, and myself, but Ila would at times bite off more than she could handle. She was young then. . . . It was crazy, but we all tried to keep it under control."

Charlie thinks the pressure of those days affected his marriage, which later ended in a divorce. "I'd come home at eight o'clock, and my wife would have a fistful of phone messages from all over the country."

If Charlie was affected by the intensity of the press coverage, so was I. The media attention during my prep years had been local and fairly benign. Now there was nowhere to hide. Maybe if I had been out of the closet, I would have handled the media attention better. I thought of Roger Maris, the New York Yankees right fielder whose successful pursuit of Babe Ruth's home run record in 1961 had evoked an insane level of national media attention. No wonder his hair started falling out from the stress.

Ila-mania also introduced me to journalistic dishonesty. One sports-caster reported that for my historic first game all of my teammates had worn adjustable caps in support of me rather than the traditional fitted caps. It is an important distinction. Adjustable caps are for Little Leaguers, fans, and wannabe ballplayers. Fitted caps are the professional standard, the serious cap. In high school, I always wore a fitted cap, cutting a hole in the back to accommodate my ponytail. The claim that my teammates wore the adjustable cap in solidarity for my ponytail problem was untrue. The truth was that our shipment of fitted caps had not arrived in time for the game, so we wore what we had. When the fitted caps arrived, I cut a hole in the back for my ponytail, as I always did. No big deal. But to this day, people believe that the Vanguards wore adjustable hats for me—they've seen the clip on YouTube.

When I first learned of this account, I naïvely thought, *How can sports-writers make up anything they want and say it's true?* It drove me nuts. Rumors spread that Whitey Ford—*Whitey Ford*, the ace of the New York Yankees pitching staff during the 1950s—called, claiming he had seen a

TV segment of my pitching and had spotted a flaw in my technique: it was my habit to keep my index finger out of the mitt. It turned out that Ford had indeed left a detailed message with Pat Guillen's office, urging me to keep my finger inside the glove to avoid a broken bone.

I saw that some in the media worked hard to do their jobs well. Richard Dunn, who covered sports for the *Orange Coast Daily Pilot*, was one. And I remember talking a lot with Mike Penner of the *Times*, as he wrote regular updates on my season. Penner seemed to understand my side of things and always tried to get the details of his stories correct. And then there was former major league catcher Joe Garagiola Sr., the childhood pal of Hall of Famer Yogi Berra. Joe's interview on March 17 for NBC's *Today Show* was a blast. Joe, known for his humor, wanted to know the weirdest question I'd been asked by a journalist. My answer: Did I wear a cup or a jockstrap? But Joe's questions were primarily about baseball. He had me throw him a few pitches—he cut his finger on one. Afterward, he said, "You have what it takes, you have good stuff. Don't let anybody tell you that you need to throw the ball harder." Then he gave me his business card and said to call if I needed anything. Wow, that was my first interview with an ex–major leaguer who thought I had a shot.

If a woman plays hardball, people figure she's likely gay. Despite the values espoused by the NAIA, opposing players and their fans often told me so. "The [t]aunts are vicious and vulgar, laced with profanity and sexual innuendo," *Sports Illustrated* reported. "In sum, ignorance surrounds 19-year-old Borders."

The ignorance, though, was not limited to irate fans or ballplayers, many of whom like to attack whatever chink they can find in your facade. Some interviewers pursued me about the boys in my life, who I was dating.

"Are you a lesbian?" a New York radio interviewer asked point blank.

I wasn't ready for that question.

"No," I replied. "I like men and I love baseball."

For Richard Dunn's "Borders(s) lines," I elaborated, explaining that "I want people to know that I'm still feminine." I wanted to send the message that I liked dating guys.

Well, journalistic dishonesty has two sides.

I could not understand why reporters dragged sex into the conversation when I was there to talk baseball. I usually tried to bring an interviewer back to the game. People have a certain image of what a lesbian looks like, and with my long hair, I did not fit the stereotype, so reporters dutifully wrote that I was straight. I conspired in this, wanting to present myself as a good straight role model, despite knowing that I could never live up to that image. I also regret that I was deeply ignorant of my small place in the history of women athletes and the whole gay rights movement. The very year I entered college, *SportsDykes: Stories from on and off the Field* was published. It was an anthology filled with information written for someone like me. I wish I had found it. Had I read it, I would have learned that I was not alone. I would have learned from Betty Hicks's essay "Lesbian Athletes" that "a major portion of lesbian athletes' fortitude and energies must be directed toward maintaining straight façades." And that "women athletes are perpetual targets of homophobic attack, most of it from straight males." And these comments by Lynn Rosellini, in her essay, "The Lesbian Label Haunts Women Athletes": "To most lesbian athletes . . . coming out is not yet worth it."

To this day I beat myself up over my ignorance and my falseness. But back then I was not ready to speak the truth, and I remain certain that my professional career would not have been possible had I come out. In 1994 few in baseball—or in the country—were ready to accept a gay player, male or female.

The rest of spring semester was a blur of people and events that spun me around, faster and faster. I threw out the first pitch for the California Angels in Anaheim and did the same for the Los Angeles Dodgers. On May 30, I flew up to San Francisco as the guest of Dusty Baker, the manager of the San Francisco Giants. Dusty had heard the tale of my seeing him hit a home run at Dodger Stadium and invited me throw out the first pitch of the game against the Atlanta Braves at Candlestick Park.

Barry Bonds came over to talk with me about workouts: Was I lifting? he wanted to know. He gave me his phone number, with an offer to help. I became a fan of Bonds that day and remain one, despite his later fall from grace over performance-enhancing drugs. I shook hands with the Braves pitcher Greg Maddux and met the team's first baseman, David Justice, and his wife, the actress Halle Berry. Fun stuff but not exactly in the rhythm of ordinary campus life. That rhythm was gone. With no gates or security guards, the campus was open to anyone who wanted to visit. Occasionally strangers would pound on my dorm room door to say, "Hi, please sign my ball."

A bus full of Japanese tourists stopped by to visit Vanguard Field, see my dorm room, and meet me. One afternoon a stranger came up to me at lunch in the cafeteria and snapped my picture. Sitting in the auditorium for my general psychology class, I would see professional photographers making their way up to my row for a quick snapshot. At first my professor thought it was pretty cool, but when it kept interrupting our class it became not so cool. I was mortified. Some of the encounters were good, though. At practice one afternoon, I almost collided with a man who had bent to pick up a baseball that had rolled off the field. He scooped up the ball, looked up at me, and said, "Ila! It's you! I'm a fan of yours. Good luck!"

This fan was an actor named George Gerder, who had appeared in Lee Blessing's play *Cobb*, about Hall of Famer third baseman Ty Cobb. Gerder, a huge baseball fan, drove down from Los Angeles on the days I pitched.

With little privacy left on campus, surfing became my release from the pressure. On my board in the Pacific, I could be alone. The waves challenged me, washing away some of the anxiety, and I found peace in the water. Sometimes spectators followed me there, and I would look at them on the beach, cameras in hand, and think, *Take pictures all you want, but out here you cannot get to me.*

With the intense attention, my newly discovered sense of freedom evaporated. One night six of us met for a study session for English class when the media showed up. I know my friends felt uncomfortable about this, and it made me feel disconnected from them. I felt the old loneliness returning and began to revert to the aloof, stone-faced girl I had been in high school. Despite being raised in an abusive home, I was at heart a fun-loving kid, but the fun was fading. I wished for a protector, but Charlie seemed to be on a media high, so I did not feel like I could go to him for help. And Dad would just tell me to stop being a wuss or tell me to quit, so I never told him how bad it got. Dad had taught me to control my emotions. This worked great for baseball, and I felt like I could do anything in life because I had confidence in my body and brain. But I had trouble with female friendships. I didn't want to talk about my emotions, or cry, or go out to dinner and talk—I wanted to go hit a bucket of golf balls and have a beer afterward. If I wanted my emotional stuff fixed, I took it to God.

That spring I heard about the all-female baseball team, the Colorado Silver Bullets. A man named Bob Hope (not the comedian) had gathered a team of mostly softball players sponsored by the Coors Brewing Company, in Golden, Colorado. Under the coaching of Phil Niekro, the Silver Bullets had begun playing men's college, semipro, and minor league teams across the country. They played their first game on Mother's Day. My reaction was dismay. Their sponsor was Coors Lite beer, and their level of play felt like baseball-lite. Here were mostly softball players trying to play hardball. I would have felt the same if I had tried to switch from baseball to softball.

One day as I walked on campus, I saw her. For reasons that will become clear, I have changed her identity. "Shelley" wore her black hair long, had piercing blue eyes, stood about five feet eight, and was skinny. She did not look like she belonged at scc—she looked like she belonged in a rock band. I had never met anyone quite like her. I knew right away I wanted to get to know her better. I also knew I wanted more than friendship with her.

The attitude toward homosexuality at scc was curious. Everyone had been raised to believe that it was wrong, but I do not recall hearing it discussed in chapel or in class. Yet it was whispered that in our midst were gay coaches, instructors, and students. Things operated in a "Don't Ask, Don't Tell" sort of way. As Shelley and I spent more time together, I was careful not to outwardly show my attraction to her. Even so, rumors began to spread that we were lesbians. The fact that I was at a Christian school did not protect me from the snarkiness of other girls. I noticed that some Christian girls had a tendency to focus on the appearance of how godly they were, rather than the reality of who they truly were. I started to see that Christians didn't have the lock on good works and that the good works I saw done by secular people sometimes seemed more genuine, as they came from the heart rather than a desire to look good. I managed to avoid some of the girls' accusations, because I was also spending a lot of time with the guys on the team, but the snarky girls gave Shelley a hard time and told her to dump me.

"They're just jealous," I told her. To others I said, "God forbid you have two people of the same gender who get along, have a good time, and enjoy each other's company. It doesn't have to be sexual."

But deep down I knew I was in love for the first time and that I was loved back. I also feared that nothing would come of it. We talked it out, over and over. Our conversations showed how young we were.

"I love you."

"I love you, too."

"If you were a boy I would marry you in a second," Shelley would say. "But I can't. I want marriage and a family—and not to live that life."

I had never felt this way before and was not thinking straight. "Why can't you just wait for me? I'll find a way to make some money—and then I would give up everything for you."

"Maybe you could dress like a guy," Shelley suggested. "Then we could be together and no one would know."

But she was torn. If we did not have to worry about going to jail for being gay, as in Victorian times, we knew we could lose everything if we gave in to our feelings—our families would disown us; I could be kicked off the team; heck, we could be kicked out of college. Yet, there it was: love. We held each other close and Shelley would kiss me on the cheek, but that is as far as we ever went. Our physical attraction was painfully real, but we never acted on it—we both were too scared.

As the season got under way, another problem arose. The guys I played against had always given me flak; now some of my teammates began to do it. They resented all the media coverage coming my way. (I agreed and wished that things could be handled like Coach Rolland Esslinger had in junior high.) Rick Homutoff tried to mediate. He clued me in that two of our teammates did not believe it was biblical for women to be on the field. I know he told the guys to give me a break. Then Charlie broke the tradition that freshmen pitchers don't start conference games. True, he was out of available starters that day, but some of my teammates held it against me. (I went six innings that day, giving up three runs, two earned, seven hits, and three walks). What also concerned me was that our assistant coach, Jim Kale, was close with Jeff Beckley, our jackass ace, and I sensed that Kale was less than happy with my being on the team. During pitchers fielding practice, Beckley would hit the ball as hard as he could at me. (This practice covers moving your feet, covering first base, and following the track of the ball.) When I shagged balls in the outfield—whoever was pitching the next day shagged balls—and turned to put them in the bucket, Beckley sometimes nailed me in the back with balls thrown as hard as he could. Charlie's memory differs somewhat. "I remember guys throwing at her, but they all did it to her when we took batting practice and the shagging pitcher was behind a screen from the hitters, and players would throw balls like it was hockey. I would assume guys threw more at her to see if she could handle it and see how tough she was. If it was during a drill I would have run all of them until they threw up. I did not tolerate people messing around during fundamentals."

But I don't think Charlie was aware of a lot of the stuff that went on. And I was convinced Beckley had it in for me.

Dad recalls standing alone near the right-field fence one afternoon when a ball whizzed by his ear. He turned and looked around: Beckley, who was warming up nearby in the bullpen, grinned sheepishly and shrugged. Dad walked up to him and began a one-sided conversation that went something like this:

> "You can throw at my daughter—she can take care of herself. You can throw at me—I can take care of myself, too. But I'm six-two, two-forty. So the next time you want to buzz me? I'll take the ball and shove it down your throat so far you'll be shitting baseballs for a week. Got it?" Beckley got it. He never threw at me again, but it didn't stop him from going after Ila. . . . Do we hold Beckley accountable for how he was at twenty-one? I think if he just said he was sorry sometime, that could help.

At the end of my freshman year I had gone to SCC's president, Wayne Kraiss, to ask for financial help. I explained that on a partial scholarship I could not meet my academic and baseball responsibilities and still work. He had been kind to my father and me when we first met with him, and he quickly understood my dilemma. President Kraiss agreed to pay my full tuition. It was a relief to know that from now on I would only have to cover my living expenses and books. I looked forward to next season. I had gone 2-4, with a 2.92 ERA over forty-nine and one-third innings. Not bad for a freshman.

In Japan I had become a player of interest. Japanese reporters flocked to watch me play all season. That was surprising, as I had always believed that the Japanese, despite not having a Southern Baptist tradition, saw women as subservient to men. But that would not be my experience at all. When freshman year was over, I was invited to quit SCC to play for Tokyo University. Instead I accepted an invitation from the World Children's Baseball Fair (WCBF) to go to Miyazaki, on the island of Kyushu, Japan. At the college and professional games I attended, I saw that baseball in Japan is like football here or hockey in Canada. Every pitch, every batter, and every inning, people were on their feet and sounding off with their hand-held clappers. They appreciated the game like I always had, and they accepted me. I loved Japan, with its culture of family, baseball, fun, strong work ethic, and good citizenship.

The WCBF was founded in 1989 by Sadaharu Oh, Hank Aaron, and Dr. Akiko Agishi. Each summer about two hundred children from nations like Switzerland, Germany, Israel, Canada, the United States, Australia, and Spain, are invited to attend for a week. Each morning ten coaches teach the game's fundamentals to their group of kids— pitching, hitting, base running, and sliding. Afterward everyone takes part in various events, the idea being to promote a better understanding of different cultures through baseball. You do not need to speak the same language to have fun with baseball and develop friendships by playing together. I pitched forty-five minutes of batting practice to the U.S. and Japanese All-Star Legends, including Lou Brock, Dock Ellis, and Harmon Killebrew, in hundred-degree heat and 70 percent humidity. I also threw in the bullpen. Given my large hands, a number of players tried to teach me the knuckleball; but, like many pitchers, I never could master it. Ozzie Virgil Jr. went out of his way to encourage me. I think it was Ozzie who told me, "You have enough speed to make it. You just need one more pitch." Ozzie showed me a straight change and I tried it with a twist and so began to develop a screwball. When I returned home, I showed the pitch to Dad, who worked with me. I moved my thumb up on the side of the ball and put a different spin on it just before release. That pitch would become my out pitch in professional baseball.

That first trip to Japan was a kaleidoscope of fish farms, rice paddies, green mountains, and tiny cars. I got lost in the subway system, attended a tea ceremony, and learned a few Japanese words. On one occasion we were in downtown Tokyo and someone left their camera on a street-crossing pole. When we returned one hour later it was still there. I admired the Japanese values that allowed that. One night I ran a mile through a horrific rainstorm to an Internet café to check my e-mail in hopes that Shelley had written. She had. I thought about staying on to play baseball in Japan, but with Shelley back in California I could not accept living there without her. I also worried about living my lie there. They would surely get rid of me if they learned I was gay. Had I thought I could be accepted there, I might have stayed.

To me, baseball and running have always gone together, not just because speed is one of the game's five tools, along with hitting, hitting for power, throwing, and fielding, but also because the game gave me a great escape from our family's troubles and, when I was on the field, an escape from the worry over my love for a woman. Maybe that's why Japan, an ocean away from these worries, was so appealing.

At the beginning of sophomore year came a material bonanza for the whole team out of all the media hype. The Japanese baseball equipment company ssk took an interest in my pitching. They filmed two commercials, with most of the team participating. They couldn't pay us (eligibility rules), but our team got new uniforms, gloves, and cleats. Charlie was delighted, as he usually had to scrape up money out of the college's budget for equipment.

Over the summer I had pitched only about twenty innings. It was not nearly enough, and it showed up when the season began. I was slated to be the number three starter and in my first game faced last year's nemesis, ucsd. In three and two-thirds innings, I gave up nine hits and six runs (four unearned). It got worse. On my twentieth birthday I pitched at San Francisco State. In the worst outing of my life, I got rocked for seven runs and thirteen hits. Alone in my hotel room I bawled my eyes out. The bad streak continued. My mechanics were off—Charlie urged me to pitch inside more—but the competition was tougher and my confidence was low. Opponents were hitting .406 against me, and my era was 8.80. I made fourteen appearances, twelve of them starts, without a win. The drought finally ended at home with a ninety-six-pitch, 11–7 win over Claremont-Mudd.

But by then, Charlie Phillips was on his way out. In a game at Point Loma Nazarene College in March, Charlie had been ejected after arguing with an umpire. Charlie did like to chatter during games. As he told the

Los Angeles Times, "That's baseball. . . . You have to protect your players and gain their respect."

Charlie's college coach had been Rod Dedeaux, known to be a maestro at teaching his players how to get into the heads of the opposing team. Bench jockeying, it's called. (In 1976 Charlie had won the team's Vic Lapiner Award, also known as Captain of the Bench). Likely the constraints of the NAIA code were tough for an award-winning bench jockey. But on this particular day at Point Loma, Charlie was in the clear as far as I was concerned.

At the Point Loma game, during their argument, the ump had shoved and sworn at him. Back on campus President Kraiss called Charlie into his office to discuss his use of profanity, which was in violation of the NAIA code. Charlie explained that the ump was the only one using profanity. Pat Guillen, our sports information director, backed him up; I hadn't heard Charlie swear either. Charlie considered the matter closed. But early in May, President Kraiss, who had definitely not trained with Rod Dedeaux, mailed Charlie a note, stating that he "should not anticipate receiving another contract," according to the *Times*. President Kraiss told the *Times* that "he and Phillips had some philosophical disagreements, among them a dispute whether coaches should badger umpires."

I thought Charlie's treatment was unfair. To me he handled himself well with the umpires. Charlie knew rule-wise we were not supposed to be able to bench jockey like he had in his college days. In the NAIA, you could ride your opponents, but if the ump heard, you were usually warned and then ejected. I think SCC wanted a more passive coach who didn't question the school's position. But Charlie came from USC and pro ball, and that's how things went. He went to bat for his players, and we appreciated that. The school, on the other hand, did not. The players on our team came from different states and from very different backgrounds. I can't speak for them, but I never heard them complain about how Charlie conducted himself on the field.

After making the playoffs four years straight, we had failed for the second year in a row, so maybe that was a factor. President Kraiss was a formal and proper man who dressed in suit and tie. I had never known him to attend one of our games, and I had to wonder if he knew how much swearing goes on in the game of baseball, even in the NAIA, and if he was aware of the language that had been directed at me: blunt references to female body parts and threats of rape.

That spring relations with some of my own teammates improved. It came about because of a midnight phone call in February: three of our players had gone to Tijuana and got drunk. For some reason they had no ride back and called, begging me to pick them up at the U.S.-Mexico border. I did what a good teammate does—snuck out of the dorm, hopped in my car, and made the ninety-mile drive down the San Diego Freeway. I found the guys at the checkpoint and piled them into my car, where they slept all the way back to school. We didn't discuss the adventure at the game we played that afternoon, or ever, but they started backing me up more.

One of the highlights of that season came away from the diamond. One afternoon I picked up my mail and found a letter from Cooperstown, New York. A new exhibit was to be added to the *Diamond Dreams: Women in Baseball* wing at the National Baseball Hall of Fame and Museum. My SoCal (no. 25) jersey, along with my glove, cap, and baseball, as well as photographs, would go up on the wall. I thought it was a joke at first and had to read the letter over and over to accept that it was true. I was beyond thrilled. I showed the letter to Charlie and to Pat Guillen, who gathered the requested equipment and mailed it off to Cooperstown. I did not have the money to travel there to see the exhibit for myself but would hear from friends who did.

All through sophomore year, Shelley continued to be pressured by friends who wanted to set her up with guys. She resisted, which only fueled more gossip. So if Shelley was there when I went to the cafeteria, I sat somewhere else. And all the while, I would be looking to catch her eye, wanting her to agree that this was all so stupid. As for stupidity, consider this: earnestly complying with the media's portrayal of me as the poster girl for the all-American Christian athlete, I did an interview for a magazine called *Youth 95* for its March–April 1995 issue. The Worldwide Church of God published the magazine: "Because we care about teenagers around the world. We're dedicated to showing that God's way of life is relevant, interesting, and helpful to today's teens." The issue opened with an article titled "Would the Real Christian Please Step Forward?" The writer wanted to know: "Just what is a real Christian, anyway? And how can you tell the phony from the real?"

Flip the page and there was a photo of me, smiling through my lipstick. The headline read, "Will she wind up in the big leagues?" Listed was my "personal stuff: Goal—to make the majors; PE major; writes 'Psalm 37:3–5' on every ball she signs," and "fave saying: Don't judge a book by its cover."

I was struggling mightily with Psalm 37:3–5: "Trust in the Lord and do good; dwell in the land and enjoy safe pasture. Take delight in the Lord, and he will give you the desires of your heart. Commit your way to the Lord; trust in him and he will do this."

That was just not happening. And "don't judge a book by its cover?" That's just what I was seeking—to be judged by my "cover," given that I was, at heart, gay. I felt like a fraud.

On campus I was easy prey for anyone who wanted a piece of my life. Letters crammed my mailbox at school until the administration gave me a separate post office box. Men in the military proposed marriage. I also received a letter from a man in prison. He signed the letter "Dracula." I cannot recall what he had done to land in jail but he now offered a marriage proposal—we would meet up when he got out. Because I tried to respond to everyone, I wrote back to Dracula, thanking him for his support and wishing him well. I thought that would be the end, but his letters continued for several months. I always worried that he might show up on the field or at school. I also heard from Bible-thumping women who berated me for sending the wrong message to girls and boys. A woman in Alabama was especially incensed with me: here I was at a Christian school, and ladies were not supposed to be playing baseball with men. To clear my head, I gravitated to the field late at night. One of my fondest memories of SCC is those quiet moments there. I'd lie down on the mound, look up at the stars, and reflect on the beauty of this game. Other nights, when I needed to burn off energy, I ran the track. Usually I did not wear headphones so I could be heads up—paranoia doesn't mean somebody isn't after you—but one evening I put them on anyway to drown out the negative comments that too often played through my mind . . . Lap three: I'm into the music and beginning to break a good sweat when suddenly someone grabs my right shoulder and throws me to the ground. Two other guys are with him—I recognize one—he's a teammate. I pull my knees to my chest, and wrap my hands around my head in defense. As they yell and kick and rip at my clothes, I remember thinking, *Oh, God, I'm at a Christian college and I'm about to get raped.* Then I go into a white rage. I start kicking back and screaming. I know my teammate wants me to see him, that he wants to put the fear in me so I'll quit the team. Suddenly they leave, running, and I'm left on the ground. My virginity intact, I stand on shaky legs and hurry to my dorm room. No one is there. I feel like an idiot—Dad would have said, "It was your fault for not being heads up."

When my roommates walk through the door, they know something is wrong by the dirt on my clothes and the odd look on my face.

"Why are you acting so standoffish?" they want to know. "Why is your face all ashy?"

"Oh, I just got spooked by someone," I say. I want to tell them the truth but know they would make me report it, and then it would be so easy for the administrators to say, "See what happens when you put a female in a man's role?"

The attack hardened me. I took kung fu lessons and tried to bury the memory.

Because so many guys had threatened it, I figured that I was probably going to be raped at some point in my quest to play professional baseball. Perhaps this sounds harsh, but I decided to not let anyone break me by taking my virginity—if it were to happen, I would not let the rape mean anything to me. Only the person who captured my heart mattered. I was, and still am, able to turn off a switch in my head in order to endure a lot of pain. Just like that time freshman year when my roommate saw where the baseballs had left bruises and imprints of their seams all over my back. So I borrowed a friend's dildo and took my own virginity. I remember seeing blood and wondering what I had done. I just didn't want anyone to take anything from me that was precious, so afterward I felt relief. It was a solitary act I now find sad.

I was between role models. Growing up it had been Madonna—strong, confident, and independent. As in high school, I turned to a teacher. Most of the faculty was encouraging and worked with my baseball schedule. Then, during sophomore year, I signed up for the mandatory Western civilization class taught by John Wilson. Professor Wilson was open-minded, a Democrat like me in a mostly Republican school, and a lover of baseball. He usually sat in the stands for the games. I could tell that he was pulling for me, and I enjoyed talking with him. We kept in touch after the semester ended. Otherwise I could think of no one to turn to except God, and that was not going well. For the first time I questioned my spiritual beliefs. If Christians had to be straight, why had He allowed me to be gay? I wanted to be seen as a child of God, not a reject. But I did not fully accept that He was in control; I wanted control, perhaps because there had always been so little stability around me. I had been attending Calvary Chapel, a nondenominational megachurch, in Costa Mesa. I liked hearing Greg Laurie preach there, though always with the dread of hearing a comment about the abomination of homosexuality. I never did hear it, but I knew where the church stood, and it excluded someone like me.

Campus gossip and the media's scrutiny of my sexuality had lessened, though my own uncertainties still tore at me. Here I was at a Christian school, where people were expected to be kinder than in the secular world, but much of what I saw involved greed for publicity and judgmental attitudes. What did it mean that the same teammates who harassed me one minute spoke of their Christian faith the next? I would pray, *I am relying on You to get me through this tough time and help me be a good example and represent You, but I am failing, and these Christian people are treating me like shit.* That was another struggle: I had developed a full repertoire of swear words, which I used liberally on the diamond; I prayed that God would change me. Meanwhile, I tried to remember to not swear so much, or I could wind up gone, like Charlie. My poor numbers—1-7 with a 7.20 ERA over fifty innings pitched—the attack at the field, and my heartbreak over Shelley had sunk my confidence. I had let my personal messes affect my schoolwork. I wish I had had a safe outlet for the turmoil inside. Even so, I refused to consider quitting baseball. My dream was central to who I was; I would stubbornly hang on to it.

For the summer of 1995 the World Children's Baseball Fair invited me back to Japan. I turned it down. Should I have gone? Maybe, but I just couldn't see myself over there alone all summer. Going home was not a happy option, either. Mom continued to hide from the reality of her failing marriage, and the atmosphere in our house was thick with tension. I had some hard lessons to learn about life, but at this point, except for Dad's teaching me to be self-sufficient and successful, my guideline was mostly to do the opposite of what my father would. That was why I did not smoke or drink or lie, aside from hiding my gayness. I tried to live by the motto "Always leave things—and people—better than when you found them." So, better not go home for the summer. Besides, after putting up lousy numbers my sophomore year, I needed to develop another pitch, work on getting left-handed hitters out, and get my head together. Where to run to now? I signed on to play ball in Canada with the Swift Current Indians of the Saskatchewan Major Baseball League, a five-team league of collegiate and other amateur players from throughout the United States and Canada.

SUMMER 1995, SASKATCHEWAN. Sometimes you go through a time in life and just think, *What the heck was that?* That was Canada. I got off the plane in Calgary, a city girl, a surfer, arriving in another country. The sky was so clear and blue it looked as if I could reach out and grab it. I was in the plains, seeing for the first time vast stretches of open land, farms with cornfields, and horses alongside the road. Getting out of the car in Swift Current, I met Saskatchewan's "official bird." I had never seen so many mosquitoes. They welcomed me.

Shelley had promised to come up in a few weeks, and I couldn't wait to see her. Together, out of town and away from suspicious friends, maybe we could work things out. Mom came up with Uncle Ray. Dad and my brother Phillip watched me pitch in Moose Jaw. They had to use a towel to wave off the mosquitoes. The temperature was about a hundred degrees, but I wore leg tights, two pairs of socks, two long-sleeve shirts, a jersey, and tons of Off! insect repellent, and still got eaten alive. Dad and Phillip ended up watching the game from inside their rental car, but the mosquitoes swarmed through the vents and continued the attack. I never have heard of a game called for mosquitoes, but this one should have been. Even the locals said it was crazy that day. That summer, not only did I lose ten pounds, but I also looked like I had chicken pox.

I was failing miserably at getting left-handers out. Usually left-handed pitchers have greater success against lefties, but I had faced mostly right-handed batters throughout my years in baseball and had developed successful pitches against them. In Canada I now faced mostly left-handed batters. The Indians wanted me to win, not work on a new pitch. I also had to make time to earn money. I lived rent-free in the basement room of a family's home in town, and for transportation I borrowed the family's bike. But I still had expenses, like three meals a day. From nine in the morning until one o'clock in the afternoon I worked for minimum wage at a sod farm. I hand-pumped water uphill from the reservoir to the sprinklers. Then I cut the sod, rolled it up, stacked it in the truck, delivered it, and unloaded it for the customers. I think my forearms nearly doubled in size that summer. The other cool thing about the job was driving the tractor all over the place under the big blue sky. When there was no work at the sod farm, I painted houses and fences. After my work was done, I bicycled several miles to the ballpark.

I liked being in Canada. I got to know the locals by going to dinner with different people in town. The people here loved hockey—baseball was second—and everyone looked out for one another. I appreciated that. Still, there was the constant loneliness I endured. One of the hard things about a female playing baseball is spending time and bonding with your teammates without their girlfriends or wives getting mad. So I hung out with the guys and played cards but kept a certain distance. That way there was never a problem. These guys were cool. Unlike my college teammates, it was no big deal to them that I was a girl.

We played all over the prairie, from Oyen and Kindersley to Moose Jaw. Our team traveled on a red-and-blue bus with yellow bench seats and a round table in the back, where the guys usually played poker. The players called it the bubble bus, a party on wheels. I remember one guy, Steve, trying dip for the first time. The guys were all over him for not chewing or dipping. They gave him a tin of Copenhagen, he put in a dip and within twenty seconds he had thrown up and fallen asleep—or passed out, I'm not sure which. The coach was pissed and made us live with the mess.

I laughed. I am either blessed or cursed, I do not know which, with a male sense of humor. I don't know what it is with guys, but they love to make you do gross things. Girls' humor can be demeaning and cruel; guys' jokes are disgusting and funny. They would not let me avoid the pranks, so I gave in to the less invasive ones: for twenty bucks I ate a worm, and for ten dollars I tried the hottest hot sauce. I turned down gulping a box of doughnuts and cup of milk—not worth the money offered—and the full-body shave. But it sure was funny to watch the guy who did the shave scratching himself all the time. He was always squirming, and maybe it gave him a new appreciation of what women go through to look good.

Traveling on the bubble bus was an adventure. Returning from a game around two in the morning, we drove into a huge thunderstorm. The lightning was practically nonstop, making the middle of the night seem like day—the driver did not need his headlights on. Everyone was nervous, remembering the rumor that a player in the league had been killed while he was just standing in center field. A bolt of lightning hit him and traveled to his metal cleats. I wanted to stick my head out the window and breathe in the fresh storm air but thought better of it. On another night, the bus struck a deer; the collision took out the front windshield and a fender. On yet another night, the bubble bus broke down forty-five miles from home, so a few teammates trekked to the nearest town to call for a tow. A few hours later, we were on the field for the next game.

Later that summer came a jolt of heartbreak. Shelley called to say that she was not coming to visit. While I was playing ball, she had found a boyfriend. "I can't live your baseball dream with you," she told me. "I have my religion, and I want to get married, have kids, and fit in."

I had no answer for that old argument. Shelley could not see the pain on my face or the flood of tears that came upon me. After we hung up, I cried like I had never cried before. The family I was staying with came downstairs to see if I was all right, and I told them that one of my friends had died. Well, something had died. I felt my heart close around the grief I felt. At the end of the summer I left Canada with an ache where love had been and having learned not near enough about baseball.

Back on campus for junior year, change had come to scc. In my freshman year, the student body numbered nine hundred; this year there were twenty-seven hundred. I felt bad that Charlie Phillips was gone. With my nemesis Beckley graduated, I was pleased to have a new coach, Kevin Kasper, until I found out he had a different role in mind for me: I was to pitch out of the bullpen in a setup role. But I felt I had the makeup of a starter: I put the ball in play, did not strike out a lot of hitters, and did not throw in the nineties. Pitching in relief meant that I was not going to get a lot of innings, and scouts want to see innings. My pitching continued to be lackluster, in part because in losing Shelley I lost the laser focus I had during freshman year. The season looked like it was going to be a washout, but it was too late to transfer. I ended up going 1-1, with a 5.18 ERA over twenty-four and a third innings.

Off the field, I fit in even less than I had the previous year. Wanting to be with Shelley, I had neglected other friendships, and seeing her with her boyfriend almost every day brought me down. She tried to reason with me, saying that it was for the best. "You know I want a family, and you can't give me that. You have to live your baseball dream, so it's best if we go our separate ways now."

She wanted me to get on board with dating guys too, but that was not going to happen. Even getting my degree wasn't a priority. My determination to make it in baseball, despite my declining performance on the mound—call me stubborn—remained my driving force, though it caused me to neglect other aspects of my life. I looked at my options. Transferring schools seemed the best answer. While I had problems with the baseball program, the main reason I left SCC, though I didn't admit it at the time, was to get away from the pain of seeing Shelley every day. I looked for a school where I could find the backing of a coach and get in a lot of innings. I got lucky.

Whittier College, a small liberal arts school, was just a few miles from my family home. The school was founded by the Religious Society of Quakers in 1887, and to me its campus felt peaceful and quiet. It is named after the abolitionist and Quaker poet John Greenleaf Whittier. I loved the school mascot: a fierce-looking patriot dressed in circa 1776 garb and three-corner hat, on the run, a book under one arm and grasping an oversized pen inscribed with the nickname of the team, "The Poets." Richard Nixon, the school's most famous alumnus, ran for student body president. Campaigning on a platform to end the bans on smoking and on-campus dances, he won.

Playing in the Southern California Collegiate Conference, the Poets' baseball team had gone 8-26-1 the year before. Coach Jim Pigott was delighted to see me, as he had lost four pitchers from that team to graduation. He, the staff, and the players were used to seeing me on the mound when the Vanguards competed against the Poets, which made my transfer an easier transition. I was blown away by the friendliness I found at Whittier. The first time I stepped onto the field, six teammates greeted me and told me that I was to come to them if I needed anything. I think this attitude came from the top. As Mike Rizzo, the assistant coach, later said:

Coach Pigott didn't care whether she was a girl—if she can pitch, it was okay and my message to the team was: judge her as a baseball player, not a girl. One thing that stood out was her work ethic. Back when it used to rain in Southern California, I'd go out to the field—practice would have been canceled—and she'd be working out. She'd be the only one out there. To this day, I use her as an example. If we'd had twenty-five players with her work ethic, we could have gone far. She was as fierce a competitor as you can imagine, a pitcher who consistently got outs, and she could make [a batter] look bad.

But the language coming from opposing team's dugouts bothered Coach Rizzo: "She heard things coming from the dugouts that no one should ever hear, but her teammates here had her back. We had a transfer catcher on that team, and when the language got to a certain point (meaning personal), the next hitter needed to be light on their feet if you know what I mean!"

Coach Rizzo has his own opinion about the razzing, though. "Today," he said, "You'd never get away with that kind of language. But I think the players back then were a little bit more mentally tough because of it. The players today are much more sensitive—they get hurt feelings, and I tell them, they'd never have made it back then."

I pitched for the Whittier College Poets with body, soul, and heart. Here I perfected the straight change-up I first learned in Japan. I now had a reliable screwball. At five feet nine, 140 pounds, never having taken steroids, and topping out at eighty-one miles per hours, I had a hard time drawing scouts. I watched soft-throwing major leaguer Jamie Moyer pitch, and tried to emulate him. So many in Organized Baseball have a prejudice in favor of hard-throwing, hunky pitchers. (After the Los Angeles Dodgers signed Pedro Martinez in 1988, manager Tommy Lasorda said that at five feet eleven and 170 pounds, Pedro's officially listed height and weight, he was too small for a starter—look how that turned out.) From my time in Japan, where I was taller than many of their professional players, I knew I was big enough. I remembered freshman year when I met the Atlanta Braves pitcher Greg Maddux, in San Francisco, and that we stood eye to eye. I also knew I was built for the game, with a wide back; strong, big legs; and huge hands. I just wish I had lifted weights more—ten or fifteen more pounds of muscle might have caught the eye of someone in Organized Baseball. But Dad had always warned me off weight training—he was from an era that didn't believe in bulking up for fear of becoming muscle-bound. He also wanted me to look feminine. Teammates and friends warned me, too, saying that I already looked like a guy because I was big-boned. In the closet as I was, I unconsciously accepted the message that I must look feminine. So I only did cardio workouts. Foolish. After I left baseball, I began to lift. Today I feel stronger than I ever did back then.

Spring of senior year was an edgy time of waiting to see whether a professional club was willing to sign me. I was in touch with Akiko Agishi, who had connections in Japan through her work with the WCBF. We talked about my playing there, but it didn't come to anything. Meanwhile, rumors circulated about major league clubs that might draft me. Randy Youngman, a sportswriter for the *Orange County Register*, reported that the Anaheim Angels intended to draft me in the late rounds. Tim Mead, then the Angels assistant general manager, recalled "the discussion making its way around the Baseball Ops area." Bob Fontaine, the club's scouting director, also remembered the discussion "because it was interesting," he wrote in an e-mail. "I know we talked about it & tossed it around & had we decided to draft her it would have been late. But we never came to the conclusion that we intended to. As I remember she had a decent breaking ball but didn't throw real hard."

In May of 1996, *Sports Illustrated* ran this comment from the Cincinnati Reds owner, Marge Schott: "I've got my scouts looking for a great girl. . . . Wouldn't that be something? Her coming in and striking all these boys out, honey?"

Dad recalls that one of the club's cross-checkers told him that the Reds were interested in drafting me. (One of a cross-checker's duties is to vet the scouts' reports and recommend whether to sign a player.) But just before the draft, Marge Schott was suspended from MLB. I would not have been the first woman drafted. Carey Schueler, a left-hander like me, had been drafted in the forty-third round of the 1993 MLB Players Draft but never played professionally. She was also the daughter of Ron

Schueler, the general manager of the Chicago White Sox. Dad knew about Carey and now asked around, "Why not Ila?"

When Dad spoke with Steve Fuller, a scout for the Chicago Cubs, he said Fuller replied that he "did not have big enough *cojones*. And whoever does draft her will have to have the biggest *cojones* of all time . . . because it would be the biggest story in baseball ever!"

But with a 5.22 ERA my senior year and velocity in the low eighties, the clubs passed on me. I hadn't expected to be a top draft pick like pitchers Jon Garland (first round), Jeff Weaver (second round), and Tim Hudson (sixth round) in the 1997 baseball draft, but the draft went into the ninety-second round, and toward the end the Tampa Bay Devil Rays drafted a slew of pitchers, mostly out of high school. Where was the harm in giving me a tryout at spring training? Dad had shared in my dream of getting a shot in Organized Baseball. I know that he was as disappointed as I was when an invitation to spring training did not come.

Then there were the Colorado Silver Bullets. Julie Croteau had played with them after college, and popular opinion seemed to be that I should, too. Early in May, Daryn Kagan interviewed me on CNN's *Morning News*. She wanted to know, "Why not play with the Colorado Silver Bullets. A lot of people are familiar with this team. It's a professional baseball team featuring all women who play against men's teams. What [*sic*] not go with them?"

Kagan also wanted to know why "not play softball like other girls?"

I explained the difference between throwing overhand in baseball, which I had done successfully, versus throwing underhand in softball, which I never mastered.

The Silver Bullets' owner, Bob Hope, had left a couple of telephone messages for me, urging me to sign. But Dad had watched their games on TV and felt there was little percentage in my playing with them. He did not believe—and I agreed—that playing against teams at that level would help me develop as a pitcher. I worried that somehow my signing with the Silver Bullets would seem like a gimmick. Besides, I just didn't see the Silver Bullets as a promising stop along the route I'd have to take to achieve my dream of making it to the major leagues.

To keep the pressure off, Dad led the Silver Bullets to believe that I would come to their spring training camp. They sent me a plane ticket. But since the Silver Bullets were a professional club, he asked that they not announce that I would join them while I was still playing college ball, to avoid any issue of eligibility. Dad says this was the only way he could think of to keep the club and me apart.

A soft-spoken Southern Californian named Barry Moss had played eleven seasons of minor league baseball and later stayed around the game as a coach, manager, and scout. What I remember most about meeting him when he scouted me were his kind blue eyes and Robert Redford good looks. Barry had great baseball smarts and knew the local baseball scene well—he scouted for the Los Angeles Dodgers and also recommended players to the Northern League, an independent professional league in the Upper Midwest. I didn't know that late in March a chain of telephone calls had begun. Mike Veeck, the son of the legendary baseball entrepreneur Bill Veeck Jr. owned the St. Paul Saints of the Northern League. Mike had heard of me and asked his manager, Marty Scott, to check me out. Marty then phoned Barry Moss, who recalled:

> I showed up for a Saturday game at the University of La Verne—I believe Ila pitched the whole game. I saw a good curve, seventy-five to eighty mph velocity, and good control. They tried to bunt on her, and she handled the plays well. She showed a variety of skills. I liked her pick-off move as well—she kept the runners close, which a left-hander must do. After the game I introduced myself to Ila's father, and we talked. After I got home—this was in the pre-cell-phone days—I called Marty with a positive report.

On the verge of signing, I got nervous. I was to start my final college game at home against my old school, scc. So close to the next step of my dream, I thought, *What if I get injured?* I talked with Dad, who said, "Don't take the chance."

Hours before the game, I officially withdrew from classes. I told the press that I was close to signing a contract and might have to leave town at a moment's notice. Besides, if I agreed to a contract it would end my college eligibility. What I did not say was that I was afraid of getting hurt. Coach Pigott told the *Times*, "It's about the only disappointing experience I've had with Ila. . . . I wish she would have waited [to withdraw]. I think the guys would have liked to see her pitch one more time. I would have liked that too."

Looking back, I wish I had finished out the season—and it would have been great to win that last game against the Vanguards. It's a regret. It would have been the right way to repay Whittier College's hospitality, which continued—even after I turned pro, I had a key to the gate to the field and was encouraged to return to practice there. As it was, I finished the season with a 4-5 win-loss record and a 5.22 ERA over eighty-one innings.

After Barry's conversation with Marty Scott, the St. Paul Saints confirmed on May 5 that I was invited to spring training camp. A few days later, I received a letter from the Saints' general manager, Bill Fanning. Enclosed was my airline ticket to Minneapolis–St. Paul. "When you arrive in St. Paul," Fanning wrote, "please give me your return ticket and when it is time to return home I will have another ticket ready for you."

Time to return home? Never, I hoped. I was so damn excited. The Northern League is not part of Organized Baseball, but it has an awesome reputation. It takes in anyone it cares to, from rookies who need more experience to veteran major leaguers who need to rehab an injury to their bodies or their reputations. In the year I joined the league, J. D. Drew was the Philadelphia Phillies' number two pick in the first round of the 1997 MLB draft but felt he was being offered too little ($2.6 million). Drew decided instead to showcase his talents with the St. Paul Saints for a year, did well (hitting .341 and eighteen home runs), and signed the following year with the St. Louis Cardinals for nearly $7 million. Steve Howe, the Dodgers pitcher who had tested positive several times for alcohol and cocaine use, pitched what would be his last season for the Sioux Falls Canaries. Darryl Strawberry, dogged by drug abuse and marital and tax troubles, had been released by the New York Yankees in December 1995. Mike Veeck and the Saints chairman of the board, Marv

Goldklang, took him in. Strawberry went on a tear—batting .435, with eighteen home runs and thirty-nine RBIs, in twenty-nine games—and landed back with the Yankees. After his last game as a Saint, Strawberry told author Neal Karlen, "It goes so deep down inside, what the St. Paul Saints mean to me. . . . Those players gave me the energy and lift to go out there every day. We became a unit together."

When Barry said that Mike Veeck was all about opportunity, it was real and true. I had not been offered a contract, just a chance to make the team. Best of all if I made the Saints, no one could say it was because they needed to fill their ballpark. Over the past three seasons, their home games had sold out. But the idea of bringing in a woman ballplayer had long been in Mike's mind—he says he had talked it over with his father in the 1970s. He was just waiting for the right time.

Well, all I ever wanted was a shot, and now I was going to get one. I will always be grateful to Barry Moss, Marty Scott, and Mike Veeck for their open minds. Sportswriters said that my invitation into men's professional baseball was history-making, but that's not accurate. Others had gone before me:

1898: Lizzie Arlington became the first woman to sign a minor league contract, with Reading of the Atlantic League. She lasted a season.

1931: Jackie Mitchell struck out Babe Ruth and Lou Gehrig in an exhibition game for the Chattanooga (Tennessee) Lookouts.

1936 and 1937: Frances Dunlap played two games of Class D minor league baseball in Fayetteville, Arkansas, going 1-for-2 and 1-for-3.

1952: Eleanor Engle signed with the Harrisburg (Pennsylvania) Senators but never played. George Trautman, president of the National Association of Professional Baseball Leagues, banned women from playing Organized Baseball.

1953–55: Mamie "Peanut" Johnson, Connie Morgan, and Toni Stone played in the Negro American League. (Stone played for the Indianapolis Clowns in 1953 and the Kansas City Monarchs in 1954. Johnson and Morgan played for the Indianapolis Clowns in 1954–55).

1994: Julie Croteau and Lee Anne Ketchum, of the Colorado Silver Bullets, played for the Maui Stingrays in the Hawaiian Winter League. Kendra Hanes played for the Kentucky Rifles of the Independent Frontier League, going 0-for-10.

1996: Pamela Davis pitched one inning of an exhibition game for the Class AA Jacksonville Suns against the Australian national team. She won the game. And Mike Veeck had tried to recruit Carey Schueler. She had no interest.

I hoped to last longer than one inning, one game, or one season. But lasting in the lower levels of professional baseball means a vow of poverty. If I made the cut and became a Saint, I would earn 750 dollars a month. And then I remembered the deal Dad said that he made my sophomore year. After SSK filmed the commercial at SCC, he met with Akiko and negotiated a deal: when I turned pro, the Japanese baseball equipment corporation would pay me three thousand dollars to use their mitt. That was fine with me—I had had been using their gloves ever since Little League. But Dad held out. He wanted fifty thousand.

"Wow," I said.

When SSK agreed to his price, I was shocked. If I made the team, this money would set me up financially. I had few bills—no cell phone, no computer, and no car payments—only student loans that were deferred and auto insurance on my blue 1985 Mercury Topaz, which I planned to leave at home. With fifty thousand dollars in the bank I would not have to worry about living under Dad's rules at home when the season ended. I was rich, I was free.

4

MIKE VEECK AND
THE ST. PAUL SAINTS

GAME DAY: FOURTH INNING. In the top of the fourth, we score another run on three successive singles. While we're at bat, the guys in the dugout joke around, but they continue to leave me alone. There are so many superstitions in baseball, one being that when a no-hitter or a shutout is going, don't talk about it with the pitcher. Superstition counts for a lot in this life. To keep a streak going or to break a slump, players rely on ritual. Some players have special shaving rituals. One guy shaves with a razor, doing alternating strokes on each side of his face and then does his chin last. If they're on a good streak, some guys won't shave until they go hitless or give up a run. I've been told, though I am glad to say I never saw it, that one teammate always whacks off before he pitches, so he won't be jittery on the mound. Others pop greenies like sunflower seeds or need their special dip or chew. We have one player who is like Nomar Garciaparra—at the plate he tightens his batting gloves, zipping and unzipping them I don't know how many times. We give him so much crap for that. My own ritual is fairly minimal: Before each game, I put on my uniform in exactly the same way. Then I eat a Snickers bar and drink a can of Mountain Dew. I wear the same holey undershirt for the season but wash it after every game. Whatever it is, it seems like most of us need to have a ritual.

I head out for the bottom half of the inning to face the heart of the order (the third, fourth, and fifth batters in the lineup), for the second time around. This is a huge inning. Coaches tell their pitchers that what we do after our team scores is pivotal. It's about momentum. I need to shut down the opposing team fast and give us a chance to put more runs on the board, boosting everyone's confidence while killing the RedHawks' spirit. They'll start to feel the pressure not to lose to me. They'll swing at bad pitches, thus making the strike zone bigger. Well, I need every little edge I can get, not because I'm a girl but because I am small for a pitcher who wants to make it in professional baseball.

I look to the sky as I face home plate, grateful it's a night game. During day games in Fargo, the center fielder and pitcher get no relief from the sun's glare in their faces. It's so bad that if a pitch is lined straight back at the pitcher it would be hard to react fast enough. That very thing happened in May, when the Baltimore Orioles pitcher Mike Mussina was hit in the face by a line drive and fell to the ground, bleeding. He didn't move for nearly two minutes. Mussina's nose was broken and he had a cut above his eye, but he didn't lose his eyesight—every pitcher's fear. Any time I throw an outside corner pitch my mitt ends up by my melon. I learned that lesson—to always be ready—from Dad when I was ten years old.

I throw my last warmup pitch, and the catcher throws the ball around the horn. Chris Briller underhands the ball to me, then approaches the mound from third base. Covering his mouth with his glove so people can't read his lips, he gives me an order: "Fuckin' kill 'em."

I give him a devilish smile back. I feel the positive energy around me. My shortstop and second baseman are toe-tapping the dirt because they can't remain still. It's like they're saying, "Hit the ball to me. I want it." My first baseman stares toward home, all business. I look back at the outfield. Everyone's ready to go.

After Steve Hine flies out to left and Johnny Knott flies out to right, I decide to go after Marc Fink. I throw a two-seamer fastball away, and he hits a high chopper between first and second. Base hit. Oh, well, I figure—he's slow and unlikely to steal. He just pulled an outside corner pitch, and it got through. Tip of my cap to him. I can sense his relief as he stands on first, a big smile on his face. The crowd starts to chirp.

Chris Coste is up next—he has smeared black under his eyes. He pushes his helmet down on his head and checks down the third base line for the coach's sign. To keep the guy at first honest, I throw to first but make it look like crap. The first baseman doesn't even try to tag him. Soon as I get the ball back, the runner takes a bigger lead. And I think, *Okay, you fucker, keep doing that.* I hold the ball a little longer and give a better move to first.

Even though I know I am not going to throw the ball to home, I look in for the sign. Javier flicks his thumb toward first again. It's all about rhythm. So I come to the pause in the stretch, and hold the ball until the hitter finally calls time. I want the runner to feel a little heavy in his legs. The fans start to boo. Someone screams, "Throw the ball, Sally." Others yell, "Turn the other page . . . She's scared . . . She's done . . . Pull her, coach."

Seated just behind the visitors' dugout is a woman of about fifty, dressed in red and waving a small flag, who has not shut up the entire game. I figure she buys a ticket just so she could heckle the RedHawks' opponents. Every town has a fan like that. She is all over our team when we hit. She screams, "Go back home," when I run into the dugout.

A regular ball of fire. Now she sits quietly. I think to try something that a lot of pitchers do, but it's dangerous. I call Javier out and tell him I want to hang a curveball inside and let this guy rip it foul. We have done this before, so he says, "Okay, whatever you feel comfortable with."

Why does a hanging curve go foul? A lazy curve, one without a good break or spin on it, thrown up in the zone goes inside. When the hitter connects—and he usually does—he will try to blast it and it can only go foul. If he does hit it fair, he's somehow missed it and it's an easy pop-up. But most of the time he gets a long foul drive for his trouble. As the ball approaches the plate, I can see Coste's eyes getting big. As expected, he rips it foul. I imagine everyone is thinking, *Holy crap, what was that?*

Javier and I look at each other with one thought: *Cool.* He comes out, hands me a new baseball, and says, "Nice pitch. We know this guy will be looking away. He's seen everything you have. Let's trust your stuff and give him what he wants."

I agree but say that I first want to throw my two-seamer off the outside corner plate, so he can't whale on it, as well as to set up the screwball away. Agreed. Javier heads back to the plate, puts his mask on, and signals "no sign." I throw my two-seamer, putting it close to five inches off the outside corner. Coste leans in with his entire body, watching it all the way in, but takes it for another ball: 2-2. He figures I'll come after him with my best pitch for a strike. I will, but it will be a ball. I throw my screwball as hard as I can right down the middle to where it looks like it's going to be a strike, but at the last moment it tails away and sinks. He swings and taps a harmless grounder to third. No runs, one hit, no errors, one left on base.

Our bench erupts with praise. It's only the bottom of the fourth and we have a lot of game to go, but there's a stillness in the crowd now. The RedHawks and their fans are thinking, *Holy crap, she might beat us.* For that they can blame the man who was not afraid to take a chance on me, Mike Veeck.

MAY 14, 1997, ST. PAUL, MINNESOTA. As the plane descended over Fort Snelling Pass, I saw Midway Stadium, home of the St. Paul Saints, set against the city's skyline. In the distance was the Metrodome, home of the Twins. I could not believe I was getting to play at Midway, a ballpark that held the immense (to me) number of seventy-six hundred people. I had spent the flight evaluating my readiness for St. Paul. Baseball-wise I was arriving in town with a seventy-something fastball, a good curve, a screwball-like change-up, and precision control. Mentally I felt prepared, having dealt with pressure situations from Little League through college. I had even prepared myself emotionally by taking my own virginity with that dildo in college. Spiritually, I thought I was okay. I am all right with failing as long as I did my absolute best, figuring it wasn't something that was supposed to happen. I would have done my part, and the rest was up to God. I saw God as my best friend, though

I would come to learn I also needed to learn to be my own best friend. And financially the SSK contract represented freedom and a break from my fiscally starved past. Now, about ready to start spring training, I felt like nothing could break me. I was going to find a way to get to where I wanted to be: a professional baseball player who helped her team get wins. No publicity gimmicks, no media games, but a woman who would stand the test of time in professional baseball.

After I picked up my big red suitcase from baggage claim, I walked outside to find my ride. Holy crap, it was cold. I was a California surfer girl, used to living in board shorts. Growing up, our family never traveled outside Southern California We usually vacationed at Big Bear Lake in the San Bernardino National Forest, a two-hour drive from home. But through baseball I had been to Japan and the plains of Canada from Calgary to Winnipeg. Now I was in beautiful, green, but frigid Minnesota. As I stepped into the fresh air, I remember thinking, *It's May, why so cold here?* All I'd packed were summer clothes. I made a quick U-turn and ran back into the airport to buy a sweatshirt at one of the shops. I pulled my new gray sweatshirt, with "Minnesota" on it, over my one pair of jeans, and quickly spotted my driver, who was holding a sign that read, "St. Paul Saints—Ila Borders." He greeted me with a handshake and said, "Welcome to St. Paul, Ila." I thought we would wait for the other players to arrive, but he loaded my suitcase into the trunk of the sedan, and we took off. "We're going to stop by the stadium to meet Mike Veeck," he said. "He wants to talk with you before spring training camp starts tomorrow."

Cool, I thought. *Here I am, on my way to meet the president and co-owner of the Saints.* Along the way I got lost in the greenness of the landscape, filled with cedars, hemlocks, and firs and ash, maple, and oak trees. I saw several lakes—a great novelty to a Southern Californian—and the architecture of the old buildings downtown spoke of culture. I could not wrap my mind around the fact that the houses had no fences around them—everything was open. There were still patches of snow on the ground, but people were out Rollerblading, running, and biking in the parks. Lakes and trees, four seasons, open space, culture—this was Grandma's state, and it was, I decided in a moment, a good place to be.

As we turned off Energy Park Drive into the parking lot, I saw train tracks behind the left- and center-field wall and a fire-training center with a burn tower behind the right-field fence. A state-of-the-art scoreboard loomed over left-center. Inside the ballpark, as I stood at the front desk, a man emerged from his office, dressed in black slacks and a black trench coat. Mike Veeck was taller than I'd anticipated. After we introduced ourselves, he said, "Hey, let's take a walk." I followed him into the parking lot, where, Mike told me, people liked to tailgate before the game. We talked for maybe twenty minutes about relaxing, having fun, making the most of the experience, and how the people here were for me. Mike talked about expectations, believing in myself, and how I was going to have to earn a spot. It is very tough for rookies to make it here. Playing in the Northern League is like skipping rookie ball. People compare it to Class A minor league ball. This was a hitter's league. If I made the Saints and survived the first year, that would mean success to me.

"Anything you need," he said, "Just ask."

I mentioned that in college the media attention had driven my joy in the game away. Mike replied that I would not have to say yes to every interview request. I quickly saw a man who wanted to see me succeed— he reminded me of my junior high coach, Rolland Esslinger.

"All I want is a shot, sir," I said. I wanted to make this man proud for taking a chance on me. Not a lot of people are that gutsy, but that's Mike Veeck. I would come to admire Mike as a husband and father, a smart businessman, a funny though quiet guy, and a great communicator. It felt good to talk with him about spring training camp and to have a chance to chill out before the big day.

I thought I'd be staying at a Motel 6, but it turned out to be a Radisson, ten minutes from the stadium, in Roseville, right next to some train tracks. When I got to the hotel, I decided to go for a jog, popped on my headphones and listened to Sarah McLachlan as I ran alongside the train tracks. I am never more at peace than when I'm hiking by myself, listening to music. It's my way of calming down. I visualize myself being successful on the mound, having the correct release points, hitting the correct spots, and watching the hitters swing and miss my pitches. On game days, though, I want Metallica or AC/DC blaring from my Walkman, and I go from feeling peaceful to wanting to rip my opponent's head off and shove it down his throat. I always had to be careful about flipping that switch when competing. Still do! Then, when I want to sleep or relax after a game, I'll tune into slow music and it works every time. And when I get upset, I'll play a song in my head, usually "Dancing Queen." Then I calm down and smile.

On the way back to the hotel, I stopped at a convenience store. I had been told that each day a bus would pick us up for practice and take us home afterward, but for anything else we were on our own. Because I would not get paid these two weeks, I didn't have much money for food—ten dollars in my bank account and fifty dollars cash. Before I left California, Dad had explained that he didn't want me to worry about anything while I was in Minnesota, so he would hold on to my fifty thousand dollars, pay my car insurance, and settle up when I got back home. Now I called to tell him I was broke and needed some money, but he replied that he didn't want me to blow it all. "Go," he said. "Play ball, and give it your all."

I suppose it's hard to understand why I didn't continue to argue with Dad for my money. I just knew from my childhood days that it was an argument I would never win. So here I was, ready to play ball but hungry. So it was a couple of jars of peanut butter and jelly, bread, packaged sandwiches, cereal and milk, and anything else that was cheap and filling. After I ate, I sat down with my copy of the Saints' preseason roster. Fourteen pitchers would compete for ten spots. Each club in the league was required to include six rookies on their roster. I looked over the players' names and marked those I thought would make it and those who would not. I left the space by my name blank. That night I barely slept. Spring training camp runs pretty much on military time. The handout we players were given was hour-by-hour and detailed. Baseball was my life at this time. I staked my value on how I did in the latest game, not on who I was as an individual or a child of God. What if I overslept and missed the bus? What if I didn't read the weather right? What if I failed at spring training camp? I would let down not just myself but also my family, Mike Veeck, sports, and everyone else rooting for me. I had no backup plan; this was it. I used to be able to shove the pressure to perform behind me and go forward, but this time it felt more difficult to do that. For one, the media attention was even more intense, more international.

I was also getting flack about the Silver Bullets. The day I showed up at the Saints spring training camp was the day the Silver Bullets had expected me at theirs. Dad had fielded the angry phone call. He said he just stayed quiet and let them vent. A woman—I can't recall her name—from the Women's Sports Foundation phoned, urging me not to play men's baseball. She feared that if I failed in St. Paul, I'd set back the cause of women's sports by sending the message that women's sports weren't good enough. But I wanted to play at the highest possible level of the sport I loved, and that was not with the Silver Bullets; it was in men's professional baseball. I also remember being asked by a female reporter, a Christian, the old question of whether it was biblical for me to be competing with men in a man's game. I hated that question. I believed in God; God had been answering my baseball prayers and opening doors for me at each point in my career. If my playing baseball was good enough for God, why should other Christians object? I was glad to learn that a former big leaguer, John Dettmer, would be at spring training camp, which would likely take some of the attention from me.

MAY 15, 1997. When I walked onto the field, I saw that the fences were close in, there was little foul territory, and the wind tended to blow toward the outfield. A hitter's park. I looked around anxiously, but no one seemed to be making a big deal out of my being here. Awesome. Rookie and veteran alike, the players came up and introduced themselves. They were friendly. Doubly awesome. These guys were a little older than most of the other teams in the Northern League and had been through a lot to get here. The first part of our day was called "Meet the Media," and a lot of the reporters, thankfully, did focus on John Dettmer. Compared with my media experiences in college, it was a more balanced and controlled scene.

Sixteen of us lined up behind the mound while one guy stood on the rubber, faked a throw to home, and either fielded comebackers or bunts, covered first base, or turned a double play. These drills were different from what I saw with Charlie Phillips's assistant coach, Jim Kale, who during practice liked to try to rip our heads off with his own power. But you cannot train for reactions that way. I had always found Ping-Pong to be the best drill for hand-eye coordination and reaction time. Now I was thankful to be around people who knew the game and weren't trying to be assholes. It was all about getting into baseball shape with quick moves, setting up your feet with your body, and communicating with your teammates.

It must have been forty degrees on the field, but with the wind chill it felt more like thirty. I wore two pairs of knee sox, a pair of compression shorts and long compression leggings under my baseball pants, a gray Saints T-shirt, a black long-sleeve Saints turtleneck, and a Saints sweatshirt. And still I was purple with cold. First off, we took PFP (pitchers' fielding practice). There's this great photo of the guys and me freezing our butts off. It was fun, kidding around with the guys—they towered over me, most being over six feet tall. Most of the jokes were about how cold it was. One guy said, "Ila, you're out here with mostly women right now, because our balls have shriveled up."

Everyone laughed at that one.

"Well, I have no boobs, so we're even," I replied. Everything I did, though, I gave a 110 percent, as I fielded the comebackers and bunts, and covered first.

Some said, "Slow down, Shorty"—Shorty being my new nickname, given by Dwight Smith—"You're making us look bad."

After PFP was done we were to throw bullpen or do running sprints. This first day, I wanted to loosen up my arm and calm my jitters, so I volunteered for the bullpen. My speed was seventy-five miles per hour, ten miles per hour behind the guys'. But my control was good; I was hitting all my spots and had good movement on the ball. The guys had speed and movement, but their pitches were all over the place. I was lucky because I had just finished college ball, so I was in good shape and my accuracy was right on. Our manager, Marty Scott, was a bearded, very heavy Texan, who could be stern. But he was sensible about the game and my place in it. As he pointed out to one reporter, "There's a lot of guys who throw 90 mph and never get anybody out because their ball is straight. . . . She's got a little bit of movement and she knows how to pitch." I noticed that there were few left-handers, which meant better odds of my making the team. Afterward we headed to the outfield to run the warning track between the foul poles. I felt shy, not wanting to invade other players' personal space, so kind of let them come to me if they wanted. I tried to be friendly and smile but also tried to be as invisible as possible, wanting to show that I was here to play and not for any other reason. At first I ran by myself, until a veteran came alongside. He had a lot of questions. I figured all the players were trying to figure me out: Could they joke around with me without being called for harassment? Trust me to not spill the beans to their wives that some of them had a girlfriend, or a drug or alcohol problem? What was my background, and would I play the rookie role, which means sitting double on the bus and carrying all the bags when needed? Was I looking to hook up with them or did I prefer girls? And how was I going to change the game for them or crimp their style? So I shot the breeze with him, laughed at his funny blonde-girl joke, and dropped an F-bomb to make him feel comfortable. He seemed to relax, and from that point on we talked about pitching. I was excited to learn from veterans like him and loved listening to their stories. After we had run twelve poles, he was ready for the showers, but he said something that, coming from him, meant a lot. "We all know what you went through to get here, and despite whether we are for or against you, we have the utmost respect for you."

I smiled at him, shook his hand, and ran four more poles. Everyone else had gone to the showers, and it gave me an opportunity to take everything in. I was living my dream, so overcome with thankfulness that I didn't know how to contain it all. As I ran, I praised God, saying, "Thank you, God, for everything—for my legs to run, my arms to throw, my body, for this opportunity. Thank you for giving me life. Thank you, thank you, thank you!"

When I was done running, I grabbed my cleats and mitt, and, still in my sweaty practice clothes, headed for the hotel bus. Because I hadn't showered, I was first in, and when the next four guys appeared they were surprised I hadn't changed. "Why didn't you take a shower after we were done?"

I said, "Have you seen this tossed salad under my cap? It takes forever to shampoo and dry this hair. Plus, now I get to give you crap for a girl having to wait on you guys to get ready."

"Well, next time take a shower, because you stink and we wanted you to come out with us for dinner."

I laughed and said, "Okay," but knew I wouldn't. I was broke and embarrassed about it. I was also afraid that people would read too much into my hanging out and having a beer with the guys—a photo of that scene could be taken all wrong. Looking back, I wish I had gone with them. But I did not want anything out there that would jeopardize my chance to play pro ball. It's hard to trust when everyone wants your job, and will do anything to set you up to fail. A good friend told me a story that reminded me to be careful: "Frankie" had been drafted by the Chicago Cubs and was the starting catcher in rookie ball. Another starter on the team had a best friend who was backup catcher; and the two came up with a plan to get rid of Frankie. Curfew was midnight, and no one (as in women) was allowed to be in the players' rooms. At 11:50 one night, a girl showed up at Frankie's door.

FRANKIE: "I think you have the wrong room."

SHE: "No, I have the right room, and I want you."

Even though he was nineteen years old and a beautiful girl was knocking on his door, he said, "Come back tomorrow," explaining that he couldn't have anyone in his room after midnight. She started to make a scene just as Frankie's manager was making the rounds. Frankie tried to explain the situation, but the following day he got a pink slip. He had done nothing wrong—and who knows what the full explanation for his getting cut was—but he was gone and the other catcher was in. Baseball may be a team sport, but it can be cutthroat in the minors. Everyone is scrapping for a job and some will do anything to get it, while some managers will release you for no reason at all.

Soon as I got back to the hotel, I phoned the family. Everyone was treating me great, I reported. The Saints were a very classy organization. Minnesota was green, green, green, and beautiful. As excited as I was, though, after I hung up the old loneliness started to creep in. It felt sad and familiar. With it came the feeling of being isolated, with my family and childhood friends far away. Isolated . . . Dad had named me "Ila" because he liked the sound of it. "Ila" means island dweller, and he had come to see that I sort of lived like I was on a deserted island. He was right.

I didn't know how many other players were staying at the hotel, probably about five, but I felt apart from them. I took out my journal and began to write, hoping to relieve the loneliness. After a shower and a dinner of a peanut butter and jelly sandwich with a banana, I was off to bed, where I could escape into my dreams. I dreamed of finding someone I could trust and love and laugh with; and I dreamed of succeeding in baseball.

During the first week, the pitchers were split up and we pitched to the position players. I did well again, hitting my spots and getting good movement on the ball. I was throwing a little faster, but still not close to eighty-five miles per hour. I had to stick with what I was best at. If I threw harder I'd lose control and spin on the ball. What was different in professional ball was that batters could foul off my hanging curve and simply wait for the next pitch. Then I had to go with my new pitch, the screwball I developed during senior year in college. Without the screwball, I wouldn't have made it into professional baseball.

Each afternoon, after we threw, I'd go for a run with the guys. Most of them had funny baseball stories to tell, but I had to tell them that mine were kind of depressing. They said that if I made the team I'd start to have funny stories in no time. Boy, were they right. In the meantime, we talked about working out, motorcycles, and surfing. I love reading, but nobody else really talked books. So I quoted some funny movie lines. And I'd run along, listen, and laugh with them when they were around.

And when they weren't, I'd talk to God, begging Him to be with me or to send me someone.

Week two of practice. We were now in game situations. The pitchers were trying to get the hitters out, and the hitters were trying to get on base. On May 19, my first appearance came in a simulated game, with most of the guys playing out of their usual positions and some pitchers playing defense, due to our short roster. In a game like this, as Mike Augustin wrote in the *St. Paul Pioneer Press*, "The score didn't matter. Yet it was Borders's first live performance in a professional setting. It mattered to her."

Augustin was right; it did matter to me. But Lamarr Rogers, the first batter, beat out a slow roller to short. Then Scott Leius, a former major leaguer, singled sharply to left. A fly ball to right field was misjudged and landed for a double. The fourth batter singled through the middle. It got worse. After a fly ball out, a potential double play ground ball was thrown away. Mercifully, the next guy hit into a successfully executed double play. The following inning, after giving up a double, I got three quick outs. Marty Scott pointed out that only once did I go to three balls on a batter. "I don't put much stock in simulated games," he told the *Pioneer Press*. "But Ila made adjustments in her second inning. I am amazed at her poise, her mindset, her mound presence."

But I knew that I wasn't fully on my game: my fastball wasn't catching the outside corner of the plate. Even so, there would be another chance. Marty told me I was slated to pitch a couple of innings in the Saints' first exhibition game at Midway Stadium against the Duluth-Superior Dukes.

MAY 22, 1997. As we pulled into Midway's parking lot, I saw a mass party going on, hours before the game started; it was the tailgating Mike Veeck had mentioned to me. I had always thought that tailgating was a part of football culture, not baseball. But here it was, Minnesota style: The gates had opened at four o'clock for the night game, and people had planted their lounge chairs; their barbecues, which they fired up; and even their inflatable plastic swimming pools on the grass. Beer flowed and games of corn hole, with beanbags, were being played. People mingled, visiting with other groups—it was like a huge neighborhood party.

Because I avoided the clubhouse, I had to enter the ballpark through the front gate and make my way down the third base side, where there was an entrance to the field. Some fans tugged at me, others shoved baseballs at me for autographs. Grateful to Mike Veeck for my being here, I tried to sign them all. For my first appearance the ballpark was packed. People stood in the fire tower behind the right-field fence. The bullpen, where I sat, was down the left-field line, with a three-foot chain-link fence separating us from the fans. One guy wore a baseball cap with a streamer coming out the back. It looked like my ponytail coming out of my cap. Boy, that fad caught on fast. We ended up calling for a security guard because people were coming up left and right poking me in the back to sign stuff for them.

I was glad to be pitching middle relief, which gave me time to study the batters. Besides, I'd be spared the extra pressure of starting or closing. When the signal came to get ready to pitch the top of the seventh inning, I stood up, left my jacket on the aluminum bench, and grabbed a ball. As soon as I started to throw, people all over the stadium stood to watch, just to catch a glimpse of me in the bullpen. People started to chant, "Ila, Ila, Ila." Then a train passed by the stadium, going very slow. Its horn whistled twice, and I saw a big sign on the side of a boxcar: "Go, ILA!"

Was this Ila-mania all over again?

As I jogged toward the mound, the Doors' "Love Her Madly" boomed over the public-address system. I could barely hear the music because the fans' cheers echoed off the metal and concrete of the stadium. What was this? The good vibes were confusing. I was used to rejection, and here they were cheering. I was used to being the underdog. How did I react to love? Thank goodness I was on the mound, because I felt comfortable there. Even so, I felt the pressure of possibly letting a lot of people down. But I knew deep within that I would rather take a chance and fail than not take one at all and never have the chance to succeed. Maybe being willing to take that risk, not just talent, is the biggest difference between success and failure.

First batter up was Jeff Jensen, a left-hander, number three in the line-up. The stadium continued to rock, and I could not hear my infielders. I faced home plate. I got Jensen to 2-and-2, then threw a change-up. When he struck out swinging, the crowd went nuts. A ground out, a walk, another ground out, and I was out of the inning. Beautiful.

The eighth inning was not beautiful: I coughed up two singles and a walk—bases loaded with nobody out. Another single brought in a run before I notched a strikeout. And then a drive to left field went for a two-run double when Chris Evans, our left fielder, fell down, and two more runs came in. By the time I got a called third strike for the last out, I had given up five hits, two walks, and five earned runs. I was tagged with the loss. And still, I walked off the mound to an ovation. I felt the team and the local media behind me. As the *St. Paul Pioneer Press* reported the next day, our catcher, Sean Delaney, said, "She did a whale of a job. . . . She kept the ball down for the most part. It was exciting catching her. The fans got into it. If she stays around, it will be like that all the time." The paper also quoted Barry Moss, who managed the game. Barry was a player's coach, always backing us up. Now he told the reporter that I'd had a great first inning. "She was very nervous, but she threw well," he added. "She was real effective with her change-up."

Privately Barry told me, "Let's work on this. You started getting the ball up." I took his advice gratefully; I trusted Barry. After the game, which we ultimately lost, Jim Wadley, the owner of the Dukes, and some of his players came over to say hello. (One of their pitchers, Steve Maddock, had played against a woman named Kendra Hanes in 1994 in the independent Frontier League. Hanes played outfield for the Kentucky Rifles.)

After the game ended, the fans were all around, and I signed autographs for about an hour and a half, until the last ball was signed. I had once been a fan of George Brett and Brett Saberhagen, and remembered their taking the time to sign a ball for me. It meant so much. It was late when the last ball was signed, and I caught a ride back to the hotel from one of the grounds crew. When I got back to the hotel the guy at the front desk had waited to get an autograph. My pockets were jammed with scraps of paper with phone numbers of both men and women, beseeching me to call them. I did not call any of them. My focus was on making the team. Besides, I was too scared to date a woman, figuring that if we were seen together it could end my career. As for dating a man, I didn't want to lead anyone on or be thought of as possibly there for the easygoing sex that colors baseball.

When I got to my room I called home. Dad answered and went over some pointers. He had listened to the game on the computer. Any questions I had about a certain pitch, I always asked him. Then Leah got on the phone to say that while I was pitching, Dad had paced back and forth, chain-smoking about half a pack of cigarettes. He thought I was going to get up to bat and they were going to hit you again, like they did in college. According to my sister, if I had been hit he was going to hop on a plane and nail the guy. To my family, it seemed liked Dad was pitching and not me. With all his faults, I knew he was pulling for me big time, worried about me, and loved me. After every game I pitched I called him.

I still had a few days to prove I belonged here. We were divided into two teams and competed against each other. Everyone was doing well, but I knew I was right there. On the last day of practice they were going to announce the roster for the season. In the clubhouse was a sign, "GON' FISHIN'". Whenever a player got cut from the roster, the tape with his name was ripped from his locker and pasted onto the cinder block wall below the GON' FISHIN' sign. Nerve-wracking.

Preseason practice grew more intense as the deadline neared for making the roster. I have never been the sort of player who could joke around before a game—most starting pitchers aren't. To get ready I focus by remaining quiet and concentrating. It also fuels my anger against the other team. I wasn't here to make nice. After we suited up, I went out to warm up. Everyone had a partner to throw to but me and this other guy. Joe Miller was cool with me and very talented, but no one seemed to want to play catch with him. I learned very soon why. For one, he was left-handed also, but he threw more than ninety miles per hour and had a killer knuckleball, which is hell to catch. On his first throw he blasted me with a fastball from about sixty feet. *What the fuck?* I said to myself. Players usually tested me at first but not like this. I should have said something but didn't want to come across as a wuss or a whiner. So I moved two fingers out of my mitt instead of one to create more of a pocket to catch the ball. Next throw, same thing. The guy next to me said, "Watch out, he's a dick."

So I threw the crap out of the ball as hard as I could back at him. After we warmed up and played long toss he came back in, and said, "Wow, your ball has a lot of movement on it."

"Wish I could say the same," I replied, "but I couldn't see the seams on the ball it was coming in so fast. Next time I will get a catcher's mitt if you want to throw a bullpen instead of warming up."

Joe laughed and said he was only trying to win a spot on the rotation—he didn't want to play the outfield anymore. I figured this guy wasn't trying to see if I could handle a ninety-plus-miles-per-hour at my ankles; he was trying to impress people. Instead he was making himself look like an ass. Too bad, I thought, because he had great stuff. I played catch with this guy only one more time, because on the second day of practice he said he was going to throw a fastball and then he threw a knuckleball. He was about sixty feet away and signaled with his mitt by waving it forward that a fastball was coming. As soon as he released it, I saw a nasty knuck-ler coming my way. I managed to catch it, but it hit the tip of my right thumb, pushing it backward. I thought, *Oh, great, my thumb is broken because of this idiot.* The pain was excruciating, and it took a month to get the feeling back, though I hid it from most everyone. No one played catch with Joe anymore, so the bullpen catcher got stuck with him.

MAY 29, 1997. Last day of practice. We play another simulated game today. Marty Scott came up and said, "You are going to pitch against all left-handed hitters."

This was bad news. I had usually been a starter through high school and college and so had developed out pitches only for right-handed batters, because the lineups are usually stacked with them. My stuff was great against them, but I did not have a slider to use against the left-handers. My ball likes to sink and tail away from right-handers, but it goes right into a left-hander's wheelhouse. *Great,* I thought. *I need to learn a dialed-in slider or a cut fastball right now.*

This was not a formal game—a step up from batting practice but not an intrasquad game. Facing the feared left-handers, I struggled; the batters feasted: one inning, three hits, three runs. When I was done I went for my usual run in the outfield, cussing myself, furious that in a mere thirty minutes I had blown it. No one was harder on me than I was, not even Dad. Then I stretched out on my stomach in left field, staring at the blades of grass. I looked around at the ballpark, pondering what I went through to get here and what I had been a part of at Midway Stadium. I had learned a lot in these two weeks. I'd sat on the bench next to John Dettmer, listening to his experiences pitching for the Texas Rangers. From John and other pitchers I'd picked up mechanical nuances, like how to get more spin on the ball. I'd learned to read hitters better, and when to slide step to home and when not to. Now I wondered whether this was my last day here. I cannot remember who came out to me in left field to say that the coaches wanted to see me. Had the name "Borders" already been posted under the GON' FISHIN' sign? I got up, brushed the grass off my uniform, and said, "Okay, where are they?"

"They're all behind home plate," he said. "In the shed where the ground crew stashes their stuff."

Why there? I wondered. *Probably because they don't want to tell me the bad news in front of everyone in the clubhouse.* My stats for the four-game exhibition season were not good: I had given up six runs and six hits for an 18.00 ERA over three innings. So the jog to the shed was the longest three hundred feet I had ever done. Inside were Barry Moss, Marty Scott, and the pitching consultant Marv White. Marty started by asking how I felt today. "I sucked, I was nervous," I replied. "I want this so bad, but I felt good the other days. I just need to relax, and make my curveball more like a slider to the lefties."

"Yeah," he said. "I agree with you; it was not your best outing. But we see a fit for you here. Congratulations. You made the team."

My heart rose. Did I hear correctly? "I promise to give you everything I have and more," I babbled. "I will do better next time."

Barry Moss gave me a huge grin as Marty nodded and said, "Okay. Because we don't have a lot of left-handed pitchers, you'll be used in relief. You'll come in when we are behind and need some innings out of someone." Marty didn't hold back. He went on to say, "In any other given year, if we had a stronger rookie staff to draw from you might not have made the club. But based on what we have here and what you've shown, combined with your desire and your work ethic and your love for the game, you're going to break with the team."

I wanted to cry out, jump up and down, scream at the top of my lungs, and hug every single one of those guys, especially Barry Moss. But in my head I heard Dad's voice: "Show No Emotion. Control yourself and never let anyone see what's going on inside."

Okay, I told myself. *Keep it together. Don't be a girl.* I had learned well how to mask my emotions, but right now I was a rock star at it.

Barry told me later that they all wondered why I didn't react more. Looking back I should have showed them what I felt. They deserved that! Instead I smiled, shook hands, thanked them, and proceeded out of the shed. When I went to go grab my glove and cleats out in the outfield where I left them, they were gone. Great. I had no money, and now I had no glove and no shoes. SSK was going to be pissed because they supplied the mitt to me for free. I would have to borrow my pitching coach's mitt. Eventually I borrowed money from my friend, Kelly Deutsch, until I got paid, so I could buy a pair of cleats. I knew Dad would hold it against me if I asked for some of my money. It was easier to borrow from Kelly.

Back at the hotel, I called home. I could hear everyone scream—Leah, Phillip, Randall, and Mom. We had our shortcomings, but we all pulled for each other. I could tell Dad was excited, but like me, he kept it inside and simply said, "Congratulations, Ila."

Mom later said that she'd never seen him so joyful. After we hung up I cut loose. I jumped into the shower, singing loud the way you do when you know nobody else can hear, then got into my thermal pajamas, and put on my headphones. Heater blaring, I danced around the room singing. I was filled with so much excitement I did not know what to do with the emotion. I was almost laughing at myself, and was thanking God in my weird way. Metallica was playing, but I was singing for God, my best friend. I was ready to kick some ass. I don't recall falling asleep, but I woke up the next morning on top of the covers with one headphone still in my ear.

The next day, I went to the stadium to pick out a uniform. Most all of the numbers had been chosen, and I had a choice between one and fourteen. No way would I choose number one—it would send the wrong message—so the club added my name to the back of number fourteen. When I returned to my hotel room that afternoon I snapped lots of pictures of my team jersey.

When the news broke that I had made the team, reporters called from all over the country, along with Japan and Canada. I think I ticked off a lot of sportswriters, because I followed Mike Veeck's advice and did not say yes to every phone call or request for an interview. The comfort was that Mike Veeck and the Saints management understood my approach to all this: to just get along and play ball. I should add that a writer named Neal Karlen was hanging around. He had arrived in town the year before to do a hit piece on the "real" Bill Murray for *Rolling Stone* magazine. (Besides being a comedian and movie star, Murray was the Saints' co-owner). But Karlen instead got caught up in a transformative story about the characters of all stripes on the Saints staff and team (as well as himself) that would evolve into a book. Neal was an Ivy League graduate, smart but a real rebel. He was short and skinny, with black curly hair, and sometimes smelled of alcohol. I appreciated that Neal was respectful of the space I tried to keep with the media. But knowing he was working on a book, I was wary of opening up to him. I'd hide from him, but persistent journalist that he was, he'd come find me. I did show him one of my journals, in which I poured out my emotions about making the cut. In *Slouching toward Fargo: A Two-Year Saga of Sinners and St. Paul Saints at the Bottom of the Bush Leagues with Bill Murray, Darryl Strawberry, Dakota Sadie, and Me,* Neal recorded my reaction:

"I FUCKING MADE THE TEAM! I FUCKING MADE THE TEAM! DREAMS COME TRUE! DREAMS COME TRUE!"

Hardly a profound line in baseball literature, but there it was: real and true and good. I had fucking made the team.

I continued to stick to my approach of shying from the media, which I hoped gained me respect and trust from my teammates. I think they understood by now I was here because playing ball was my dream, just like it was theirs. And Marty wisely set a policy of refusing to answer any media inquiries about me unless I was pitching that day.

Mike Veeck's Saints made the ballpark a great place to spend the evening. Shoot, sometimes I wanted to be in the stands. Mike's philosophy, "Fun Is Good," showed up everywhere. I was surprised to see in the seats behind third base a nun named Sister Rosalind, who administered massages. She was known, of course, as the "stress reliever." Behind the left-field seats was a hot tub, where college kids liked to enjoy their beers while watching the game. Between innings were dizzy bat races for prizes, or two people in sumo wrestling costumes who would try to knock each other down. I always wanted to try sumo wrestling but never got the call. And the pig. In his first year of ownership, Mike had begun the tradition of having a pig—actually a piglet—dressed in an apron with big pockets that delivered baseballs to the umpires. This year's piglet was named Hamlet, and over the years Mike would have a wonderful time naming each season's piglet, from the Great Hambino (1998) to Bud Squealig (2006) and Boarack Obama (2008). Mike's personal favorite was Hammy Davis Junior (2000).

Mike's creativity runs right up to and sometimes over the edge of propriety, and he had paid dearly for it. As a young man working for his father, Bill Veeck Jr., with the Chicago White Sox in 1979, he had thought that a promotion to "kill" disco music might be a fun diversion between a doubleheader. But Disco Demolition Night resulted in a riot and a rare forfeit; and Mike found himself shunned by Major League Baseball. It would take him years to get back into the game. Once he was back, Mike unrepentantly engaged in promotional schemes that challenged conventional thinking. In 1996 he signed Dave Stevens, the legless ESPN producer, to play in the Saints' exhibition season. He would go on to promote Snake Oil Salesman's Night and, for his Charleston, South Carolina, RiverDogs, Free Vasectomy Night for Father's Day—at least until the Roman Catholic Diocese of Charleston protested.

Mike liked a good laugh, but he had known plenty of tears, too. His six-year-old daughter Rebecca suffered from a rare eye disease, retinitis pigmentosa, for which there is no cure. She saw the world in shadows that would grow dimmer until eventually she would become legally blind. The bright side of the publicity buzz that surrounded me was that that young girls like Rebecca learned that I played the game of baseball and it inspired them. I like to think that it helped to widen their view of the world and what they themselves might accomplish.

I had hoped the attention would wane after I made the team. It did not. The majority of the letters from fans were positive, but the ones that were not were disturbing and I tended to obsess over them. Surprisingly, many of those who sent angry letters and e-mails were women. Men were more supportive, if you discounted the weird ones. One guy showed up at my parents' house claiming he was my husband and the father of my child. Child? I told my parents to call the cops if he ever returned. Another man got hold of my home address and began corresponding with Mom. She respected that he was in the military and thought it would be okay to respond to him with information about me. She has no idea how crazy this world can be.

At the ballpark, I tried to be fan-friendly, but one time I failed. Finding the space to chill before a game was always tough, and I often used a women's restroom in the stands. As I sat inside the stall, a woman shoved her camera under the door and snapped a picture. I came out flaming, grabbed her camera, pulled out the roll of film, and threw it into the sink. From that point on I used the umpires' or staff restroom inside the offices.

I also worried about finances. Once I made the team, I started making 750 dollars a month. I thought about doing commercials but did not want to take on anything that would make me too busy to concentrate on baseball or look like I was out for the notoriety. I tried to get a sponsor to pay for my cleats. The responses came back: there is no market for a female playing baseball, plus you have no guarantee on a contract. The Saints could drop me the next day for any reason, and no one wanted to take a chance on that. I found that curious, since American entrepreneurs are all about risk.

It was time to find a place to live. Most of my teammates rented as trios in a one-bedroom apartment and shared a car. After he arrived in town J. D. Drew would sleep on the floor, because his two roommates took the one bedroom. The Saints put me in touch with their groundskeeper, Connie Rudolph. Connie and her husband had three young kids and offered me the use of their basement. I could also hitch a ride with Connie to the field. What a blessing! Living in the basement gave me the privacy I needed, while being part of their active household warmed my heart: I could see the love in the Rudolph family and how well they all got along. I read the book *Saint Mudd*, by Steve Thayer, and learned about the history of St. Paul during the Depression and gangster times. I wanted to explore my grandmother's home state and went downtown to visit the science center, the cathedral, and a club owned by Prince; I attended the first collegiate female hockey game ever played, at Minnesota State; and I biked through various neighborhoods.

Connie Rudolph was a godsend. Not only did she provide a roof over my head; she became a friend. On one of my days off, she took me to the St. Croix River at Taylor's Falls for my first canoe adventure. The river is on the Minnesota-Wisconsin border, and as we paddled, with me endlessly gawking at the scenery, other boaters passed by, always greeting us, always friendly. I remember thinking that I could get used to calling this place home. It was warm that day, and when we spotted a tire hanging from an overhanging tree, we had to stop. We were like two little kids—swinging out over the river and letting go, and swimming back to the canoe, laughing like crazy.

On another off day, Connie organized an outing to Quarry Park, near St. Cloud. As we followed the dirt path through what felt to me like a rain forest, we came upon a large water-filled former rock quarry. College kids floated on inner tubes, laying bets on who would be gutsy enough to jump from the top of the granite rock into the chilly waters and grading the ones who tried. Connie's kids, who had done this before, jumped first, from four feet up. But it was another forty- to fifty-foot hike to the top of the rock for the big jump. Of course, I had to try it. Connie's sons hiked up with me. They told me to wear shoes, so I would not slip; get a running start; and jump far out toward the deep water, away from the rocky outcroppings. I watched while they jumped first; the daredevil in me was nervous. I stood for ten minutes, listening to the voices in my head that advised against jumping. I could get hurt—that was Dad's voice. Then my own voice kicked in—Go for it! I tightened my bikini top, took a running start, and jumped out as far as I could. I'd been told to not look down, which I immediately did. It felt like my stomach came up into my throat, and I had to bear down with a grunt to push it back down. I pulled my head up, pointed my toes, and hit the water. When I surfaced, the crowd was clapping. Mostly guys had been jumping. What a rush—I wanted to go again, but it was cold that day and we packed it in. For a few hours, the adventure had taken me far from baseball and the cares that went with it.

Back at Midway, Connie was there when I experienced my first Midwestern thunderstorm. A rain delay had been quickly called—the club didn't hesitate when a storm threatened—and when Connie looked up and saw the strange color of the sky, she said, "Oh, no. This is gonna be a bad one." Remembering the tale of the ballplayer who was struck and killed by lightning in Saskatchewan, I didn't hesitate either. While my teammates hung out in the locker room, Connie and I took cover in the maintenance shed behind home plate. As the storm swept through, we watched as cars, including Connie's, floated in the parking lot and on Energy Park Drive. It was the worst storm she'd seen here. I continued to be in awe of Minnesota's landscape—and now its powerful weather.

MAY 31, 1997. I looked forward to pitching in my first regular-season game. It would be on the road against the Sioux Falls Canaries. (I was also happy to be receiving my first paycheck, as I was down to six dollars.) I like to think that determination has been my biggest strength throughout my life. Doors have been shut in my face, and I have failed miserably at times, but I brush myself off and keep going. I would have to draw on that after tonight's game. I was warming up in the bullpen when Barry Moss came down and said, "You're coming in for the sixth inning. Watch out for the home plate umpire. He has a big ego and loves to call balks."

I couldn't recall ever being called for a balk and didn't think much about it. I came into the game in the bottom of the sixth inning with two outs and a runner on third. My first pitch, a curveball, hit Paul Cruz. Watchful of Cruz, now on first, I threw to the next batter, Michael Dumas.

"Balk!" yelled the umpire, which allowed the runner on third to score.

What the frick? Are you kidding? A balk? I stood motionless on the mound, making my opinion of the call apparent: One, why so damn late in the call? Two, I had not balked. *Maybe my biggest concern should be the umpires,* I suddenly thought. *If they don't like me, they can make my life hell.*

When Dumas lined a full-count pitch right at me, I knocked it down but overthrew my first baseman, allowing another run to score. When John Tsoukalas doubled for another run, Marty Scott yanked me. I had faced three batters, hit a batter, balked, committed a throwing error, and given up three runs. I left the mound fuming and embarrassed, knowing the news would be broadcast everywhere. Then Barry Moss came up and said, "Be ready to go tomorrow. You have to let it go and be ready for the next day. Your confidence is way down, and the quicker you get out there, the better it will be to regain it." In his own way Barry was saying, "Go get 'em, Ila. It will be okay."

He always had my back. But I remained down until, after the game, one of the Dukes came over. "I don't know how we got out of that one," he said. "You didn't balk at all. I just wanted to say 'Hi,' and good luck to you."

After facing up to the postgame interviews, I wanted to disappear. The following day, in Japan, Australia, and throughout the United States, sports pages announced "Borders Rocked" and quoted me as saying this was the worst day of my life.

JUNE 1, 1997. Just like Barry said, the next day came. Marty Scott handed me the lineup card, and I carried it to home plate before heading for the bullpen. When the signal came to get ready to pitch the eighth inning, I knew—everyone knew—that if I pitched badly today, I was done. I remember praying, "Lord you know how much I have worked for this, you know how much I sacrificed for this, how I picked myself up off the ground. Please be with me and bless me, even for this one inning." I ran out to what was becoming my theme song: No Doubt's "I Am Just a Girl in This World," but the music inside my head was AC/DC's "Hell's Bells." *Give it your best shot*, I said to myself. *One hundred and ten percent of everything you have. If you do that and fail, hey, you gave it your all.*

It started out rough: a hard smash off our third baseman's glove for a single; the next batter struck out on a curve in the dirt, but the runner took second; and then a walk; another strikeout and another walk. Consistency—walk, a strikeout, a walk, a strikeout—where the hell was consistency! Bases loaded, two out. I faced John Tsoukalas, a left-handed veteran. He swung and missed the first pitch, took a called strike, and then another on a curve ball. Even though we were playing out of town, the crowd had been behind me. Now it went nuts. That pretty much sums up baseball—and my life. When I fail or something really awful happens, I come back fighting and end up becoming a better athlete or person. Coming back in, I spotted a huge grin on Barry's face. The guys high-fived and slapped me on the back. After the game, the *Pioneer Press* reported this moment: "As she was getting ready to leave the park, an elderly gentleman approached Borders.

"'I would be honored if you signed my scorecard,' he said.

"'Where should I sign it?' asked Borders, experienced in the practice.

"'By the eighth inning,' the man said, 'where you struck out the side.'"

Then the Canaries player–pitching coach Steve Howe came over, shook my hand, and said, "Good job. You have great stuff. Don't let people say you have to throw harder. Keep at it."

That meant a lot, coming from Howe, who knew a few things about coming back from adversity. He had been a star pitcher with the Los Angeles Dodgers but had been suspended seven times for substance abuse. After the game I thought, *Cool. I had guaranteed one more day with the Saints. My name won't appear under the* GON' FISHIN' *sign tonight.*

JUNE 3, 1997. In my third professional appearance, on the road against the Sioux City Explorers, I got the call to pitch the sixth inning. I ran to the mound to the tune of "I Am Just a Girl in the World," and so I was. I pitched two innings, allowing a run on two hits, and notched another strikeout. Fireworks and more cheers from the opposing fans! I still felt uncomfortable about this sort of attention, concerned that it could turn my teammates envious, as it had in college. Of course, the adulation was not unanimous: Before we entered the game, the Explorers' radio announcer asked Sioux City manager Ed Nottle his opinion on the Saints' roster. Nottle's reply was memorable: "There is one thing on it I hope they get rid of pretty soon. Besides that, I don't know much about it."

The "thing" he was referring to was me.

So I appreciated Marty Scott's comment about my part in the game. "I thought Ila showed tonight she has as big a heart as any ballplayer around," he told the *Pioneer Press*. "Did she go out there and compete and try to keep us in this thing? Yes she did. She deserves more respect than she's getting."

Heading back to the bus after the Sioux City game was an education in a whole new way. Groupies were lined up outside the locker room, waiting for someone, anyone, to come out. There were fifteen or so women, some flashing their boobs at the players to seal the deal. A few of the players drove off with a woman, and others arranged to meet at the hotel later. The girls who hadn't hooked up continued to flash the guys on the bus. Some even tried to get on our bus for a quickie in the back restroom. I don't know how many times guys had sex in that bathroom, but I learned to avoid that place. I was amazed at how aggressive these girls were; but for the guys it was better than a frat party. There were guys who were faithful to their wives, but not many. At first the guys were a little worried about me: "Holy crap, I'm married but have girlfriends in every town. Is this girl going to talk?" But they learned fast that I would keep their secrets. I did not care who they slept with, as long as they were ready to play ball and do it well.

If my teammates were concerned about what I saw, I soon learned that their wives and girlfriends really worried. Each of these women would single me out, stare, or try to get the scoop on me. I tried my best to put their minds to rest. I wished everyone knew me better, that no matter what, I would never do anything like that. But I came to understand why most guys got into trouble. You are stressed out, on the road, lonely, and near broke, and now you have these women throwing themselves at you, wanting to make you feel good.

I adapted to the groupie scene by trying to make myself invisible. On game days I showed up in my uniform and went back on the bus that way to avoid the locker room. For road trips, when we'd be on the bus for up to eleven hours, I wore an awful-looking jogging suit that was way too big. When my back hurt and I needed to lie on the floor of the bus, the spilt beer cans that rolled to a stop next to me didn't bother me. Guys dressed to the max, but I downplayed everything I had. I wore no tight clothes, used no makeup, and showed no skin, all to avoid drawing attention to myself. I never talked to my teammates about dating. Why? So no one would hit on me and the wives would not worry about me. At one point a religious teammate told a reporter that it would be nice to see me in a dress on the bus. Are you kidding me? Obviously he had no daughters. The next day everyone on the bus said he was a freaking idiot. They tried to get me into a pink tutu and wear it at practice or on the bus. Gee, just for the fun of it, I wish I had.

I was happily settling into life in St. Paul. Each night I set extra alarms so I'd be sure to wake up in the morning for the early bus ride. After every game, my muscles ached all over. I put my trust in God to take the abilities He gave me as far as they could go. ssk had come through—every time my mitt was stolen, they sent me another one. They probably thought I was selling them. I felt good in St. Paul, knowing that Mike Veeck and Barry Moss had my back. They had been true to their word about the media. If I didn't want to do an interview, they didn't care—they just wanted me to be at ease. And I tried to do everything I could for them.

After every game I signed autographs until everyone was gone or the team bus was about to leave. Maybe that boy I sign a ball for will someday have a daughter who wants to play baseball, and he will help her. Maybe that girl doesn't have a mom or a female role model but now sees me doing something that people predicted she could not do. The memories of the hard times I'd had with some of my teammates at Southern California College began to fade. Most of my teammates and opposing players accepted me. So did most of the fans, though sitting in the bullpen was an adventure. One woman reached down with a pair of scissors to try to cut a piece of my hair. Others threw beer or food on me. All I wanted was to concentrate on gaining my teammates' respect and helping us to win. Before one of the games I read to a bunch of kids in front of the stadium as part of a program called the Reading Tree. On the outside of Midway Stadium, an artist had begun a mural of Wayne Terwilliger, the Saints' seventy-two-year-old assistant coach, and me. "Twig," as everyone calls him, is a beloved baseball figure in the Twin Cities. The mural was the first thing you saw when you pulled into the parking lot. What an honor to be next to Twig on the stadium wall! I wished I were getting more innings, but the Saints were in first place, heading for the pennant, and tended to go with their veterans. Still, I was surviving as a rookie.

JUNE 10, 1997. The first regular season home game I pitched in was a wild ride. Just as it had during spring training and the exhibition season, the train, with its "GO, ILA" sign, blew its whistle as it passed by the left-field stands. I came into the game against the Sioux City Explorers in the top of the ninth, with the bases loaded and two out. I gave up a two-run single before getting the third out on a fly ball to center.

JUNE 15, 1997. In a game against the Duluth-Superior Dukes, I was brought in during the eighth inning with one out and the bases loaded. I faced catcher Bryan Mitterwald, a left-handed batter. He swung and missed on the first pitch, fouled off a couple of pitches, then took an inside fastball off the plate. He fouled off a couple more pitches, and then, on a 1-2 count, I got him to hit into a rally-killing double play.

Mitterwald told the *Pioneer Press*, "She threw me some breaking balls and I just tried to stay back on them, but I didn't do my job. . . . She didn't throw nothing by me. . . . But she got me out on a good pitch, a curve in on my hands."

The Saints swept a doubleheader from the Thunder Bay Whiskey Jacks. In the first game, I pitched the bottom of the seventh, giving up two singles, a walk, and a run, with one strikeout. Back at Midway, I pitched the ninth against the Winnipeg Goldeyes and gave up three unearned runs. And there I sat. The Saints were in first place, contending for the Eastern Division again, and I was seeing little playing time.

JUNE 26, 1997. And then it was over. When I showed up for practice, Marty Scott called me into his office. "We really like you here," he said. "But you should be getting more innings." He told me he valued my work ethic but that my stuff was not up to par for a pennant contender. My record was seven games, six innings, eight runs, eleven hits, four walks, five strikeouts, 7.50 ERA. The club wanted to free up space on the roster for a hard-throwing pitcher. At first I figured I was being released. And then Marty said that I had been traded to the Duluth-Superior Dukes. That team needed a left-handed reliever and had a rookie spot available. Marty expected that I would get more work there. I had not seen this coming, but that's life in the Northern League: you're up, you're down, you're out. Last season, after Darryl Strawberry lit up the league, he returned to the bright lights of New York, where he played three more seasons with the Yankees. After Jack Morris threw a complete game shutout, the Yankees offered him a place on their Triple A roster. He declined. Instead, Morris finished out the first half of the season in St. Paul with a fine ten-inning performance, then quit to return to his ranch in Montana. And I was moving not exactly sideways but a step down to a smaller-market team, where Marty thought I would do better away from the ever-present Twin Cities media.

My six weeks with the Saints had been crammed with people who became dear to me. I would miss Barry Moss and Marty Scott and Mike Veeck. I'd miss the loyal and forgiving and enthusiastic St. Paul fans. And what about Connie Rudolph and her family? I felt a close bond with Connie and didn't want to lose it. Yet baseball-wise, the trade seemed like a win-win-win for both teams and for me. Both teams were looking to strengthen their rosters, and I definitely needed to pitch more innings. But a couple of individuals expressed their unhappiness with the trade. When Mike told his daughter Rebecca that I had been traded, she reacted in true Veeck fashion—she turned to the media. "When my daddy told me Ila wasn't going to play for the Saints anymore, I cried," she told Mike Augustin of the *St. Paul Pioneer Press.* "Ila was my favorite player. She came to our house. I followed her all around."

Keith English, the utility infielder I was traded for, wasn't excited either. "I will probably be the most hated person in St. Paul—they're losing their Ila," he lamented to the *Duluth News Tribune.* "I got traded for a girl. It can't get any worse than that." (English, who was batting .091 at the time of the trade, was quickly shipped to the Frontier League, another independent league.)

I did not care if I was traded for a box of baseballs; I just wanted to play. Yet as I threw my clothes and gear into my luggage, I had to wonder how married ballplayers with kids dealt with having to suddenly move. People have romantic ideas about pro baseball, but both of my Little League friends, Mike Moschetti and Frankie Cicero, draft picks just a few years ago, were out of the game. The life is hard. Airline ticket in hand, I said a quick good-bye to Connie and the Rudolph family and caught the last flight of the day to Duluth.

1. Starting out: in 1975, it was Dad, Mom, and me. (Courtesy of Marianne Borders)

2. In my first year of Little League, the determination shows in my face.
(Courtesy of Marianne Borders)

3. At age twelve came my first big media interview. Rick Lozano from KABC-TV in Los Angeles reported on the Little League game I pitched, when I struck out eighteen of eighteen batters. (Courtesy of Marianne Borders)

4. At my high school graduation in June 1993, we look like a happy family, on the outside. Despite everything, I've always stayed close to my siblings. *Back, left to right*: Mom, me, Dad, Leah; *middle*: Phillip; *front*: Randall. (Courtesy of Marianne Borders)

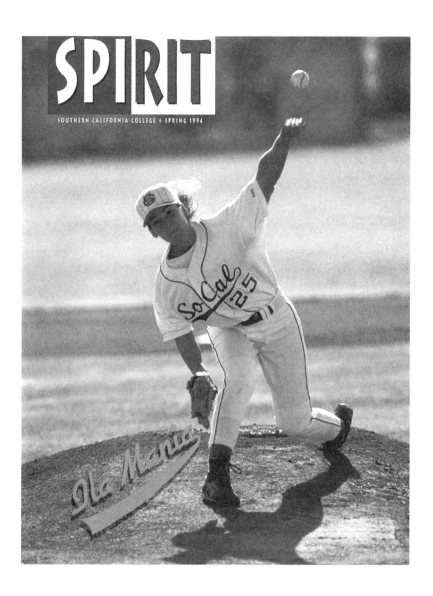

5. The spring 1994 cover of Southern California College's magazine *Spirit* captures the beginning of "Ila-mania," the intense media scrutiny that continued throughout most of my career. (Courtesy of Vanguard University Archives, Costa Mesa, California)

6. This shot shows so well my anxieties in college. (Courtesy of Lois Bernstein)

7. (*above*) After sophomore year in college I spent the summer in Canada, playing for the Swift Current Indians. Life there was always an adventure as we traveled to games throughout Saskatchewan on the "bubble bus." Pictured are my teammates and me in the back of the bus. (Courtesy of Ila Borders)

8. (*left*) My rookie card was a baseball dream come true. (Courtesy of the St. Paul Saints)

9. (*opposite top*) Being on the mural with the Saints' much-loved Wayne Terwilliger at Midway Stadium was a huge honor! (Courtesy of the St. Paul Saints)

10. (*opposite bottom*) In my few weeks with the St. Paul Saints, their groundskeeper Connie Rudolph provided hospitality and so much more. A friendship began then that continued through the years. Here we are biking in Arizona in 2008. (Courtesy of Ila Borders)

11. (*above*) Waiting to interview me as I pitched for the Dukes, Mike Wallace stood up for me in the stands over an umpire's call. (Courtesy of the *Duluth News Tribune*)

12. Mike Veeck always had a hug for me whenever I returned to Midway Stadium. (Courtesy of Connie Rudolph)

13. My Duluth-Superior Dukes teammate, pitcher Dave Glick, was my biggest supporter and closest friend throughout baseball. We were best buddies who looked out for each other. (Courtesy of Ila Borders)

14. Photographer Annie Leibovitz relaxed with Dad and me at Whittier College during our photo shoot in 1997. Talented, humble, and giving, Annie inspired me to live my professional life with integrity. (Courtesy of Annie Leibovitz)

15. It blew me away when I arrived for the opening of Annie Leibovitz's exhibit *Portraits, Profiles, and Progress: Celebrating Women of the Twentieth Century* at the Corcoran Gallery in Washington DC and saw my image in lights. (Courtesy of Ila Borders)

16. (*opposite top*) After retiring I continued to coach for the World Children's Baseball Fair. Here I am with Sadaharu Oh, Japan's Babe Ruth, in 2000. Oh founded the organization with another home-run king, Hank Aaron. (Courtesy of Ila Borders)

17. (*opposite bottom*) If Annie Leibovitz showed me how a woman can thrive in the world, Shannon Chesnos taught me how to love. Here we are by the Mississippi River in St. Paul, Minnesota, on the tenth anniversary of my debut with the Saints. (Courtesy of Ila Borders)

18. (*above*) Bill Murray, the actor and St. Paul Saints co-owner, was always easy to talk with. We reunited in 2014 at the last game ever at Midway Stadium. (Courtesy of Ila Borders)

19. I found myself in a friendly new league when I joined the Cornelius Fire Department in the summer of 2015. To my left are Steve Black and Keaton Card; to my right, Jordan Shepard and Ben Sletmoe, the B shift crew. (Courtesy of Dave Neimeyer)

20. Jenni Westphal and I celebrate being together in winter 2014, Flagstaff, Arizona. (Courtesy of Ila Borders)

February 24, 1994

Ms. Ila Borders
Baseball Office
55 Fair Drive
Southern California College
Costa Mesa, CA 92626

Dear Ila,

I read with great interest in USA Today's <u>Baseball Weekly</u>
recently about your memories of me hitting a home run at a
Dodgers game you attended as a child.

While I may have provided the inspiration for you on that
particular day, it sounds like you're the one providing the
inspiration these days.

I'm sure your pursuit of a pitching career has taken
tremendous courage and determination. I commend you for your
achievements and I wish you well in your future challenges, both
on and off the baseball field.

When your schedule permits, I hope you will consider
visiting Candlestick Park this year and be a guest of the San
Francisco Giants and myself at a Giants game. We would love to
see you at our 1994 home opener April 4 against the Pirates.
Please call Bob Rose or Jim Moorehead in our public relations
office (415-330-2448) and they will be happy to make arrangements
for you and your family.

Keep up the good work, and remember: throw strikes!

Sincerely,

DUSTY BAKER
Manager

21. Dusty Baker's letter of encouragement meant a lot during my hectic
freshman year in college. Dusty was one of many African Americans in
baseball who had my back—not surprising, as they knew so well the
barriers one could face in the game. (Courtesy of Dusty Baker)

5

DULUTH-SUPERIOR DUKES
Being "Babe"

GAME DAY: FIFTH INNING. "You can't, you can't, you can't . . . Do softball instead, and you'll be great."

How many times have I heard those statements, while in my head I held on to the conviction *Yes, I can . . . Just watch me . . . I'm not taking the easy path; I'm taking the one I love.*

That's what I'm thinking as I get ready to pitch the bottom of the fifth inning: *I am not too small; I am not the wrong gender. I can get another win in men's professional baseball.*

I pick up the ball behind the mound and toss it into my mitt. They say negative self-talk is bad, but it fuels me. I think about what one of the Silver Bullets starting pitchers did last June. Pamela Davis pitched the fifth inning for the Class AA Jacksonville (Florida) Suns against the Australian Olympic men's team. The press reported, "She is believed to be the first woman to pitch for a major league farm club under the current structure of the minor leagues."

My reaction had been, that's not real, one inning of exhibition baseball. It's just one more notation of a woman who made a brief appearance in men's professional baseball and moved on. I was lucky to not sign with the Silver Bullets. The season they invited me to camp turned out to be their final one after Coors Beer pulled the money plug. I also think about how my local high school refused to have me play, and how God always put into my life people who were willing to help at the perfect time—Rolland Esslinger, Charlie Phillips, Jim Pigott . . . Then Mike Veeck took a chance on me, and now owner Jim Wadley and the Dukes are behind me. I want this win bad.

Warming up on the mound. I feel confident. My stuff is still moving really well. We're leading 2–0, our team is jacked, and so am I. But I also know this RedHawks team just needs a little momentum, and it will make me pay. *Just keep pitching smart,* I tell myself. *Stay focused, and quit thinking about anything else until this game is over.*

Forry Wells digs in at the batter's box. First pitch is a fastball outside, which he fouls off into the stands, igniting a scramble among the fans to capture the prize, the ball. Strike one. The ump throws me a new ball, and I grab hold of it and feel the seams. The new ball feels good and isn't too glossy. Forry takes my next pitch, a fastball inside, for a ball. I try a curveball that cuts sharply to the outside of the plate. Wells swings and connects, but not with the barrel of the bat, and so a towering fly goes to middle right field. "Here we go, Ila," says an infielder. "One down, one down."

With Ruben Santana up, I fall behind in the count and end up walking him. I was nibbling at the plate instead of going after him. *Motherfucker, Idiot.* Maybe by cursing like this I am being like Dad, and that fuels me to shut him up by pitching well. *Oh, cut the psychology, Ila.*

The walk brings manager George Mitterwald to the mound, along with Javier. With the tying run coming to the plate, I spot one of our pitchers in the bullpen taking off his jacket and starting to stretch. *Shit, one mistake and I'm out of here.*

George wants to know how I'm feeling. "I feel great," I reply. *You are going to go down scratching to stay in this game and help win it,* I say to myself. *No way am I coming out.*

George looks at Javier. "What happened with that last batter? Do you agree that everything is still looking good?"

Javier says that everything does still look good.

George looks back at me. "Ila, you're better than that. You cannot walk someone with a two-run lead. Make them hit the ball."

"I fucked up," I say. "I get it."

David Francisco, the RedHawks' number seven hitter, steps up to the plate and hits my first pitch for a long fly ball to center.

On the mound, I'm still talking to myself, *One more out to go, Ila. Man on first, and the number eight hitter up. But Smith is a good hitter. Whatever you do, stay ahead, or you're gonna get smacked. Think about it and be smart.*

Cory Smith finds the hole between short and third for a single to left field. The crowd stirs, and I can see George and my coaches getting antsy, directing the fielders to reposition a little more back. Two outs, runners with speed on first and second—concentrate on the batter. Chad Akers is up again. I tell Briller at third that I have that side if Akers bunts. With two outs, that's unlikely, but Chad is fast and the infield is back, so it's a possibility. The scouting report shows him hitting to the left side. (Earlier he singled between third and short, and grounded out to short.) So we all shift in that direction. He's also a first-pitch hitter. I throw a screwball away, and he hits a sharp two-hopper to Brito at short, who underhands it to Switzenberg for the force out at second. No runs, one hit, no errors, two left on base.

As I head back to the dugout, I pass Maury Wills, the Fargo-Moorhead first base coach, who looks me in the eye and says, "Nice inning, Ila."

His words catch me off guard. I look up, smile, and say, "Thanks."

Well, maybe I am changing some minds. I take a seat on the bench and think back to what it was like when I first got to Duluth.

JUNE 26, 1997. During the short flight from Minneapolis–St. Paul, I had looked out of the plane window at a placid landscape of forests and water. I was coming from the Saints, a classy organization from the top all the way down. Now I was starting over. What would this club be like? Would I fit in? Where would I live? But hey, I still had a job in baseball.

After landing in Duluth I headed toward baggage claim, wondering how I would get to the stadium—life at this level of baseball tends to be one foot in front of the other, with little planning. But Jim Wadley, the club's owner, and Bob Gustafson, the general manager, were there to meet me. They grabbed my bags and put them in the car, and we were off in a hurry—the game was about to start and they wanted me there. Mr. Wadley was a trim, white-haired man, well but casually dressed (he owned the Mr. Big & Tall clothing store in Norwalk, California), outgoing, and talkative. He was interested in baseball and history. He told me that he liked to be called "Jim," and that he was happy to have me in Duluth, and I felt it.

The Dukes' ballpark is a real throwback. The façade of the stadium is built of old bricks that had once paved nearby streets. From the top of the stands you can see Lake Superior and the loading docks of the won-derfully named Duluth, Missabe, and Iron Range Railway. Wade Stadium was a collaboration between the Works Progress Administration and the City of Duluth. Grandma would have been eleven years old when the Wade opened in 1941. Maybe she had walked those brick-paved streets.

Wade Stadium is a pitcher's ballpark, with lots of foul territory and 340 feet down each foul line. Even better, the wind usually blows in off the lake. *Great,* I thought when I first saw it. *This is more up my alley.* But because of the lake's proximity, games are sometimes delayed or even called when the fog rolls in. And when the wind kicks up, it can freeze you to the bone. During my weeks with the Saints, I wore foot and hand warmers whenever we played in Duluth. In early May the field had been covered with snow, the sunken dugouts buried in it.

By the time we pulled onto the field that served as the parking lot, the game had already started. I hustled into the merchandise store to get my uniform—the only one available was number three—and then to the umpires' locker room to change. I felt anxious about how things were starting out. I had hoped to arrive well before game time so I could mingle with my teammates. Now I would have to go through the clubhouse to get to the field, and I hesitated, all suited up in my number-three uniform, until Jim Wadley said, "They're expecting you. Go on in."

I opened the door to the back of the clubhouse. The showers and bath-rooms were there, then a wide doorway opened to the lockers alongside the walls, with benches in front of the lockers, a whirlpool, and trainer's table off to the side, and finally an office right before the stairs down to the dugout. Just as I was about to creep down the stairs, a guy came out of the shower room. I felt like a kid caught stealing, and my face probably showed it. I stopped and said over my shoulder, "Sorry, man. There's no other way to get to the bullpen."

Remembering to make eye contact when I meet someone, I turned around. He came up close, a towel wrapped around his waist, looking like he was going to rip off my head. He was about my height but must have outweighed me by fifty pounds.

"What the fuck? You think you can just come on in here, like this is your place without putting in your time? You're a fuckin' rookie. I could have been naked, and my wife would have been really pissed off. How would I explain that to her? You tell me."

Not knowing that this guy had no wife, I pondered the question.

"Sorry . . ." I said, but he cut me off with a huge laugh, wrapped his arm around my neck and gave me a shake, while a couple of guys in the background giggled nervously.

"I'm just fucking with you," he said. Then he pulled back, eyed my uniform, and said, "Welcome, Babe."

That's how I met Tony, one of my fellow pitchers. It took me a minute get it. My uniform number was three, so apparently my nickname was no longer "Shorty"; it was now to be "Babe," for Babe Ruth, who had worn the same number.

I smiled back at him. "Wow, that's a step up from 'bitch.' Sounds good."

I escaped into the dugout, grateful that most of the Dukes were on the field, and introduced myself to George Mitterwald, my new manager, and Mike Cuellar, the pitching coach. Both were friendly. As I stepped onto the field to head for the bullpen, the crowd erupted with applause and began to chant, "Ila, Ila, Ila!"

Great, no chance of being invisible here. As I jogged to the bullpen, I saw the pitchers on the bench there, watching me closely. I figured they were likely to give me hell for getting applause just for going to the bullpen. *Think of something witty to say,* I told myself, but nothing came to mind. I went up to each of them, looked them in the eye, shook their hands, sat down and waited for someone to speak. Everyone was nice; everyone smiled, but then, silence, which made me more nervous. *Uh-oh*, I thought. *They have no clue they can joke around with me.*

Then here came Tony toward us.

"Why the hell is he coming out here?" someone said. "He's a starter now."

They tried to wave him back to the dugout, but he ignored them and sat himself down right next to me. Nodding toward the guys, he looked at me and asked, "Did you tell them your nickname?"

I smiled and shook my head.

"It's Babe," he announced. "You cannot call her anything else. It is Babe."

Another guy wanted to know if Tony had told me his nicknames. No? Well, he was known as "Dickwood," "Fatso," and "Shorty." Tony, officially listed at five feet eleven inches, was actually shorter than I was, at five feet nine. No longer would I be Shorty.

"No," Tony replied, in stock ballplayer fashion, "but I told her your wife was good last night."

A guy down the bench said, "Ila, watch out for Tony—he's a little whore, even though he has a girlfriend."

And so the banter went. One of the guys confided that his wife was upset about him being on the road with me, a woman.

"Well, just tell her I'm gay," I told him, and we both laughed. We both knew his wife should worry not about me but about all the women lining up for the guys after games. Then the binoculars came out. We were way down the right-field line and there was no bullpen phone here, so I figured they were looking to pick up the opposing team's signs. Finally one guy handed me the binoculars.

"What do you think of that girl right there?" he said, pointing out someone in the stands.

"What do you mean?"

"I mean I am going after her. How much will you pay me if I sleep with her tonight?"

"Nothing," I said. "I see how they all fall for you guys, and I don't get it."

"Hey, if you saw what I have, you would get it."

While the guys on the bench were still laughing, I grabbed the binoculars and carefully scanned the stands. "Ah," I said. "I found just the girl for you."

"Where?"

I pointed above the visitors' dugout. "There—five rows up and fourteen seats to the right."

He grabbed the binoculars and looked. "Nice," he said. "Now I know to never rely on you to do my scouting."

The lady was about seventy years old and very overweight.

Over the season one guy in the bullpen kept his binoculars handy. We would lay bets as to which woman he would go with. It did not seem to matter to him that he was married—all during the game all he worried about was finding the hottest girl in the stands. I came to wonder why he had gotten married. I felt sorry for his wife.

Not all the antics were limited to our bullpen. I first met Bill Murray, the comic actor and the Saints co-owner, after I was sent to the Dukes. We were playing in St. Paul, and there was Bill, hanging out at the Italian restaurant near the visitors' bullpen. I liked his look of a large, friendly, rumpled jokester, usually in a Hawaiian shirt. Murray had grown up in the Midwest, and maybe he found St. Paul a normalizing haven from Hollywood. He did seem to genuinely enjoy being with the club, sometimes taking batting practice and playing catch before the games. That night he was in his element, flicking spaghetti noodles and horsing around with the diners and us in the bullpen.

I began to relax, not expecting to be called in to pitch—down by three runs, we were hitting in the bottom of the eighth. Then we noticed pitching coach Mike Cuellar.

"What the hell is he doing?" one guy said, seeing him give an unfamiliar sign.

Mike would put his hand on his head to indicate he wanted the tall guy up. Or use a side arm signal, for the side-arm guy. He would point to his left arm for the other left-hander and to his right arm for the right-hander. Now he was doing this waving motion. No one in the bullpen knew this signal.

Finally one of our teammates, Al Barsoom, ran over, and said, "Ila, start warming up."

As I was taking off my jacket, a guy asked, "What's Mike signaling?"

Al replied, "He's doing the hourglass sign with his hands to mean the girl." Then he told me, "If our pitcher gets into trouble in the top of the ninth, you're in."

In the bottom of the eighth we went down one, two, three—and suddenly here came Mike's hourglass sign. *Geez,* I thought. *Welcome to Duluth.* I made the long jog to the mound, not knowing anyone on the field and feeling lost. Javier Rodriguez, our starting catcher, came out and asked what pitches I had.

"Two-seam fastball, four-seam fastball, curveball, and screwball," I said. "I'm working on a slider, but it sucks."

"All right," Javier said. "Shake me off. You call the pitches, because George and I don't know your stuff yet. As soon as we do, George will call the pitches, so enjoy this while it lasts." (George Mitterwald had been a pro catcher for eleven years and had his own ideas about what pitches to throw when.)

First batter up got a base hit on a fastball away. *Damn it,* I thought. *Focus.* If I had paid attention in the bullpen, instead of fooling around with those binoculars, I would have known more about the guys coming to the plate. I told myself to calm down and just get a ground ball. No point throwing to first, because they were up by three, but I changed up my cadence to keep the runner honest for a potential double play. Next batter hit a grounder, and we turned two. Right on, two outs. One more, and I could breathe again.

Javier and Anthony Lewis, our first baseman, came over to the mound to say, "This guy's a first-pitch hitter and will chase balls."

I shook off Javier's sign for a curve, then nodded at his second one for a screwball away. I threw it so it ended up in the dirt. Sure enough, he swung—another grounder. Out of the inning. The entire crowd was on its feet, clapping and chanting, "Ila, Ila, Ila!" as I came into the dugout, and that is how I met the rest of my new team. My fielders came up from behind and slapped me on the back.

"Good job," Javier said. "Great pitch."

I made my way to the bench, ducking to avoid the low roof, put on my jacket, and sat down. The bench inside the dugout was only eight feet long. There was also standing room in front of and below the bench, but you cannot see the game from there, so most of the guys liked to sit on a bucket in front of the dugout or stand, leaning against the fence. As our guys batted, I realized that if we came back I could get the win. Wow, what a great beginning that would be. My reverie was interrupted by the smell of smoke. At first I did not think anything of it until I saw flames creeping up my pants leg. As I smacked the flames out, I laughed, but the guys were loving it. They had pulled off that traditional initiation, quietly setting an unsuspecting rookie's shoelaces on fire: my first hot foot.

We never did come back in that game, but when it was over the guys came in from the bullpen to say, "Good job, Babe," before heading for the showers. Meanwhile I went outside to do an interview or two and to sign autographs. I was still there at eleven o'clock, when Jim Wadley came over to tell me that I would be staying at the Best Western Hotel until they found me a host family. The hotel was conveniently downtown, and I could easily catch a ride to the ballpark with a couple of the other players staying there. *Beautiful—privacy.* That night I slept through until one o'clock in the afternoon.

The rooms at the Best Western faced the parking lot, which was just off West Second, a busy street. The hotel was one story, so anyone coming and going was easily visible. I was afraid a stranger might show up at my door if it became known I was staying there. There were reasons for my fearfulness. While most of the mail I received was positive and included a return address, because the writer requested an autograph or a photo, others made it clear what they wanted by enclosing a condom or a bra. It was the letters with no return address that frightened me. As I recall, one said that someone needed to take me out—whether it's a broken leg or an accident, he warned me to watch my back. Another writer said that women were bringing the game down. I received a few death threats and kept the worst ones in my duffel bag in case one of these characters acted on his threat; someone would know where to look for the culprit.

Meanwhile Dad kept asking whether I was getting any weird mail, and I told him no, as I did not want him to worry—or overreact and come up to Duluth. This was my battle; I just needed my parents to be smart back home in California, where people continued to call and stop by our house. Dad promised to ship the letters that had arrived and gave me the family's new phone number he had to get. "Just be heads up," he said. His attitude had changed. No longer was it "Suck it up." Now it was "Be careful."

"Dad," I said, "the people who come after me now should be careful because of how you raised me. I am a machine and can handle anything."

Dad and I were now equals. I told him to watch out for Mom and my sister and brothers.

Later that season I learned just how careful I needed to be. One day, after we arrived in Sioux City, like always I picked up my key from George Mitterwald and went to my hotel room. When I opened the door, two men were standing in front of the bed. I was lucky to catch them off guard. I slammed the door and ran to the front desk, my mind reeling: Why were *two* men in my room? Should I report this? Request security? Or just shut up and take care of it myself? The front desk clerk ran back to the room with me, but the men were gone. We looked outside but saw nobody. Then we searched the room for clues as to who these guys were. Nothing. The clerk wanted to check the security cameras, but I turned down the idea and just asked for another room. I did not want to create a stir with the club, afraid that if I gave them any reason to think I might threaten legal action or attracted any negative publicity, I would be gone. In the end I said nothing. But from then on, I always tried to take a room next to a teammate. Even if the media caught on and reported it, I figured I would be safer. Sometimes I asked a buddy to come into my hotel room with me while I checked under the bed, in the closet, in the bathroom. Sometimes I changed rooms during the middle of our stay. Before I went to sleep I always jammed a chair against the door. I wanted to give myself a chance to fight if I had to.

Next day I woke up, put on my jeans, running shoes, my Minnesota sweatshirt, and a beanie I got from Connie. I was hungry. I went to a 7-Eleven and bought a box of Honey Nut Cheerios—not enough money to buy milk. Back at the hotel, I filled my ice bucket with half of the box of cereal and water. Lunchtime came, and the other half was gone. I got by that day on three dollars. The Dukes proved to be sympathetic toward the survival of us players who made 750 dollars a month. After home games the vendors made sure we left the stadium with hamburgers or pizza and water or pop.

One of the pitchers on our team, Dave Glick, was also staying at the Best Western. Glick, as I came to call him, drove a truck, and offered me a ride to the stadium. During our drive to the ballpark, he told me that he was from California, too: Valencia, in the Santa Clarita Valley, about an hour-and-a-half drive from my home. I liked him right away. He was tall, with dark good looks, and very much his own man. These days you see lots of ballplayers with tattoos, but in 1997 Glick was the only one I knew who was tatted. He had them on his chest, shins, back, arms, all over. He told me that he hid them from management because they hated tattoos. In 1996 the Ogden Raptors had cut him because of them, even though he had gone 3-1 with a 3.41 ERA. After his time with the Dukes, he continued pitching for another ten years, making it into Double-A ball and then back into the independent leagues. David was a strikeout pitcher with a three-to-one ratio to walks and threw ninety-plus miles per hour. To me it seemed all wrong that he did not go farther. But Glick had not received a big signing bonus—he had been drafted by the Milwaukee Brewers in the forty-eighth round of the 1994 June amateur draft; the players who do get the big bonuses tend to get mulligans again and again.

When we got to the clubhouse, Glick said, "Aren't you coming in?"

"Hell, no," I replied.

He wanted to know why, so I explained that I was not here to change things up for the guys; I just wanted to play. Glick said that the guys already got that; they just wanted to get to know me.

"Uh-uh, not in that way."

He laughed, and said, "No. This team is so relaxed. We like to joke around and have fun."

"I do, too, but not when I am pitching. I need to focus."

"The guys are going to joke with you to see if you take it, and there is no one here that will fault you for dishing it back. But they will if you don't come back with something. Everyone here is part of the team. There is no rule about rookies having to do everything."

"Okay," I said. "Thanks for the info—hope you're right."

"Hope you take my advice," Glick said. "It will go a long ways."

After changing in the concourse bathroom, I headed for the dugout, where I sat, waiting for someone to come out to play catch with. I looked out at the field—I loved the old red brick schoolhouse atmosphere of this ballpark—thankful I was playing here. Then the door to the clubhouse opened and one of my teammates said, "Ila, George wants to see you."

George being the manager, I thought, *What the frick have I done?* I got ready to open the clubhouse door but first knocked on it, hard. I heard a knock back, and someone said, trying to sound like a girl, "Hello?"

I knocked again

"Open the door."

I stepped through, and the guy pointed me toward George's office. When I got there, I looked in but, of course, the manager was not there. *Those little shits,* I thought. All I need is a reporter coming in now, and it would be a drama. I turned around to ask, "Where's George?" and saw one of the players approaching. He was six feet two inches tall, and I could see he was well endowed—he happened to be butt naked. Several clothes hangers hung from his penis, and he carried more hangers in his hand. In a serious manner, he asked me, "How many hangers do you think I can hang on my penis?"

Everyone around us watched.

"I have some underwear and clothes in the dugout, if you need some," I said. Then I spotted Glick in the background looking at me, as if to say, *I told you, push back.* I saw one of the religious guys coming my way, possibly to my rescue, but stepped in front of him to face the outfielder.

"Give me a hanger, jackass." I grabbed the remaining hangers from his hand and hung them on his penis. The answer to the number of hangers that fit was eleven. Trying to sound very scientific, I told him, "You must have been doing this way too often if you knew exactly how many hangers fit on your penis."

He burst out laughing and walked away. When we got out to the field he gave me a huge hug and said, "You're an awesome sport." From that point on, he was one of my protectors. He still liked to walk around naked in the locker room—he was quite proud of what God gave him—but that was the end of his trying to get under my skin.

As I headed down the stairs toward the dugout, I turned, grinned at the guys in the locker room, and said, "I found George."

When Glick came onto the field, he was all smiles.

"You passed," he said. "The guys were all laughing after you left. They feel like they can joke around with you." He added that there were two people I should watch myself around. "They like you, but they're religious and just have different views of what women should be doing and wearing."

"That's weird," I replied, "because I'm a believer, too. But I don't believe in judging others—I mean, I'm certainly not perfect myself." I came to think that the religious guys were telling the nonreligious guys to have some respect for me and put some clothes on in the locker room. But these were the same guys who screwed around on their wives, so I doubt the others paid much attention. They just said, "She's one of us, so who cares?"

From that day on Glick and I became great friends. He usually was the first one on the field unless he was starting. During warmups I hated doing sprints because it was so damn boring, but throw me a football and I would sprint all day. So we developed a ritual. We would stand in the outfield on the foul lines, and he would yell, "Go!" I would sprint as hard as I could go for about forty yards, then break left or right, and he would throw the ball. I lived to make a diving catch. Sometimes a crowd gathered to watch. Once Glick got in trouble because he dove for the football and got grass stains and dirt all over his pants. At these times, I felt playful, like when I was twelve years old and snuck out of the house at night to play football with the kids down the street. Glick loved baseball like I did. He was a talented and disciplined player, and I admired him very much.

Our manager must have known what was going on in the clubhouse. A few games into the season, Mitterwald called all of us into the locker room and laid out the rules. Unlike in St. Paul, my using the stadium bathrooms to change was not going to work here, so I was to use the umpire's room whenever it was open. I was to be welcome in the clubhouse any time, where some players would be fully dressed, some with towels wrapped around them, and some in their underwear and jock straps. I learned to announce my presence by saying loudly, "Housekeeping. Me fluff your pillows?" I do think that sometimes the guys pretended that we were going to have a clubhouse meeting, just so they could hear me say that.

It was clear that I was on a very different sort of team in Duluth. The Saints had been older and quieter; these guys were young and rowdy. (Think of the Saints as the dignified New York Yankees and the Dukes as the crazy Boston Red Sox during the 2004 season.) Stuff happened. One evening it was so cold down in the bullpen that we could not feel our feet or hands. How could we keep warm if we were called in to pitch? We dug a hole in the dirt, got a white towel out of the locker room and pieces of a broken bat and lit them on fire. We were having a heck of a good time but doing everything possible to not let the fire get too high. We ended up sitting all around it so no one in the dugout or the stands could see the flames. Toward the end of the game, who got the call to come in? Babe. I got two quick outs and joined the guys in the dugout. People were laughing as the cameras went off, though I did not understand why until I looked in the mirror later and saw that my face was covered with soot, with only a couple of patches of skin showing. The press loved it. The next day, some of the guys mocked me by wearing, all over their faces, the antiglare stuff we put under our eyes for day games. After that, management no longer sent towels down to the bullpen.

The guys could see I loved playing and wanted to win, that I was not a man-hater or someone interested in being famous as the "first woman ever." And I kept my mouth shut about those who were popping greenies like sunflower seeds or taking steroids—and about the groupies that were everywhere. I could laugh off my teammates' practical jokes. I don't know how many times I got a hotfoot, or shoe polish in my cap, or slime in my mitt. The only thing I escaped was towel whipping, thank goodness. Guys would come out with welts. No place was sacred from clubhouse pranks. The trainer might be stretching you out before a game when a teammate would come by and fart as loud as he could. It did not matter who you were—you were easy bait if you were getting stretched out. As long as they had underwear on and I did not have to see their hairy butts, it was all good. I can imagine some of you thinking how gross and rude that is, but I took it as a compliment. I wanted them to treat me like another player. Well, that is what I got.

As the second half of the season got under way, the Dukes went on a roll. We had been dead last when I came to the team; now we were moving up to second place. I say this not because of anything I contributed but because it was plain exciting to be winning. We were a bunch of misfits who happened to play well together. Wins, of course, help a team to mesh, but even before that we all got along. We were definitely the melting pot of the Northern League. We had homegrown Texas white boys, a tattooed Cali guy with chin hair, three African Americans, clean-cut though not necessarily devout Christians, an Asian, a Canadian, ex–major leaguers, *rico suave* ladies men, several Dominicans (some speaking no English), and me, the girl. Our pitching coach, Mike Cuellar, fit right in. He walked with a swagger, wore a gold necklace, and liked to have fun. He was still in great shape after his fifteen seasons as a four-time All-Star and an American League Cy Young winner. There were limits to our communication, though. Mike was from Cuba and sometimes struggled with English, especially at important moments. One day he ran to the mound to chew me out. "You Think, You Stink," he hollered over and again, spit foaming at his mouth. I fought down a belly laugh. If I was not getting as many innings as I had hoped, I was having a heck of a good time.

The bullpen was like a private community. Our conversations ranged from talking baseball (players' weaknesses and strengths, past seasons with other teams, and the use of steroids, testosterone, and human growth hormone supplements) to arguments over where we could get the best coffee—most of us agreed on Dunkin' Donuts—and how many times a week married couples should have sex. And always, the guys were scanning the stands for women. I often got cast as the judge of these debates because I was considered the fairest person.

My teammates' sense of humor helped me relax. For most of them it was not do or die, like it was for me. They enjoyed playing baseball, but most knew it was not going to be their life. If it did not work out, they planned to go back home into the family business or some other job. They felt like they had nothing to lose, because most players don't even make it to professional baseball, and they had achieved that. To move higher was often a matter of politics or good luck, so they just gave it their best and let whatever happened happen. But they saw the extra scrutiny and stress on me. And I could see that my Cuban teammate, Ariel, had a lot more pressure riding because he had to keep his job or he was going back to Castro's country.

One night at a game in Iowa we were fairly deep into a scatological discussion when Mike Cuellar gave the hourglass sign. When I got to the mound, I saw small brown frogs everywhere. The field was brand new and well groomed, but it was surrounded by farmland. August in the Midwest is hot and humid—I guess this was frog weather. Well, better this than the cold of May and June. I notched a strikeout and got out of the inning with no runs, but when I came into the dugout I ran into a plague of frogs of near Biblical proportions. When my teammates saw me dodging the frogs, I was in for it. The guys were all over me for being afraid. I denied it, saying I just did not want them all over me and did not want to kill them. No mercy. Back on the mound, I opened my glove and there was a frog, which I laid on the grass behind the mound. From the eighth inning on, I had frogs all over my gear and my body. *Dang,* I thought. *Just give ballplayers a little opening, and you are toast.*

After we won the game, I was safely settled on the team bus when I heard noises coming from my baseball bag. When I unzipped it to check, about twenty frogs hopped out.

"Damn it," I muttered, "Those little shits" (meaning not the frogs but my prankster teammates). I tried to gather all the frogs that had jumped onto the bus floor. I was all over the bus trying to get those suckers. Then I stepped off the bus and put them in a grassy place nearby. I could see some of the guys who were talking to local Baseball Annies peer around and laugh.

Other teammates just said, "Ila, what the fuck have you done now?"

Having done my deed of kindness, as I headed to the back of the bus I stuck my slimy hands out, darting at the freshly showered players as if to touch them, all of them yelling, "Get the fuck away from me."

After taking two games out of three from the Sioux City Explorers, we returned to Duluth, where I learned that the club had found a place for me to live. I had loved the anonymity of living in a hotel room and treasured my privacy, which I considered important to my mental health. The house, though, was convenient for someone like me without a car—right across the street from the stadium. My hosts were a divorcée who was a retired cook with grown kids in the area and a single woman with a boyfriend. How was I going to live with two women in a thousand-square-foot two-bedroom house? Whenever I was in town, one woman gave up her bedroom and slept in the living room. They were the nicest women, and I could tell they wanted to hang out with me, but by the time I got home I just wanted to chill. Sleep was what got me through. My hosts did their best to give me the space I needed.

As I settled into my role with the Dukes, some of my bullpen mates began asking for pitching advice. Because I didn't have ninety-five-mile-per-hour speed, I had to pitch smart, with a lot of movement on the ball. I also threw a heavy ball, according to teammates I played catch with.

They saw that I understood mechanics. (Some coaches, like Mike Cuellar, were so good back in their day that they couldn't relate to pitchers whose styles were different from theirs.)

All through August, the Dukes continued to win. The guys were happy because now even more groupies were lining up for them. We finished the season in first, one game ahead of the Saints. Now we would face them in the best-of-five semifinals. No one expected us to win—the Saints were considered unbeatable against a team like ours: fifth in the eight-team league in hitting and batting, and sixth in pitching and fielding. I started to pray, "Please God, please . . ."

I cannot recall every game of the playoffs, but I remember Game Five, played in Duluth on a frigid night with about two thousand people in the stands. Starting for us was our ace, Allen Halley—six feet one, 195 pounds, and a ball of fire. With a shaved head, a soul patch below his lip, and a ruddy face, Allen always looked like he was out to kill you. It was his habit to dip or chew, he popped greenies like candy, and he drank coffee like water. Though he had a huge temper, he was kind to me and superfunny. We also had a hot bat in designated hitter and outfielder Mike Meggers.

Before the game, we in the bullpen played our ritual game of flip. You could use only your mitt and body to bounce the baseball off you and onto the other player. If you hit another player and the ball hit the floor, he was out. Every part of the body but the head was "in." I never won that damn game. After the ball game started, the bullpen was quieter than usual. We were all ready to come in at the first sign of trouble, but that night the Dukes were on. Mike was crushing the ball, and Allen was dealing big time.

In the top of the ninth, we stood together in front of the wooden bench, jumping up and down or toe tapping to keep warm, anticipating the win. When the last batter struck out swinging, I rushed the mound with the rest of the guys. Some of us ran with our arms raised, others jumped up and down and hugged while champagne flowed. It felt great but also weird, because I still felt a sense of loyalty to the Saints.

For the best-of-seven championship series we faced the Winnipeg Goldeyes, who had edged out the Fargo RedHawks in the other semifinal. During the series, both stadiums were packed with fans going nuts. We took a game, they took a game, and then we pulled ahead three to two. We knew we had to get them in Game Six, at home in Duluth. As the game got under way, both starters were dealing, and fielders were making plays that seemed impossible. Who was going to take this game? Both teams deserved it. There was no kidding around in the bullpen that night—we all paced, ready to go if called in. We tried to do this only when the Dukes were in the dugout, not wanting our starter to think he might be coming out. We just wanted to be ready to contribute.

Top of the ninth, we were ahead. In the bullpen I hunched over, close to Glick, biting my fingers, praying to God, "Please . . ." Our closer was in now, the best in the league, but the Goldeyes had the best hitting in the league. Fly ball. One out. I hit Glick on the shoulder: next hitter up went to a full count before grounding out. Two outs. I shook Glick, who gave me the look, like "you're a freak." When the umpire motioned strike three, I slapped Glick on the back. Then the entire bullpen rushed the mound, where we transformed into a dog pile of exuberant kids. I was just grateful to be on top of the pile and not the bottom. The Dukes—the misfits of the League—had won the pennant. And I, perhaps the biggest misfit of all, had survived my rookie season. I had my own baseball card. And soon I would be wearing a championship ring. *Look at me now, all you naysayers!*

I remembered to whisper a quick prayer, "Thank you, God, for watching over me, and for teaching me to aim high and put no limits on You . . . Please Lord, prepare me to get a win next year and to go as far as I can go in this beautiful game."

Holy Shit, I kept saying to myself, *Holy Shit.*

"We Are the Champions" blared over the PA. Then we players went on the microphone to thank the fans for their support. For more than an hour we celebrated on the field, helping to make the fans feel a part of this. Finally the guys started to head to the showers, and I realized that the season truly was over.

The following day I hopped in Glick's green s10 Chevy truck and headed west with him. We both resigned ourselves to going from an ultimate high to ordinary life back at home—though I would have the security of my money from the ssk contract. With that I would have the time to train and get stronger. Trading the wheel every four hours (whoever drove got to choose the music), we wanted to see as much of the countryside as we could. The first day, we traveled through the cornfields and small Scandinavian towns of Iowa before stopping in Lincoln, Nebraska. No romance then, though we dated later that winter. If ever I was going to go hetero—and I prayed that I could—Glick would be the guy. On our dates we would talk baseball and sports, ride the roller coasters at Six Flags Magic Mountain, and talk about our futures. But we both knew we would not last together. I understood that he needed to date other girls and was not close to settling down. I knew I loved him, though not physically.

The next day it poured as we drove through Colorado, soaking our luggage in the bed of the truck. Then we entered the breathtaking red rock country of Utah. We had planned to make it home that night, but by the time we reached Las Vegas, we decided to relax for one more day before returning to the realities of our lives. No gambling, we had just enough money for gas to get home, so we people-watched as we walked the Strip. We talked about what we would face when we arrived home. Glick would go back to his job delivering pizza, because it gave him plenty of time to work out and improve his pitching skills. He still had to live at home with his parents, because he could not make it on his own financially. Sometimes he stayed with a girlfriend, so he had some independence from his parents. The next day Glick dropped me off in La Mirada before heading north to the Santa Clarita Valley.

For the first time since leaving for college five years ago, I was home. I planned to use my endorsement money to rent a place and return to college for four months. I needed to complete six more units to get my BA in kinesiology and become the first person in the Borders-Carter family to graduate from college, so this was a big deal. I would then pass the state teaching exam and substitute-teach while training for next season. I looked forward to reaping some rewards from all the hard work.

Except it did not work out that way. In my memory, I waved goodbye to Glick, rolled my luggage up into the house, and began to tell Dad about my plans.

"I'm ready for my money," I said. "It will let me live on my own, and I can work less and train more."

He had negotiated with me to keep half of the fifty thousand dollars as his agent's fee, because he had gotten more than they originally offered. I had wondered at the time about that—what agent takes fifty percent? But there was still my half, right?

"No," said Dad. His face didn't look right, a combination of fear and guilt. "I had to use my half immediately to pay off the rest of Randall's bills, plus your auto insurance for two years."

I did the math. "Auto insurance is only six hundred dollars a year, Dad. That's a total of twelve hundred."

Dad's face changed to anger, as if I didn't care about the family's needs.

"I also tithed 10 percent of your twenty-five thou to the church."

Dad tithing was news to me and, when she found out, to Mom.

All my money was gone. Dad said he would pay me back as he could afford it. In truth he went for many years without paying anything. He could not understand why I was so angry. I was told to be a good sport about it but that if I was going to be a sourpuss, then I was selfish and against the family. To me what he did was stealing, and it broke any trust I had left in him.

It was not just about the money, though—there was a much bigger picture here. Mom and the rest of the family had always invested in the pretense that things in our family were okay. Mom said not to worry, that Dad would pay it back. I was furious that she did not back me up after I had stood up for her for so many years. Our family had the habit of not confronting one another with a complaint or trying to resolve the problem; instead they talked behind one another's backs. Dad had his list of grievances: He felt disrespected by Phillip and Randall, but he was older now and too tired to discipline them, unlike when I was young. He was angry that his kids avoided him. Well, who wanted to be near him when we all lived in fear of his hitting us, kicking us out of the house, and generally making our lives difficult? He was upset with Mom's weight gain and called her lazy for not contributing more financially. He felt like he was the only one working, with three kids living here for free, eating up all the food, and not taking care of the house. Well, teenagers tend to be that way.

Mom was crushed because Dad was having an affair and everyone knew it, though he denied it. She sank into depression. My brothers were great dudes, but they were mad at Dad for his cheating and lying and had lost respect for Mom because she didn't stand up to him. Meanwhile my sister Leah complained but did nothing about anything. And here I was, the firstborn, who not only hated lying, cheating, laziness, and talking behind each other's backs but also was trying to face up to whatever problems came along. For this I was considered the black sheep of the family. Even so, I had always been the mediator. If someone had a problem, they told me. I was tired of the role. I learned that I was enabling the others to not grow. It was time to get out of the house and find a healthier way of living, but did that mean no more baseball for me? Or should I suck it up, live at home, and allow Dad to control me, so I could have more time to train?

I transferred my credits at Whittier to Southern California College and enrolled in the six units that would fulfill my degree. When I walked into one of my classes, I was in for a shock. There was Shelley. She told me that she was not seeing her boyfriend anymore and asked how I was doing.

"Great," I said. "I'm doing great." Still upset with her, I was civil but distant, as if we had never been friends.

With my degree in hand and my teaching exam passed, I began to work as a substitute instructor in high schools around L.A. I also worked as a janitor and taught pre-K at Mom's preschool. I had little time to train and was not at all sure whether I could play next season. Once again I reached out to God. "Lord, help me out," I prayed. "You gave me a gift to play baseball and you gave me a very determined spirit. If it is still your will, please give me a way to pursue my dream, and I promise to work my ass off."

After living with friends here and there, I met a woman through my sister Leah. Kelly Deutsch was a huge Yankees fan. During the mid-1970s, Kelly was among the first girls to play Little League in Passaic, New Jersey, and pitched for the boys junior varsity high school team at Collegiate School before switching to softball. By the time we met she was back to her first love, baseball, playing on Leah's women's team. I think Kelly loved the game more than anyone I have ever met. She would listen to the Yankees on the radio and would race home on her motorcycle from her work as a producer in Hollywood to catch a game on TV. Kelly also was out-of-the-closet gay, light years ahead of me that way. She understood this difference between us. We dated a couple of times, but I think she knew I was not emotionally ready for a relationship. By mutual agreement we agreed to continue as friends. She became my confidant, the one who knew stuff about me. I admired her in so many ways.

Kelly invited me to move into her apartment in Hollywood, covered my share of the rent, and gave me food. In return I cleaned the apartment and coached her in pitching and hitting. We lived for the weekends, when we drove to Beverly Hills High School and practiced baseball for hours. We also watched a lot of baseball on TV, and I would explain the game to her and what was going on. She showed me around Hollywood and Los Angeles, and got me a job as an assistant producer, even though I had not a clue what I was doing. Because of Kelly I was able to train hard for the upcoming season.

That winter photographer Annie Leibovitz called. She had been taking pictures of various women for a book she was working on with Susan Sontag, and I was someone of interest to her. She wanted to come to California and take pictures of me pitching. She arrived in town with a bunch of assistants and three large trailers of equipment. She did her usual amazing work, shooting one overcast afternoon on the field at Whittier College. What I remember most about Annie was her kindness. I had always been a fan of her work; now I became an admirer of the woman she was: talented, famous, and gracious. The off-season had started with a bitter financial disappointment, but it ended on a high. Sure, there were people like Dad in this world, but there were also people like Annie Leibovitz.

Then a letter dated November 6, 1998, arrived. The Dukes wanted me back. *This time,* I told myself, *I'm taking two suitcases and lots of warm clothes and packing like I'm not coming back. I am determined to get a win.*

6

THE DUKES
Nailing a Win

GAME DAY: SIXTH INNING. Three up and three down for us in the top of the sixth. People are talking at me, cameras are in my face, but in my head there's a calm rage to win. My veins feel like they're bubbling with fire. I'm still in the zone. I know exactly where the ball is going. This is crunch time. I also have a health worry that I haven't dared to mention to anyone, one that makes me wonder if this will be the last game of my life. So I tell myself, in this sixth inning, to give everything I have and more.

Steve Hine comes to bat. I'm aiming to get a ground ball. I throw a fastball to the outside corner of the plate, which he hits between first and second for a single. Well, I got a ground ball, and it was a good pitch. Still, it doesn't stop me from swearing. Now their hottest hitter is up: Johnny Knott. I throw to first a couple of times to keep the speedy Hine honest. I offer Knott a screwball, which he grounds to third—could be a double play. Chris Briller bobbles it in his desire to get the lead runner at second, then has to throw to first, barely getting Knott for the first out. *Dang—we can't give this team opportunities like this.* Instead of two out and nobody on, it's a man on second and only one out.

Our catcher, Javier Rodriguez, comes out to the mound again, along with our manager, George Mitterwald. I tell them that with first base open I want to put Marc Fink on and pitch to Chris Coste. I know that puts the winning run at the plate, but I feel like I have Chris's number today. I tell George I feel good and to let me get out of this. George leaves me in the game, saying just don't give Fink anything good to hit. Javier takes his place behind home, and gives no sign. My straight change begins to tail beyond the outside corner, and Fink swings: a high pop up to short. I count to forever, waiting, until the ball lands in Brito's glove. Sweet, two outs.

Chris Coste comes up, and Javier suffers a passed ball, letting Hine take third. I don't care about the runner, but I do care if Coste gets on. The count goes to 2-and-2 before Javier waggles three fingers, the sign for a screwball. Coste swings and misses—strike three—and slams his bat into the dirt. I jog toward the dugout, unashamedly wallowing in the praise coming my way. Javier: "Holy shit, that was a nice pitch."

Mitterwald: "Way to go, Ila."

Jackie Hernandez, our hitting coach: "Girl, you are on fire. Good job!"

I put on my jacket, take my place on the bench, and let the sweet sense of relief wash over me: no runs, one hit, no errors, one left on base.

I think back to a game earlier this season and how we came together as a team. I don't recall who we were playing, but our shortstop, Tyler Bain, was fielding the throw to second base when the runner slid into him—actually it was more of a tackle than a slide—and dislocated Bain's shoulder. He was out for the season. Our pitcher offered payback: his first pitch hit the next batter. Both dugouts cleared, and the brawl began. I hadn't been in a good fight since sixth grade and was happy to wade into the middle of this one. I was going to stick up for the injured Bain and all my teammates. After the umpires restored order, I felt a tap on my shoulder. "Whoa," said one of my teammates. "I thought you would just sit back on the bench and watch."

I could tell he was impressed I'd joined in, and so I smiled at him as if to say, "Of course." After that the guys on the team treated me differently, with more respect.

Now, with *60 Minutes* filming every pitch, and Doug Simunic spitting his distaste for me, I've pitched six scoreless innings against his first-place team. That makes a string of twelve consecutive scoreless innings.

After we make the first out in the top of the seventh, George comes over to me and says, "Great job, Ila. You made a believer out of me. I'm going to bring in our setup guy for an inning, and then Giron to close it out and get this win for us. You did your job. You can stay here and watch or get cleaned up if you want."

I had no idea George had someone warming up in the bullpen. I say what a pitcher is supposed to say to the manager: "Okay."

But being a starting pitcher, my opinion differed. I want one more inning. Sure, I would be going through the lineup again, but I would give them something different to swing at. In my head, it's one inning more and then Emiliano Giron, our closer and the best in the league, will mow them down. When Maury Wills gets to his coach's box at first base, I smile at him from the dugout, in thanks for the good word last inning.

So I watch the game unfold from the bench, where I am utterly powerless, the outcome being out of my hands. To avoid obsessing over it, I reflect on the season. Progress has been made. I had started in pro ball as a spot reliever facing left-handed batters, gone on to long-distance relief (three-plus innings when the starting pitcher gets into trouble early), and now am starting—and winning—games. Maybe the confidence I brought into this season began when I realized I was not just a one-season novelty.

MAY 1998, DULUTH, MINNESOTA. As I had vowed, I packed plenty of warm clothing for my second season in Duluth. Reporting to camp, though, brought a chill in several ways. The weather was still cold, but I was prepared, with tights, long sleeves, short sleeves, and a jacket. What I didn't anticipate was losing our MVP of last season's championship team, Allen Halley, who had died after a seizure in March at age twenty-six. We loved Halley and his fierceness, and his death devastated us. Our team was different now. Some of the guys were new, and there wasn't the same mesh as last year. After dating last summer, my relationship with Dave Glick changed, too. We were back to being just buddies. The team started out well, though I wasn't getting many innings. And then, on July 24, I was tapped to start the game. Excited, I went deep into the zone that day. And here is the bizarreness of memory. I remember speaking to Javier Rodriguez and to pitching coach Mike Cuellar. After the game I remember going on the radio via a hookup with my parents. That's all I can recall. I had won my first professional baseball game, and I had little memory of it. I pitched six shutout innings against Sioux Falls, giving up three hits and two walks, and notching two strikeouts. Of the seventy-three pitches I made, forty were for strikes. The game went into the books: a 3–1 victory.

The people of Duluth were friendly, die-hard fans who reminded me of Green Bay Packers football fans. They knew to show up with blankets and parkas to night games, no matter how warm the day had been. They wore replica jerseys. Some locals started the Ila Borders Fan Club. They showed up at the park for every home game and even followed the team on some road trips. The flip side to the adulation came as we began to lose more games. On the road in the visitors' bullpen, our backs were usually to the fans and up against the beer garden—easy targets for drunks to dump beer on us. Others would ride us hard, commenting on our looks, family, baseball, or anything else they could think of to get a reaction. If that did not work, there was always more beer to spill on us.

Stalkers were another problem. Duluth is a small town, and people knew where I lived. Jim Wadley had arranged to move me to a remote farm owned by the Lothenbach family. My teammate Chris DeWitt saw guys hanging around my car in the parking lot. One night I noticed a car tailing me as I drove home. So Chris made it a practice to walk me to the car, and then he and his wife would follow me home. At six feet five and 215 pounds, Chris was an intimidating deterrent, but he could not be there every moment. I did not call the cops or tell the front office about these incidents, for the same old reason: doing so would feed the argument that having a girl in baseball caused too much drama. I had always handled threats and stalkers by myself. The difference now was that I had guys like Chris DeWitt at my back.

Ever since I was a kid, I had tried to prepare myself in every way possible for a life in baseball. What I had not prepared well for was romance, which gets confusing when you're in the closet. I had always gotten along with guys as friends, but whenever one tried to hit on me, I would send the vibe that I was not interested. Guys hate being rejected, so with varying degrees of success, I always tried to present that I just wanted to be friends. I hadn't read much about being a gay athlete, so I didn't fully understand the dynamics. As Carol Berendsen wrote in *Loving Women*, "Women athletes will rarely achieve an egalitarian relationship with a heterosexual male, because once the average straight male has perceived that a woman doesn't need stud service, it's scary for him."

That left only women to date, and I was not doing it well. I knew the sort of woman I liked—someone smart and independent who enjoyed music, art, and books—but had not grown up with a clear understanding of how to treat a woman I cared about. I had a lot to learn about what a healthy relationship looked like. Besides, playing baseball allowed little time for dating. When people tried to set me up, it was easy to say, "No thanks, too busy."

By my second season with the Dukes, I was scaring myself because I felt most myself when alone.

So I could see why the guys often went for one-night stands rather than a steady girlfriend: convenience. But I had to wonder, *How am I going to find love that way?* Being in the closet only made it worse. If you have ever tried to keep secret the person you are seeing, you know how exhausting it is to plan a date. You are on edge, stressed out, and telling a lie or sidetracking questions to move the conversation to other subjects. I never understood why the media wanted to know about my romantic life—I didn't want to know who *they* were dating.

Living in the closet also complicates finding someone available to date. When a woman I liked asked me out during baseball season, I had to fake that I was not interested or flat out say, "No, I date men."

Talk about sending mixed messages. When I dated in the off-season, I would avoid being seen in public twice with the same person. I would say, "I cannot hold your hand in public, you cannot go to special events with me, and if we go out to a banquet, you cannot sit with me."

Since most of my dates had been in the closet, too, that was okay; but by the late 1990s more gay men and lesbians were coming out and resented having to be hidden. I came to see that my skittishness was unfair to the women I dated. It was one-sided and selfish on my part. I once attended an athletic ceremony with a woman I was dating. It was killing me not to sit with her, but I did not want anyone to take a picture of us together. When I received my award, I would not openly hug her—we ended up hugging in the women's restroom. We both laughed at that, but I could sense her frustration. My secrecy and untruthfulness got to her, and eventually she was gone. I put my career in baseball above love, over and over again.

My love life was a sorry contrast to many of my teammates', who seemed so carefree about their heterosexuality and showed little restraint in enjoying themselves. The groupies who chased after them seemed to feel much the same. After a night game in Sioux City, a girl who had way too much to drink stood by our team bus. No guy had picked her up, so she opened her blouse, pushing her breasts against the bus window. It is hard to erase a memory like that. I think a rookie finally ended up going home with her. I never did get over how crazy the girls were for these guys. All I could think was, *If you only knew how many times they do this in every town.*

One teammate had such smooth moves that he got a girl almost every time we went out of town. We reaped the rewards of his talent. It went like this: On the road he would find a girl the first night we got in and make it known that his birthday was the next day. Invariably the team got his birthday cake. In each town, we would wonder what birthday gifts he would get this time. One woman gave him a watch, but we still got the birthday cake. You would think this guy would have a warped sense toward women, but he was one of the nicest to me. Before games, he made sure to bring me a piece of cake.

On another road trip, we were in Thunder Bay, Ontario, staying at a hotel with a beautiful location on the water, though it was old and smelled musty. Coming back from dinner downtown, I was walking to my room when I heard some crazy noises down the hall. The floors creaked, so I tried to tiptoe past without looking because I had figured out what was going on.

But I had been spotted, and I heard the call, "Hey Ila, look at this!"

The doors were wide open to showcase it all—I guess the hotel knew to keep the ballplayers on one floor, so the other guests would not complain. One guy was behind a woman having sex with her, another was in front having sex with her. Two other guys were cheering her on. The girl was smiling. I swear: if I had been straight, this sort of stuff could have turned me gay. To be one of the guys, I gave a quick thumbs-up, fled to my room, and escaped into the book I was reading.

Living in the closet surrounded by rampant sex was one kind of stress. More universal was the physical stress of playing baseball day after day. You want some meat on you to see you through the season. Even though 140 pounds is pretty solid for a girl, it is underweight for a guy. Many people think I weigh 115 or 120, but that's usually because I'm standing next to a six-feet-two-inch, two-hundred-pound teammate. I have no problem, however, eating like someone that size. During the season, I tended to consume lots of the leftovers from the game—an entire pizza, hamburgers, pasta, and an occasional beer (being cheaper than wine). Oh, and I loved my Snickers bars. I was always hungry. The joke was that if someone asked where I was, the reply went like this: "She is probably stuffing her face somewhere." But I had to eat like this to keep my weight up. The extra weight also kept my stamina up. I figured I'd enjoy eating that way as long as I could.

GAME DAY: SEVENTH INNING. As I sit in the dugout with the Dukes carrying a two-run lead into the seventh, I continue to distract myself with the thought that I am having the best season of my professional career. I have a win and twelve scoreless innings going. Coming into this game, my ERA is 4.88, which puts me in the middle of our pitching staff. I am now in the rotational mix of things: a starter. My confidence is up. I'm also getting along well with everyone—I am a part of this crazy team.

I watch as Narcisco Febles, a Dukes left-hander like me, runs out to the mound from the bullpen. As Forry Wells walks to the plate I want to be out on the mound so bad. Febles strikes him out. *Sweet.* But then Ruben Santana hits a line shot down the right-field line for a double. *Hell.* The next hitter grounds to first, and Anthony Lewis tosses it over to Febles, who runs to cover first for out number two. Santana's now on third on a fielder's choice. Then Smith grounds out to first, and the runner dies on third. Cool, three more outs and no runs.

When Febles comes into the dugout, I bump his fist, and say, "Good job, man; nice pitching."

Our hitting coach tells our batters to take more pitches and make the pitcher work for it. For the Dukes it's been one-two-three innings since the fifth. Now Brito fouls out, Schmitz strikes out, and Lewis flies out to center. We took more pitches, but it was still a one-two-three inning.

EIGHTH INNING. Back on the mound, Febles walks Chad Akers. Febles's pitches are all over the plate: four straight balls. Then Hine doubles to left center, and Chad comes around to score. With Hine sitting on second, George yanks Febles and brings in our closer. I still think we have this. Emiliano Giron strikes out the next batter. *Yes.* Next batter up hits a grounder to Hine at second, who bobbles it, then rushes and throws the ball away. All during the game the infield has been bobbling balls. Hine scores on the error, tying the game at 2–2, and with it goes my chance for another win. But Giron gets Coste to ground into a double play and we get out of the inning. When Giron comes into the dugout he chews out Hine for the error. He has more seniority, so people listen to him. He's pissed. For one he wants to beat this team—we all do—but he also understands how much another win would have meant to me. He comes by, slaps my leg, and we watch as the Dukes once again go three up and three down. Our bats have gone dead, and we know we only have Giron left for one more inning.

NINTH INNING. Giron goes out there again and deals. The RedHawks have a one-two-three inning, too.

TENTH INNING. Extra innings and I'm still on the bench, waiting to see what's going to happen. Our bats stay silent once again, and with Fargo's number nine, one, and two hitters coming up, Ariel Hernandez is sent to the mound. He walks Cory Smith. *Shit.* Then Akers gets a bunt single, advancing Smith to second with no outs. Next hitter, Hine, bunts down the third base line. He's thrown out at first but gets credit for a sacrifice for advancing the runners to second and third. Next hitter up, Knott is intentionally walked. Bases loaded, one out, and Fink is up. It's lefty versus lefty, Hernandez's specialty, and he strikes him out. The stands are going nuts, and so are both benches. Base loaded, two outs, and Chris Coste is up. Last time I struck him out, and he slammed his bat on the ground. He steps to the plate as the crowd chants, "Coste, Coste, Coste." Ariel's fastball comes straight into his wheelhouse, and Coste connects. Hometown guy wins the game with a walk-off grand slam.

As we Dukes trudge off the field, my teammates come by to say, "Good job, Ila. You pitched an awesome game."

The RedHawks designated hitter, Darryl Motley, comes over to say "Nice game."

And here comes Doug Simunic, the RedHawks manager who complained about my playing to the league and blasted me on the pre-game radio show, to say, "Nice game, Ila."

Even though I got a no-decision, I still feel like I won.

I don't see the *60 Minutes* crew leave.

I went home that night with a pain in my neck and trapezius muscles that I had been ignoring for the past couple of weeks. I reached toward the pain and felt bumps. The following day, I asked Mrs. Lothenbach, the woman I was staying with, if she could look at my neck and back.

She said, "Yah, you better get in to a doctor. I don't know what it is, but it looks like something is trying to come out of your body."

Luckily, the next day we were off. I went to our team doctor, who examined me and said that the lumps looked like dead lymph nodes. They might even be cancerous, possibly Hodgkin's disease. He would not know until after he removed them and sent them for a biopsy. He wanted to remove them right away. I wanted to know how long I would be out of pitching. Two or three weeks. If I tried to pitch too soon, the stitches could pull out and the wound become infected.

I was mortified: first, I could have cancer; second, my season might be over just as I was getting into a groove. I was also scared because with no long-term contract, I could be let go at any time. The only people on the club who knew about my surgery were the doc and the trainer, Gabe Gorby. I don't know whether Gabe ever told our manager. So the doctor numbed the area and made a ten-inch incision on my upper back. As I sat there, I hoped that one week of taking it easy would be enough to heal the wound before my next start.

Seven days later, I was to start a game. The stitched-up wound had not healed yet, but a scab had formed. After my bullpen session was done, I rushed to the restroom, changed my bloody shirt, and came back out to pitch. After almost every inning I came back in and changed my shirt, afraid someone would spot the blood. My head was fogged with pain, and I kept worrying, *Do I have cancer?* I ended up getting rocked over five innings. I had gotten my ERA down, but this was going to send it up.

I had two more starts to get through, and then I could head home for the winter. But the next two starts went the same way. My ERA doubled over those three games. When the test results came back, they were negative—no cancer! But I was still down because the surgery had demolished the good season I was having. Looking back, I should have waited to pitch. It seems like I have to learn about life the hard way. But the surgery taught me a lesson that is simple but profound: control what you can control and leave the rest to God. It would take years to learn that if I did my best to focus and prepare, and then strove to go beyond what I thought I could do but failed, God wants me somewhere else. It usually turns out better if I make that change. This lesson goes against my basic nature, and I remain challenged by it. The hard part to understand is, when is this adversity a test to see how much you want to succeed and when is it a door being shut in your face for good reason?

Back in California I sank into a funk. What affected me most was being flat broke. Japan wanted me to pitch over there. I loved their culture, and they treated me well, but felt I would have been too lonely there. Instead I found work as a substitute teacher, janitor, and personal trainer. Kelly helped me out so I could make time to train for baseball. Without her, I could not have made it through to next season. But here I was again, relying on someone else while others my age were starting their careers. I was growing tired of living on a sofa, eating lousy food, and worrying whether I would get the call to return to spring training camp. People around me often said, "Go for it! Go, Ila!" They loved sharing my dream. But I was living with the stress of being broke and was finding it more and more difficult to find the fun in the game while hiding in the closet. I told myself that I would give the 1999 season my best and see how it went.

7

ANOTHER TEAM, ANOTHER TOWN

MAY 1999, DULUTH, MINNESOTA. When I got to spring training camp I learned that the Dukes had a new manager, Larry See. This was not good news. I had faced See last season, when he was a player-coach with the Thunder Bay Whiskey Jacks. He didn't like the experience. "Coming up against her is a no-win situation," he said. "I mean, if you get a base hit you're expected to off a woman. And if you don't . . . well, you look like a fool."

I hadn't liked the experience either. See tended to walk around with a scowl on his face and act like he was better than others. Now, at spring training camp, he liked to remind the players (including me) that he hit two home runs off me last year. Asked about his other at bats against me, he mentioned a few infield grounders. He also remembered a strike-out, "a called third strike on a pitch that was a foot outside," he said. "I thought the umpires in the league gave her a wide strike zone, and others agreed with me."

Actually I struck him out twice, though I knew there was no percentage in correcting my manager's memory. During workouts, I could tell that my presence made See unhappy. We had a communication gap, too. See said he invited me into the locker room when the guys were watching TV, but after I wouldn't go in, he said, "It's hard to bring a team together, to bond, when you have that."

I don't remember him inviting me in. I don't think that was personal, though. See didn't seem happy to be there. To me, he lacked a sense of humor, a quality that is important in the baseball life. "Two bad outings and you're gone," he warned us pitchers.

I told myself, *Control what you can, and let the rest be in God's hands.*

Our new pitching coach, Steve Shirley, was different from See, empathetic and approachable. "Much of my work with this team has been psychological," he explained. "Many of these players have recently been cut from affiliated clubs or are fighting back from an injury. They're not sure of themselves, and in baseball that hurts."

Steve's daughter had played baseball before switching to softball and later attended college on a softball scholarship. "How many young women are going to win a scholarship to play baseball?" he wondered. Perhaps, given what I had gone through, he wished I had turned to softball, too. He had also played ball in Japan. "There's a term they use over there, *genki*," he said. "It means feeling good about yourself. Right now, I don't see much *genki* in Ila."

I was driving myself nuts trying to adjust to the changes at the Dukes, knowing they could dump me anytime. Here I had been a part of the 1997 championship team and had done well during the past season until the last three games. The guys knew me by now, and we were all pretty close. It was a day-by-day interior battle to keep my spirits up. But Steve Shirley was right: I did not have much *genki* in me.

On the chilly night of June 7, we were getting clobbered by St. Paul, which had scored five runs, with twelve hits, off starter Rick Wagner. It got worse after that, and then See called me in to pitch the ninth. Suddenly the lights behind first base went dark for twenty minutes. Call it an omen, because I felt a sense of foreboding as we waited for the lights to get fixed. The mound had always been my territory, my domain, but as I began to pitch I felt completely lost. My fielders behind me seemed to be frozen in place, committing two errors. By the time it was over, I had given up six hits, six runs (three earned), a walk, and a wild pitch.

In two and one-third innings this season I'd given up ten hits, eleven runs (eight earned), and four walks. Larry See was true to his warning: the next day the Dukes put me on revocable waivers. I stayed up most of the night calling clubs from the Western (Independent) League. On June 10 Bob Gustafson, the Dukes' general manager, told me that the Madison Black Wolf had acquired my contract. I didn't want to go there. I would have preferred going to a different league for a fresh start, where nobody knew me. I was sad, scared, and relieved all at the same time. I could feel myself withdrawing, as I had in high school. Right now there was little that was stable in my life. I talked to God but had no flesh-and-blood friend to talk to. I found myself angry at the situation I was in—was this punishment for something? My mindset was so negative that I couldn't see the move to Madison as an opportunity to grow. I was to catch a Greyhound bus and be ready to pitch the next night, until I caught a ride with the woman who would become my coauthor. "That's hard, riding the bus all night and going right into a game," Jean said. "Why don't I drive you?"

Bob Gustafson looked relieved. He handed me a fifty-dollar bill from his cash box, and we headed toward the I-94. During the three-hundred-mile drive to Madison, Jean and I munched popcorn and swigged mineral water as we analyzed the complications of my baseball life. It was a relief to talk it out with someone who shared the common language of baseball. My nerves began to calm down. I had found it hard to keep up much with friends while I was playing ball. Maintaining a good friendship takes time, which I had little of, and requires give and take, a skill I had yet to learn. Right now it was all about me and my career. On that drive we also talked about religion. Jean was a Christian but much more liberal than the ones I had known growing up. She was not shy about pointing out what she saw as the Religious Right's deviations from Christ's teaching and example. "Do you really think Jesus gives a rip whether a woman should play baseball?" she asked me. "Isn't *how* you play, *how* you conduct yourself in whatever arena you're in what he'd be interested in?" Jean had a good friend, a devout Christian, who had recently come out as a lesbian. She had seen what it had cost her friend professionally and spiritually—the local evangelical church she attended had cut her off. Jean said she thought it odd—weird, really—that such Christians were so paranoid about what other people did in bed. I listened but didn't say anything. As far as Jean knew, I was into guys.

When I got to Madison I checked in at Warner Park, nicknamed the Wolf Den. I saved what was left of Bob Gustafson's fifty dollars for meal money rather than a hotel room. I called a friend from Whittier College, Trish Van Oosberee, whose brother lived in Madison, and asked for help finding a place to live. I had mastered sleeping in the car, on a friend's couch, and on the beer-soaked floor of the team bus, so my first night in Madison was spent on the cushioned stretching table in the smelly and chilly locker room.

In the clubhouse the next day, I encountered one of the greatest baseball characters I'd ever met: the Black Wolf manager, Al Gallagher. We players thought he was known as "Dirty Al" not because of his language, which was just normal baseball profanity when he got upset, but because of the odor of onions that always seemed to exude from him. Dirty Al's hair was uncombed, his cap was on cockeyed, his uniform was rumpled, as if he had slept in it, and his socks were pushed down. But his nickname actually went back to his college days. Being highly superstitious, he determined not to shower or wash any part of his uniform while a good streak continued. His was not the orthodox look of a baseball man, and my first impression was to wonder how I could take anything he said seriously. But Dirty Al smiled at me, and the hitting and pitching coaches seemed excited I was there. Meeting them was a good icebreaker, a welcome introduction to my new team. Al said, "How do you feel about starting today?"

How did I feel . . . ? I could not recall a manager asking how I felt about starting. To be truthful, I wasn't thrilled about pitching so soon; I hoped for some time to get ready. But I picked up my uniform—I was number six now—and suited up for practice.

The clubhouse culture here was different from what I had known in St. Paul and Duluth. If the Saints reminded me of the lordly New York

Yankees, and the Dukes reminded me of the unruly Boston Red Sox, the Black Wolf defied categories—they were just themselves. They seemed to have no core identity—everyone kind of did their own thing. Most of my new teammates were married or had girlfriends. Our shortstop Dan Grice introduced himself. After that first practice everyone went home while I stuck around and talked about my role with Dirty Al and my pitching coach, Bronson Heflin, who had pitched for the St. Louis Cardinals and, like several coaches in the Northern League, also played on the team. Gallagher wanted me to start—pitch three innings and work up to five. Then he planned to bring in our hard-throwing right-hander for a few innings and finish the ninth with our closer.

Dirty Al had played for the San Francisco Giants and turned out to be full of baseball knowledge. It was an honor to play for him. He was one of the best managers I played for, easygoing and supportive. He understood that I needed what he called a "fresh start." He handled the media like no one had since Mike Veeck.

"Too much is made of Ila being a girl," he told the *Madison Capital Times*. "But what she has to realize is what Jackie [Robinson] had to realize; where too much was made of him being black. Personally, I could care less whether she's a girl, boy, black, white, Dominican, or from Panama. It's all a matter of how they play."

Dirty Al's wife, Nancy, was supportive, too. She was always cheering for me, at all the games, and saying good luck with smiles. I began to get excited about the season. I walked out with Dirty Al and Bronson to the parking lot, aware that I had nowhere to stay for the night. I told one of the locker room guys, "Hey, I forgot something in the clubhouse. Can you give me the key, and I'll give it back tomorrow? Go ahead and take off."

I must have sold it, because he gave me the key. I gave a sigh of relief and returned to the locker room and my bed, the stretching table. I woke up the following day and sat out on the field in peace, visualizing success on the mound, until the grounds crew and the clubhouse attendant, also known as the clubby, got in. I then headed to a park nearby and waited until everyone else showed up. I grabbed some free food from the stands and got the call that Trish's brother had found me a place to stay starting the next day. Great news. Now I only had one more night in the locker room. After the game was over I hung out and waited for everyone to leave, and then, just as the clubby was leaving I stuck a piece of cardboard in the door to prop it open. I walked out to the parking lot and started to walk to a home I didn't have. The clubby asked if he could give me a ride, but I said, "No, It's okay. I like to walk—I've never seen fireflies before."

"You better watch out," he said. "It's not safe out in this area."

After he left, I headed back to the clubhouse, praying that cardboard had stayed put. This was getting old, but it was my fault. I was too proud to ask for help or money. I knew it was weird; I just didn't know any other way. Trish's brother had told me his daughter was in nursing school at the University of Wisconsin and lived in a small duplex on Milton Street. I could stay there until the end of the season. I was beyond grateful and excited—my own room to myself.

Because Madison is home to the main campus of the University of Wisconsin, it has a great young vibe to it. The city is a cyclist's heaven, with lots of designated paths for bicycles. Even in the winter people bike to work. Although we played almost every day, I tried to get out and embrace the city. I loved walking home after a game and seeing fireflies lighting the evening. I hung out on campus or walked around Second Street, watching the people pass by. The duplex where I was staying was next to Camp Randall Stadium, where the University of Wisconsin Badgers played their football games. I promised myself that before my season ended I would attend a game there. Madison is not a big baseball town, given the great tradition of its college football team. It had won the Rose Bowl in 1994 and again this year, and head football coach Barry Alvarez was the talk of the town. The team's prospects looked good for the coming season. I also came across a man who owned a store called the Shoe Box. He told me to come on in and get some free cleats and running shoes. I didn't want anything for free, but he insisted on giving a discount. I signed a lot of my rookie Saints cards and gave them to him. Maybe it's just the way the Midwest is, but the people of Madison were so gosh-darn friendly. I'd be out running, and people driving by would honk or wave. But they never got into my space. A local couple lent me their car, a red hatchback Honda Civic, so I could get from the apartment to the ballpark and back. They would not let me pay them. I was amazed at how many people were trying to help me. If not for people like this, I doubt my season would have gone as well as it did. In Madison I learned the value of giving without expectation.

JUNE 11, WARNER PARK, MADISON, WISCONSIN. I made my first start for Madison against the Sioux Falls Canaries. Pitching on three days' rest, I was kept to a strict pitch count by Dirty Al. Of the thirty-two pitches I threw that rainy night, twenty-one were strikes. Over two innings, I gave up two runs and four hits. I liked being a starter again, and I liked playing for Dirty Al.

He didn't converse much, but there was an understanding and respect there. He knew I worked better if he didn't tell me what to do all the time. With his encouragement, I improved, giving up fewer walks and hits. My velocity increased two miles per hour to seventy-seven. I credit this to the way Big Al treated his players. He knew how to get the best out of us. He didn't treat me like he treated others—he saw us as individuals and adjusted his approach. It's called being a player's manager. And I saw that when my manager and coaches had my back, as Rol Esslinger had when I was in junior high and now Dirty Al did, I tended to play better—an insight that extended beyond the diamond into my personal life. When I had support and encouragement in my life, I performed better. Yell at and criticize me, though, and I froze up.

JUNE 17, FARGO, NORTH DAKOTA. Tonight Gilberto Reyes subbed as manager for Dirty Al, who had a blocked artery and went in for an angioplasty. Reyes sent me in relief to pitch the bottom of the eighth of a game we were trailing 4–2 against Fargo-Moorhead. I gave up a walk to Cory Smith, the first batter I faced. Nerves, the relief pitcher's bane. But I refocused and picked Smith off at first. Getting an out that way is satisfying twice over: you make up for whatever mistake that let the guy get on base in the first place, and you demoralize your opponents. I got the next two outs. In the top of the ninth, we rallied for three runs, and Joe Stutz, our closer, shut them down in the ninth. There are times when I've pitched my heart out as a starter and lost the win because our relievers couldn't hold the lead. Well, the game giveth, and the game taketh away, to get biblical about it. Tonight I pitched one inning and got my first win for Madison. I just wished Dirty Al was here to see it.

JUNE 28, MADISON. On a Sunday afternoon I started against the Schaumburg Flyers. I was on: after giving up a lead-off single, I threw three scoreless innings, with two strikeouts; and no runner advanced past first base. I got some grudging support from the Flyers manager, Ron Kittle, who told the *Madison State Journal*, "I think the guys don't take [Borders's pitching] real serious and before you know it you're behind. . . . I tip my hat for her, though."

By August my ERA with the Black Wolf was a fine 1.51, which stirred up some envy among a couple of my teammates. Dad found their negative comments about private clubhouse stuff and about me on the Internet. It stunk because one of them was our catcher, as I learned when an umpire came up and flat out told me, "Your catcher is the one spreading rumors and isn't hiding it." It reminded me of college when my catcher would tell the opposing hitter what was coming. So I walked a fine line between hanging out with the guys and keeping aloof. I had plenty of time to practice walking this line, because Madison was the easternmost city in the league, and the bus trips were longer. I'd get on the bus, and a fellow pitcher might say, "Oh, here comes the person with the lowest ERA on the team."

And then there was Heflin, our pitching coach. He seemed to like me as a person but seldom instructed. Forgive me for pointing out that in the summer of 1999 my ERA was lower than his. Heflin finally called a pitchers meeting, where he told the others to stop undercutting me with petty stuff. I was there but played dumb.

And through it all the general craziness of baseball went on and on. At one point a pitcher for the team came up to some guys and me and asked us to check out his shave job because his wife was coming to town. It's called manscaping.

One night, a guy from my team came banging on my hotel room door at midnight in his boxers. I opened up and said, "What's up, Joe [not his real name]?"

"Do you have a condom?" he said. "I just met this girl, and she doesn't have one and neither do I."

I kind of laughed and said, "No," but thought, *Good for him*. He was a handsome guy with a lot of talent, but his wiener took priority every time. The following day we were to leave at three in the morning for a road trip. Joe was nowhere to be found. We waited for him for five minutes and then left. Coach said if he wasn't at the game by the time we got to the ballpark, he would be released. Stunk for me because he was the guy who would come in behind me. A teammate called him and told him he better make it to the game. I don't know how, but he found a bus headed for the town we'd be at and made it to the field in time.

There's a time to fight for how you want to be treated, but at this time and place it was about getting along and trying to stay under the radar. There were times when I wanted to pay back the guys, but all it would take for me to be dropped was to offend someone, so I just took it and laughed.

It was the same in the bullpen. Two guys got into a fight in the stands because one of them was throwing pistachios at my head, trying to get me to react, and the other guy was telling him to knock it off. Both were finally escorted out, but it was a scene. On another night, near the end of the game, a bunch of college guys bought the bullpen a round of beers. In my drink was one of those paper umbrellas, with a phone number written on it. I laughed and looked up at this guy standing up, with all of his friends pointing at him. I raised the cup to him in thanks, put the umbrella in my back pocket, but never called him. I faced a tougher decision during one of the club's promotions, "Bring Your Dog to the Ballpark," when fans could lead their canines onto the field to meet the players. I spotted her immediately. I went straight to her—a Boston terrier, a breed I love—not even glancing at the person on the other end of the leash. After playing with the dog for a few minutes, I remembered my manners and spoke with the owner. Her name was Janice, and she was a professional triathlete. Our conversation flowed effortlessly for about ten minutes, until it was time for me to leave for the bullpen. I could tell she wanted to say something more. "It was great chatting with you," I said. "Hope you can both come out here for another game."

I guess that opened the door, because she said, "Forgive me if I'm off with this, but here is my number. I would love to meet up again."

Janice's words brought a smile to my face, which quickly faded. I already felt like people were watching for who I might date. I dared not risk anyone in baseball getting wind of my dating a woman. I kept her number, staring at it from time to time but never made the call. I did look for her at the ballpark but never found her.

Al's plan was working well. I threw three innings of shutout ball in a 4–2 victory over the Dukes, then three more scoreless innings, giving up two hits and a walk but no runs. I felt in control, and I was putting up good numbers—two earned runs over seventeen and one-third innings for a 1.04 ERA—and so were our right-hander and closer. The Black Wolf were winning. I celebrated by watching the Wisconsin Badgers beat Murray State at Camp Randall Stadium. That year Wisconsin would go 10-2. I have been a Badgers fan ever since.

JULY 18. On a rainy Sunday I made my sixth straight start against the St. Paul Saints, struggling through three innings and giving up five hits and a walk. Sometimes those are the games you remember, rather than the ones where everything was in sync, because you battle through them. I picked off the Saints' lead-off batter in the first inning and stranded four base runners. As the *Capital Times* reported, "'She battled,' said former major leaguer Matt Nokes, who had two hits, including a single in the third inning off Borders. 'You have to be patient. She's tough to hit.'"

Dirty Al had my back. "She didn't have her real good stuff," he told the *Capital Times*. "That was the first time she'd pitched on just three days' rest. . . . She threw in the bullpen yesterday, which she likes to do before she pitches. We might have to change that."

As the season wore on, my teammates seemed to get more comfortable around me. Word got around that I wasn't sleeping with anyone, didn't pursue women, kept my nose clean, and was just there to play ball. Guys started coming up to me like they had in high school to ask if I would catch them in the bullpen. We had a bullpen catcher, but I would always go down there too, explaining, "Catching makes me a better pitcher," which was true. I'd let them know what was working, what wasn't, and why, as well as how much break they had on it and how much movement.

I had the best year of my career in Madison, with the lowest ERA on the team. I was gratified that my numbers had proved what I could do. Opponents hit .273 against me, third best on the team. As I left the clubhouse for the airport, Dan Grice called out, "Stay in touch."

Dirty Al and the pitching coach said, "Have a great off-season. See you next year."

I caught the plane to St. Paul for my connecting flight to Los Angeles. As the plane soared over the forests and lakes of the Upper Midwest, I leaned back and reflected on the past three years of baseball. In 1997 my goal had been to simply survive the season. In 1998 I had wanted to make an impact for the Dukes. This past season, with the Black Wolf, the goal had been to improve—and I had. Maybe my next goal would come true: an invitation to spring training somewhere in Organized Baseball. I figured that the people who decided these things could by now accept that I was the real deal, because I had just ended three years in a tough league on a high. When Kelly picked me up at LAX, I shared my excitement about the season: 1-0, 1.67 ERA, eighteen games, 32.1 innings pitched, thirty-three hits, seven runs, six earned runs, three home runs, ten walks.

OCTOBER 20, HOLLYWOOD, CALIFORNIA. Today a letter arrived from the Madison Black Wolf advising me of the club's "intent to exercise [my] one year option . . . through the 2000 Northern League season."

More good news came in a phone call. Photographer Annie Leibovitz invited me to attend the launching of her book, *Women*, at the Corcoran Gallery of Art, in Washington DC on October 26, 1999. I was *invited*—me, the closeted gay broke ballplayer. I also received an engraved invitation from the White House to honor Annie's exhibit at the Corcoran, *Portraits, Profiles, and Progress: Celebrating Women of the Twentieth Century*, where I would meet President Bill Clinton and First Lady Hillary Clinton. In her invitation Annie had included a signed copy of her picture of me. If ever there was a fire in my home, I told myself, I would save that picture and my Northern League championship ring. But I had no money to pay for an airline flight, let alone a hotel room. There was no way I was going to charge those things to my credit card instead of paying Kelly back—that was something Dad would do. So I called to thank Annie, saying that I would love to be there but could not make it. She asked why, and I said, very embarrassed, that I could not afford it. She was surprised to find out that I had no endorsement deals and was broke. I remember thinking that she also likely knew that I was hiding who I truly was.

Annie arranged for Kelly and me to fly to DC and put us up at the nicest hotel I'd ever been in. When we rolled up to the Corcoran Gallery, I was stunned. On the outside of the building was a huge image of Annie's photograph of me. Surreal. This famously talented stranger had recognized something in me and captured it on film.

Inside the gallery were portraits of seventy of the more than one hundred women of the book, including Annie's mother, Marilyn, five women coal miners from Alabama, tennis star Venus Williams, and Hillary Clinton. Annie told reporters covering the show that this had "been an emotional project over the last three years." Her guideline for selecting which images to include had been, "If it makes you cry, it goes in the show."

She said that my image "captured . . . a glamorous moment." And in the *Washington Post*'s review of the exhibit: "Then you look at Ila Borders winding up to throw a baseball in a vast twilight of clouds and distant trees, and you know you're looking at a whole picture that stands by itself, no questions asked, the seams forgotten—art."

It all struck me speechless. To be a part of something done by Annie Leibovitz, who I believe is the most gifted person in her field, was an unbelievable honor. At the reception, actors like Drew Barrymore and Gwyneth Paltrow mingled with secretary of state Madeleine Albright and Supreme Court justice Sandra Day O'Connor. I like to say that I don't get starstruck, but that night, yeah, I was dazzled. I got to meet President Bill Clinton—and yes, he is charismatic and charming—and Hillary Clinton, a lifelong Chicago Cubs fan who was warm and friendly, and went out of her way to acknowledge the importance of my career. When I approached my photograph, actor Robert Duvall came up to me and said, "Hey, that's you! So, how's it going?"

Then a woman turned to me and said, "Oh, this is you."

It was Patti Smith. "I bought this," she said, looking up at my image.

We chatted for quite a while, and I found this iconic singer-songwriter-poet sweet and charming. Then I found Annie Leibovitz and had the chance to thank her. I want people to know how gracious she is. I still shake my head and say to myself, *How in the heck can I ever repay her? Does she know how much that night meant to me?*

On New Year's Day the University of Wisconsin Badgers won the Rose Bowl for the second year in a row. I took that as a good omen for the season to come, yet something was off. I had worked hard last summer in Madison, just not quite as intensely as I used to. Baseball was all I had ever known and wanted, but the stress of having to prove myself game by game, season by season, had worn me down. The game was no longer fun.

I thought of my encounter last season with Janice and her Boston terrier and all the other chances for affection and companionship I'd passed up for the baseball life. I was tired of hiding who I was. In Los Angeles, I was learning, there were plenty of opportunities to meet women at athletic events around town. I started to date discreetly, edging out of the closet with tentative steps. Dating made me see that I had given up

Ila Borders, the person, to be Ila Borders, baseball pitcher. Somehow I was not able be both at the same time. Somewhere along the line, others—my parents, Annie Leibovitz, Kelly Deutsch, and sportswriters and fans—remained more excited about my dream of making it in Organized Baseball than I now was.

There was also the issue of finances. When I heard about people being at their wits' end from being broke, I got it. It kills your self-esteem and spirit. I was weary of living as a vagabond—staying in Connie Rudolph's basement in St. Paul, sleeping in the Madison Black Wolf clubhouse, and now bunking in with Kelly in Hollywood. Mom had made a home for us kids when I was growing up. I hadn't had a home base since I was seventeen, and I missed it.

Dad continued to seek out major league teams about my going to spring training to try out for a spot on the roster. One day he sat me down. No one in MLB was going to invite me to spring training, he explained. It was feared I would be a distraction, and they just didn't want the hype that followed me. It was suggested that I try out for a professional team in Japan and then return to try out—it would be a smoother transition. Akiko Agishi, who was working for Creative Enterprises International, in Hollywood, thought she could find me a spot on a Japanese team. On February 8, 2000, I sent her a letter of intent stating my interest in playing ball in Japan, which led to a tryout in Yuma, Arizona, where I was told they were looking for pitchers who could throw ninety miles per hour. So that wasn't going to happen either. With that, Dad and I looked at each other, knowing that our dream had died. I was not going to get my chance in Organized Baseball. Coming off the best year I'd had professionally, I sensed that next season in Madison was going to be my last.

MAY 2000. When I arrived in Madison for spring training, I scrabbled around for some sense of joy in the game. I was reverting to the stone-faced introvert of old and forgetting how to reach out for help. I couldn't go to my parents, who were now fighting all the time. My teammates, competing for their own spot on the roster, didn't seem likely confidants for a gay female athlete. And reporters' scrutiny of my off-the-field life—well, I couldn't see confiding my own true story to one of them. I began to see what my closeted life had cost me. I gave in to a major pity party for myself, disliking my own company.

Workouts became a chore, and it showed. I always believed I would make it to an affiliate organization if I just proved myself. Well, I had proved that I could endure the baseball life over and over, and last season I had put up the numbers to back it up, but the determination and drive that helped me to succeed had faded. I could see that other guys in spring training camp wanted to make the Black Wolf more than I did. I never had a bad preseason or intersquad game, but there was nothing great either. Coming off last season, I had expected to be more dominant, but I was plain outplayed. I was not progressing. I didn't know what else to do, so I kept on doing the only thing I knew—playing ball.

I did not make the roster. But Dirty Al and Bronson Heflin knew what I could do, and the general manager told me to stick around for a week or two in case someone went down with an injury. I should have stayed and would have if I had been in a better place—I could have contributed to the Black Wolf, as I had last year. Instead my pride and emotions got the better of me. I left for Los Angeles. I wish I hadn't—I should've stuck it out. It remains a big regret.

Back in California, I sat on Kelly Deutsch's couch, uncertain of what was to come next. Phone calls came in from concerned family members, college friends, and the media, asking where I was. I had no good answer. About a week later, a scout whose name I cannot recall called and asked me to meet him in Las Vegas. With nothing else going on, I roused myself off Kelly's couch and met him on June 1 at the University of Nevada, Las Vegas, for a tryout. I was the lone prospect. I headed over to the bullpen, and he tossed me a ball to throw. The scout liked what he saw. When it was over he signed me to play for the Zion Pioneerzz of the Western (Independent) Baseball League. The club, based in St. George, Utah, was in the second of what would be its three-year lifespan in a league that was farther removed from Organized Baseball than was the Northern League. I'd be playing for Mike Littlewood, who had played baseball at

Brigham Young University, in a new ballpark, Bruce Hurst Field, named for the former major league pitcher who had grown up in St. George.

There was no time to return to California for my clothes—off I went to St. George. The club put me up about forty miles away in the Oasis Casino and Resort in Mesquite, Nevada. My first reaction was, *I'm in nowhereland.* My hotel room had lights all around the ceiling, mirrors everywhere, and decor from the 1980s. I would drive Interstate 15 across the northwestern tip of Arizona to get to St. George, the landscape about as dry and barren as the place where my joy for baseball used to be.

JUNE, ST. GEORGE, UTAH. The town of St. George looked like a true Western town—people wore cowboy hats, Wranglers, and cowboy boots. The people were mainly white, though slightly older than average. I saw few people of color. It seemed that nobody smoked, and the grocery stores sold only 3.2 percent alcohol beer. (For anything stronger you went to the state package liquor store). Nightlife was hard to find, and even restaurants like Pancho and Lefty's for Mexican food and the Gun Barrel Steakhouse closed at eleven o'clock on Saturday nights. The women, primarily dressed in long skirts, all seemed to be with their kids. The locals looked at me like I was from Mars. One day I went to the movie theater to see *Shaft*, with Samuel L. Jackson. It was R-rated, but much of the dialogue was bleeped out—*what the frick?* I thought. I looked around: I was the only person in the theater.

The sense of difference continued. I saw that the ballplayers on the team were all white and young. When I went upstairs and met my new teammates, they were polite, as if my presence there was no big deal. Out in the bullpen I asked one of my teammates why everyone was young, white, and married. His face showed his disbelief. Didn't I know they were mostly Mormon?

"Okay, what does that mean?" I asked. You'd think that coming from Southern California College, I would have known about the religion, but I did not. We had discussed Buddhism, Judaism, Hinduism—I had done a report on them—but not Mormons. I wished I had studied it more.

He explained his religion, its background and its views, much like the people who knock on your door and pitch their beliefs to you. I smiled at him, and said, "I am a Christian and set in my beliefs."

After that, none of my teammates mentioned Mormonism to me. I couldn't get over that they married so young and that the women were so subservient, but they were clean and friendly and giving. Still, I could tell they hung out with their own. Talk about going somewhere I would never fit in! If anything, I was going backward. And yet the Pioneerzz had been willing to take a chance on me, so I practiced gratitude and tried to blend in. I bought a pair of cowboy boots.

When my brother, Randall, visited, we explored Bryce Canyon and hiked through the narrows at Zion National Park on my off days. The red-rock landscape attracted me, and I realized that I'd rather be exploring these trails than playing ball. On the field I could not shake feeling like an outcast. Pitching in St. George and driving back to sleep at the Oasis Hotel in Mesquite, Nevada, brought no joy. I also heard from friends that my first love, Shelley, was getting married and was in her second year of teaching. Other friends who had graduated were into their careers now. I looked at myself in my mirrored bedroom and saw "loser." The game had changed for me. Baseball had always been my outlet to freedom, peace, fun, and a release of aggression. That outlet no longer worked. Prior to my fifth outing, in a game that we were behind by several runs, I saw the coach come out to the mound, pull the pitcher, and signal for me. I wondered why he was bringing me in when the game was so out of reach. Then I remembered the type of player they brought in to finish these throwaway games, and my athlete's ego saw myself as beyond that level. Instead of fighting through my embarrassment, I asked myself what I was doing here. I grabbed the ball and threw my warmup pitches. Every pitch I threw got smashed. I tried throwing sidearm and still got shelled. By the time I walked off the mound, my ERA had shot up to 8.31. I went upstairs into the empty press box, where I found manager Mike Littlewood, the team owner, and the scout who had signed me. "I've had enough," I blurted out. "I want to retire."

They tried to talk me out of it, saying that it was just one bad game, they had seen what I could do, and my place on the team was secure for the rest of the season. The Pioneerzz were playing well—they would win the Western Baseball League championship that year—but the gleam of another ring or even another day on the mound was lost on me. Feeling like a quitter, something I never thought I'd be, I said, "My mind's just not in it—I just want to go home."

I had always said I wanted to go as far as my abilities could take me. Well, the end of the road turned out to be St. George, Utah. I was twenty-five years old. As the *Los Angeles Times* headlined it, "Ila Borders Gives Herself the Hook, Retires." In the article, Mike Littlewood said, "Ila Borders was one of the most courageous people I've ever met or seen play the game."

But I headed home with my head down, knowing I had let down the decent people who had hired me.

I realized I had made the mistake of finding my self-worth in what I did for a living, instead of who I was. So much of my energy had gone into baseball—and about trying to promote the image of me as a red-blooded heterosexual American girl with a perfect family. I could not or would not say I came from a family that was breaking down, that Dad was cheating on Mom, that he was alcoholic. Nor was I the kind of sweet, shy person I labored to present to the public. I was more of an adrenaline junkie, genetically driven to pop wheelies on a motorcycle and take up Krav Maga (Hebrew for "contact combat," a self-defense system that came out of the Israeli military). But for all my daredevilishness, I had always been afraid to say that it was nobody's business who I dated. This, I began to realize, was my greatest regret about my baseball playing days: it wasn't not making it into Organized Baseball; it was living the Great Lie of who I was. If I had been honest, I most likely would have lost my job earlier, but I would not have lived a lie. Quitting baseball now would let a lot of people down, and that weighed heavily on me. But I called Kelly and said, "I'm done. I'm coming home."

"Okay," she said. "The door's open."

8

OUT OF THE GAME

What do you do after everything you've ever known and worked for is gone? Even though I had a college degree, baseball had been the focus of my life since age ten. I pondered my list of achievements in baseball. It was a thin résumé for the rest of my life. ESPN invited me to Connecticut to train as a sports commentator, but the idea of being close to the all-seeing eye of the camera, of entering the media, put me off. Mike Veeck asked me to come back to St. Paul and be the pitching coach. But I was not thinking right and turned down his offer.

I headed for the couch in Kelly Deutsch's Hollywood apartment. I rarely showered and ate little. I read books and prayed to God to help me find a way out of the bleakness I had fallen into. Finally Kelly came home from work one day and sat down beside me. She put her hand on my back and, in the most loving, nonthreatening way, kicked my ass off the couch.

"Okay," she said. "Start asking yourself some questions. And go do what you like best, ride your bike."

I started biking the hills of Hollywood. I'd ride through Griffith Park and into funky Topanga Canyon. I biked to the wild reaches of Point Mugu in Malibu, exploring its trails and beaches. My view of Southern California had come from the standpoint of its baseball fields, those small, grassy parks that dotted the sprawling cities. Now I was discovering its fuller landscape, and it began to bring me peace. I would bike until exhaustion, then sit down and reflect. For the first time, I let it all sink in: my fricked-up family life, covering up my gayness, and along with that, my anxiety over being scrutinized by the media. I thought about the emotional parts of myself I had neglected in my single-minded pursuit of playing baseball. Now I wanted to live a fully authentic life, but what did that mean? Who was I and what did I want? Three things came to mind:

Whoever I was, I was no longer a baseball player.

I had to break the cycle of lies I had been living.

And I wanted to date women and do it openly.

Kelly encouraged me to eat more—no, "encouraged" isn't the right word. She pretty much forced me to, saying, "If you don't go out to dinner with me, you can't stay here anymore."

Thank God she had given me these past few weeks to begin to heal. Now she started to push me, asking, "What do you like to do—I mean, things, not a job in particular. What are you good at? How do you want to be remembered?"

I made a list:

Physical activity. Definitely not working behind a desk all day.

Good at math and mechanics. Like to build and repair things.

Make a positive impact on people's lives and be proud of the work I do.

Be challenged every day.

What was I good at? I am direct, work hard, and don't make excuses.

Quick learner and good common sense. Love sports!

Don't need a lot of money. Would sacrifice that for more time with family and friends.

It seemed important to be clear on what I should avoid, as in my weaknesses and dislikes: they included the computer and technology,

English and the use of words, traveling a lot and being in the spotlight, and emotional drama.

Then Kelly and I made a list of possible careers: firefighter, forest ranger, architect, teacher, golf pro, FBI agent, coach. That fall, I applied for a coaching job at Glendale Community College. But they wanted to know how I planned to raise funds for uniforms. From my history with Dad, I knew that asking for money was not a well-developed skill. Park rangers, I feared, were subject to layoffs due to budgetary cuts. I wanted a career that was more secure. I had worked as a personal trainer but wanted something steadier. I was not aware that I could have approached Nike, in Beaverton, Oregon, to work with them to test baseball equipment, or Columbia Outdoor Clothing for a similar job. So it came down to the FBI or firefighter. But did the FBI accept gay people? I wasn't sure. Firefighting paid good wages and offered job stability. Firefighters were respected, the people you called when you needed help fast—I remembered their presence when my grandmother drowned. What better way to honor her than to become a firefighter? In September 2001, I enrolled in the Fire Technology Department at Santa Ana Community College, in Orange County, California. A few days later the tragedy of September 11 underscored the importance of the career I had started.

I felt right at home in the academy, as firefighters and ballplayers have much in common: you have to be a team player but act individually, think fast and adapt, be physically fit, and have common sense. At the academy, the guys joke around with you, but if you cannot take the heat, usually they stop—fear of lawsuits now. Baseball was harsher. If you could not take your teammates' kidding, you became an outcast and they would keep it up until you broke. No mercy! There was more crude behavior in baseball where they didn't care if I was a girl (which I preferred), whereas in firefighting some were more careful around me. Some firefighters did treat me like one of the guys, and they were the ones I gravitated to. My paramedic preceptor, James Nelson, liked to chase me around the station with a hockey stick and once body slammed me. Loved that guy.

The culture of firefighting agreed with me. I came to understand that I was most comfortable in the company of men, active men. I'd always known I wasn't a traditional girl; now I could see that I wasn't a traditional gay woman who was more at ease in a woman's world—I preferred hanging with the guys. So this was what it was like to be comfortable in my skin. Kelly was happy to see that I was eating and showering regularly. So was I—I started to like who I was again. At the academy I was still in the closet—I was tentative about it getting around that I was gay and how that might be used as a reason to not hire me.

In my private life I had been dating women of all sorts since leaving baseball in 2000. Romantically I was like a caged bird set free. And then I met a woman named Karen at the academy. It was my first big relationship, and she showed me how much I had to learn. Any time we had a conflict, she'd raise her voice, and I'd flash back to Dad's anger and shut down. She called me on it, but eventually it broke us up. Karen was a good person and more mature than I was; I really blew it. I had to learn to stick around and work things out.

Learning to date women and making my way through the academy, I thought I had left baseball in my past. But every once in a while, I could see that baseball wasn't done with me. The game's historians and chroniclers continued to take an interest in what I had done. In July 2003 I was inducted into the Baseball Reliquary's Shrine of the Eternals. The Reliquary's Shrine is not the obscure Left Coast religious cult you might think but a sort of populist hall of fame that founder and executive director Terry Cannon hosts annually in Pasadena, California. It is a striking contrast to the more mainstream National Baseball Hall of Fame in Cooperstown, New York. The museum in Cooperstown had my college and professional memorabilia on display, but here, today, the Shrine wanted to present my whole person. As I listened to the words of the other inductees, Jim Abbott, the one-handed pitcher who threw a no-hitter for the New York Yankees, and Marvin Miller, whose work for the Major League Baseball Players Union began to change the financial fortunes of ballplayers, I realized that I was in good company as one of the game's outliers. The Shrine inducts people not likely to ever get into the Cooperstown Hall of Fame, like Lester Rodney, a former Communist who was an early white advocate for the integration of MLB.

At the induction, Jean Ardell introduced me, explaining that my career illustrated that "women have remained the game's last outpost regarding discrimination." She pointed out that a story like mine "embodies the classic theme of literature: Somebody wants something that is denied them and they set out to find a way to get it."

Yes, I thought, *that sums up my career.*

Then, as I approached the stage to give my acceptance speech, the audience rose for a standing ovation. An athlete's great fear is that she won't be remembered—that all the sacrifice mattered little—and here were two hundred people who did remember and seemed to care. Jim Wadley, the former owner of the Duluth Dukes, and his wife were there. So were my parents. I spoke of gratitude; I called my life in baseball "a fairy tale."

One day at the academy, one of the guys called out, "Hey, Ila. Howard Stern's talking about you on the radio. He wants to know where you're at."

I thought he was kidding until I heard Howard on the radio telling listeners to call in. I was not crazy about Howard's shock-jock reputation, but the guys at the academy loved him. During lunch break I called the station. Why, you might ask, would someone as averse to the media as I was call the reigning shock jock who was all about sexuality? Peer pressure—the guys wouldn't leave it alone, and I did so like being one of the guys. That and my own stupidity pushed me to it. I told myself, *What harm could come out of this?*

It turned out that Howard had an argument going that I could strike out "that fat little bastard Artie Lang." Artie, a comedian who was part of Stern's show, insisted he could get a hit off me. They were ramping up for a big battle of the sexes.

So I called and was asked a bunch of questions, inappropriate ones, of course, but still funny. They were trying hard to rile me up, but I didn't bite. Then the invitation: would I go to Las Vegas and pitch to Artie?

I said, "Okay, but I would bet against me right now." I explained that I had not thrown a baseball since retiring four years ago.

Howard told me to bring along a catcher. Our hotel rooms would be covered, plus we'd get five hundred dollars cash. I asked one of our firefighting recruits if he wanted to go, and he jumped at it. He was a big Howard Stern fan, and he liked the idea of staying at the Hard Rock Hotel and using his half of the cash to gamble with.

The Hard Rock Hotel parking lot had been turned into a mini baseball field on asphalt. There was a backstop, umpire, pitcher's mound, nets all around us, and tons of spectators. And I thought, *Why did I sign on to do this?* I had brought my own glove and baseball, but when I got there they had their own baseballs—Little League size balls, as if this was a kids' joke, and to me they felt softer than the ones I had thrown.

In the studio truck I met the crew. Howard Stern was tall and skinny, with lots of hair. *Hair!* I thought. At the firefighting academy, nobody's hair could touch the collar of his or her shirt, and no matter how much I gelled or moussed my hair, it grazed my shirt. For the first time ever I had cut my long hair. I felt exposed without my long hair and braced myself for the ridicule from Howard I was sure would come. But Howard in person turned out to be the opposite from his manner on the air: he was friendly and polite, and so was his entire crew. Artie, though, was swigging bourbon and talking trash. I did not talk trash—I had a hunch I was screwed by my lack of conditioning. I went out to the mound and threw about ten warmup pitches. *Ouch, it hurt. Holy crap—ten throws after four years.* Then I got the Little League baseball, and Artie came up to bat. I threw three fastballs, but high around his head. Holy crap—the ball was dragging off my fingers so badly that I tried to almost throw it into the ground to approach the strike zone. I finally decided, *Screw it, here comes a curveball.* And Artie made contact—not good contact, just a nubber, a grounder to short. But Artie had won.

Afterward, furious with myself for not being better prepared, I just wanted to get the hell out of there. I came back to the booth, said my good-byes, and headed back to L.A. My buddy, though, stayed on, partying with Howard's crew. Back at the Academy he said he was forever grateful to me for the gig. And I was a minor celebrity. Thanks to

YouTube, people still like to talk about the Howard Stern clip. Dang, everything you do really comes back to you.

I was honored to be named the first female recruit chief of the Santa Ana Fire Academy. I graduated in June 2004 with an associate of arts degree in fire technology. Along with about five thousand others, I applied for one of the twenty-four openings in the Long Beach Fire Department (LBFD). I had come in under seven minutes on the Biddle Physical Ability Test, and that caught their eye. The Biddle is a grueling test with eleven continuous events, from running up four flights of stairs with your pack and bundle to raising an extension ladder, and to pulling a 175-pound dummy around obstacles. To make the cut you must complete the test within nine minutes and thirty-four seconds. I knew of only one other woman at the academy who had come in under seven minutes. To me it was just another kind of spring training. In August 2004 I was hired on by the LBFD. I had to complete one year as a rookie on probation before the job would become permanent. I rented an apartment in the Belmont Shores area of Long Beach, right on the water. It was an active neighborhood, filled with Rollerbladers, joggers, dog walkers, and volleyball players—my kind of place. Long Beach had a good-sized gay community, but I was twenty-nine now and done running around looking for love. I liked staying home on a Saturday night, listening to the waves crashing on the shore, doing a crossword puzzle, enjoying a glass of wine, and chilling on my couch. When I did go out it was to visit a museum or attend a basketball or baseball game at Long Beach State, the University of Southern California, or the Staples Center. I was alone much of the time but didn't struggle with loneliness. I was willing to wait for the right person, whenever she came along, but I wasn't working very hard to find her.

SHANNON. On September 25, 2005, I biked to my favorite coffeehouse, Peet's. As I waited in line for my caffeine fix of choice, a medium skinny French vanilla latte, I opened a magazine to a feature about Joshua Tree National Park. I had bungee-jumped and ridden off rooftops on my bike but had never tried rock climbing. Joshua Tree, I read, was the place to go.

From behind me came a voice: "You have to go there."

I was not in a sociable mood, and thought, *Mind your own business, pal.* Then I turned and looked into a face that beamed joy back at me. A face that seemed kind of shy yet confident, and quirky. Something leaped in my heart, and I smiled back.

The woman said that she often went out to Joshua Tree. I ordered my coffee and invited her to join me. As I sat at the table, I thought, *What am I doing, inviting a stranger to hang out with me?* I took a quick glance at the rest of her. About five feet eight and lanky, all arms and legs, with blonde hair and kind brown eyes—not usually my type, which was blue-eyed brunettes. She was oddly dressed in jeans a little too short and a blue oversized sweatshirt. Her name was Shannon Marie Chesnos. We talked about rock climbing, scuba diving, and firefighting, with no sense of time or the people around us. Afterward, we looked at one another with the same idea: Did we have time to bike along the Long Beach boardwalk?

I was not thinking romantically right then—I did not know whether she was gay or straight—I just thought, *Wow, this is one down-to-earth, fun-spirited, cool person.* So we biked to the ferry and back. Laughing like kids, we competed to see who could "surf" their bike. It reminded me of my days with Grandma, when I felt so at ease. Shannon was so alive—she did not seem to care what others thought—and her laughter was contagious. By the end of the ride my eyes were watering and my stomach hurt from laughing so hard.

We exchanged phone numbers and made plans to meet the following week at the bowling alley at the Pike amusement park. I got there early and sat on a bench to people watch, wondering whether my time with Shannon would go as well as it had the first time. My cell phone rang—Shannon was calling to say she was parking. *Cool,* I thought, *she does not run late,* a peeve of mine. I turned my head, and there was Shannon—gorgeous, but what was she wearing? Lime green, way-too-short pants. She gave me her amazing smile, and I got the vibe that she was interested romantically. Then I wondered, *How is this person still single? Oh, yeah, it must be the clothes.*

During our bowling date, neither of us held back. I was curious to see how she dealt with winning and losing. I won two out of three games but felt no sense of competition, only the joy of being together. Afterward we walked to Islands, which turned out to be Shannon's favorite restaurant. Islands? I had been an island unto myself for so many years, but maybe no longer. I learned that she was an accomplished sailor and a master instructor of scuba diving. As we lingered over dinner, we discovered we were both neat freaks. While she was wiping salt off the table from her favorite french fries, I was wiping condensation from her glass of water. I knew right then I wanted to spend the rest of my life with her.

We took our time getting to know one another. Shannon had a complicated past. She had been adopted and was raised in San Jose by a wealthy couple. While Shannon felt her parents loved her very much, she also felt they were out of touch with who she was. Her father wanted her to go into a high-paying career and to marry a wealthy man, rather than accepting her as the model–computer geek–sports-minded woman that she was. I found out what was up with her baggy old clothes. Like me, Shannon did not like to be an object of attention—she had endured much of that during her modeling days. She also did not like people to know she came from money. So she dressed frumpy, in oversized, holey sweatshirts and unflattering pants.

OUT OF THE CLOSET. At age eighteen, Shannon had told her parents she was gay. Her father, she told me, had insisted that she was not. I understood. Just before I met Shannon, I had asked Mom to meet me at the track at Biola University. "Biola" stands for the Bible Institute of Los Angeles. It was a half mile from our family home, and I had been going there since age thirteen to shoot hoops in the gym or run the track. It wasn't just a place to train; it was also where Mom and I went to talk. After Randall was born she had struggled with her weight, so I often invited her to walk with me there for exercise and conversation.

I had turned thirty and was fed up with living the Big Lie about who I was to my family. Mom had faced the reality of her failing marriage and filed for divorce in October of 2003; it had become final the following year. I thought the divorce might help her better accept the truth of my own life. The only one in my family who knew I was gay was my sister, Leah, and I turned to her for advice about how to tell Mom.

"Go to the track, Ila," Leah said.

So here I was, walking the track of the Bible Institute of Los Angeles with Mom. I shook as I searched for a way to not tell her. *She doesn't really need to know,* I told myself. Her response was likely to be bad. I was her firstborn, the responsible one. Now I would be the one who let the family down.

"Mom," I began. "I'm going to tell you something you aren't going to be happy about. I don't expect you to agree, but I just cannot lie to you anymore."

Deep breath.

"I'm gay. I've known it since I was five. I have prayed hard to be straight, but I'm not. I'm gay."

Mom looked at me, puzzled. "But you've had two boyfriends."

"They didn't last very long, did they? And I wasn't physically attracted to them. I dated them because I felt that's what I was supposed to do.

"Oh, but maybe it's just a phase."

I could see why she might think that, given that I had been living a lie for so long. She started to cry. I had hoped that coming out would be a huge relief; instead I felt terrible. "I'm so sorry."

"I just worry about you," she replied. "I love you and know that people are going to be mean to you and call you names. It hurts that my child will be ridiculed."

I saw no anger in her eyes, but I did see fear. I looked at her, as if to say, Mom, I've lived with name-calling and ridicule all of my baseball life.

Mom sighed and said, "Well, I'm still going to pray that you meet a nice man."

We left it at that. Mom stopped asking questions about my personal life, and I did not offer any information. For me, the burden of secrecy had been lifted, only to be replaced by another weight. I was no longer the good daughter who upheld our family's Christian image. Yet I realized that Mom had let me down, too. No matter how much we love someone, they can fail us. Only God can supply the great doses of unconditional love that I as a gay woman so badly needed. I did feel that love but still feared that friends and family would view me differently now.

I knew I was lucky, though. Some of my gay friends had been kicked out of their homes or shunned by their families. Shannon had suffered, too. For years her father had set up Shannon on dates with men. She rebelled by moving to Hollywood, where she became a model and a singer. She got into alcohol and methamphetamines. Unable to come to terms with her family's response to her as a gay woman, she tried several times to take her life. I found it hard to believe she had lived that sort of life. Then Shannon showed me the scar on her butt, the result of an accident after she overdosed at her dealer's house. "It's all true," she said.

Eventually she quit drugs and alcohol cold turkey. Seeking a sense of community, a place where she might find acceptance and where people sought to live morally, Shannon turned to the Church of Latter Day Saints and at age twenty-five converted to Mormonism. It sounds self-destructive, but many gay people turn to the place least likely to accept their sexual orientation. It's a bargain with God in hopes of a miracle that just maybe they can turn straight. Shannon prayed that God would do just that. She dated guys. A Mormon man wanted to marry her, but she refused to pretend to love someone in what would have been, for her, a sham. Shannon also objected to the expectations put on women and their behavior. She often talked with her Mormon friend, Susie, who probably knew she was gay. Susie had explained the church's three levels of heaven. (The Mormon Church lists the Telestial as the realm for unbelievers, the Terrestrial for religious non-Mormons and Mormons who have not met the requirements for full holiness, and the Celestial for select Mormons who have kept all of the church's laws and ordinances.) Didn't Shannon want to be up higher, where Susie would be? But Shannon remained concerned with the religion's sense of exclusivity. And, like me, by age thirty she no longer wanted to live the lie of who she truly was. She left the Mormon Church. A year later, I was her first date.

Our weekends were a bonanza of bowling, rock climbing, swimming, Ping-Pong marathons, and movies. I had discovered the Southern California landscape first through the baseball diamonds I played on and later through biking the hills of Los Angeles; now I saw the area through love. It was a watery world: we went deep-sea fishing out of Newport Beach, snorkeled in Laguna Beach, and kayaked the canals near Long Beach. We crowded so much into our days and nights. Well, we had been looking for each other for a long time. If I had to come up with only one word to describe our life together, it would be laughter.

I had waited to tell her about my baseball career. When I did, she was intrigued. "You have to write a book about it," she said.

We'd go up to the field at Long Beach State, where the Dirtbags play, and I'd throw to her, though I made sure not too hard, or I'd hit ground balls to her. Shannon was a big fan of the Angels and one day surprised me with tickets to one of their games. "You know," she told me, "If you ever want back in the game some way, I'll support you."

My family liked Shannon from the start. Mom said she had never seen me so happy and stress-free. She was able to look past the gay part and appreciate our relationship for what it was. She knew I had met someone special and wanted me to be happy. Dad, though, was in denial. He and I had never had the conversation about my being gay—Mom says that she told him but he never brought it up with me.

Shannon's Mormon friends disapproved of her gayness but kept contacting her, urging her to return to the church. She stood fast but began reading the Bible, trying to find her way to God. Meanwhile, I was still recovering from my Southern Baptist upbringing. At one point, I asked what she believed in: "One heaven, one hell, and that good works can get you to heaven," she answered. We prayed together, and Shannon accepted Jesus Christ into her heart. We both wanted to find a progressive Christian church that would accept us as we were—definitely not one that taught we were going to hell for being gay. Our conversations made me reflect. God had answered my lifelong prayer to play professional baseball. Now, while I was on a new path as a firefighter, my second lifelong prayer had been answered: I had met my soul mate. Had I met Shannon earlier, I might have been so focused on my career that I would have passed her by. God's timing had been perfect. I've been asked why I give God the credit when something goes well but none of the blame when things don't. I believe that God is good and just but that there is a continuing struggle with evil in this world, and he has given us free will over our choices. I don't think God allows bad things to happen; they happen because we have free will.

In March of 2006 Shannon and I decided to move in together. If someone had ever told me that I—independent and aloof as I was—would do such a thing I would have said, "Hell, no." The idea had always scared me—lose my independence and privacy?—no way. Now I felt no hesitation. We had differences—I was more of a fighter, a competitor; Shannon was more peaceable. I had built up emotional walls; Shannon was a great communicator. When we disagreed, we talked it out and compromised, never trying to change one another. She was fearless, too. She liked to bake brownies and take them over to the gang members who hung out near our apartment. Our differences were part of our strength together. She had a way of taking away my fears, anxiety, and tension. No one had ever been able to do that. I felt that whatever came our way, we could get through it.

In April 2006 we made our commitment official. She gave me a leather ring—we could not afford an expensive engagement ring, and I wore it all the time. When Shannon had to be away from home, though, she wore it. She was my family now—no longer did I feel like the island my name represented—and this ring meant a lifetime commitment. But we had a few things to address. We had started spending time as a couple at Mom's house, with my siblings there. They accepted our relationship, but Shannon's parents held out. I had met her mother a couple of times but not her father. I knew what they thought of me: a gay firefighter? Not for their daughter. We decided to keep our living situation to ourselves and my family.

We began to look to our future. We loved Long Beach but were living in a condo in a rough area of town. We wanted a good school district and a safe town where our kids could someday play the way we had growing up. A friend of mine was working for the Gilbert Fire Department, a suburb outside Phoenix. He told us that Gilbert had a low crime rate, good schools, affordable housing, and a fire department that was supportive of women candidates, with one openly gay woman already working there. Living in Arizona would also give us some distance from our families. We drove out that summer and took a quick look around. It felt right to both of us. But to have a chance at firefighting in Arizona, I would have to go through extensive testing and a five-weekend internship—kick-ass boot camp.

Unfortunately, we were broke. I had just enough money for airfare to Arizona, where I was to take a written exam for the Gilbert and Mesa Fire Departments in October of 2006. I took my backpack and folding Razor scooter, like a skateboard with handles, and flew to Phoenix Sky Harbor International Airport, unaware that the area around it is not pedestrian (or scooter) friendly. I waded into the traffic. Horns honked, and I flashed my red lights as I made my way through the cities of Tempe and Mesa. The testing center at the Mesa Convention Center was farther than it looked on the map. It took more than two hours to travel the twelve-and-a-half miles to get there. I arrived with my pink shirt soaked through with only minutes to spare. We applicants were told to leave our belongings at the front door before going in to take the test. I went up to a Mesa firefighter and explained why I could not leave my scooter unattended—it was my way back to the airport.

"You rode it here from the airport?" he said.

"I did. I just need someone to watch my scooter while I take the test."

"No way. I could not live with myself with you riding back to the airport on that scooter. I'll watch it. Come find me when you're done."

Others gathered around. "That's the kind of person we need," someone said. "Somebody who really wants the job."

I got a ride back to the airport.

During my time in baseball, I'd nearly always had a nickname. After the story spread about my wild ride to the interview, I became known as "Razor Girl." After I made it through the six-week intern academy, we flew to Arizona in January 2007 to take the next step, my interview with the Gilbert Fire Department. Shannon waited in the parking lot, while I interviewed with three fire department personnel. When it was over, I told Shannon, "The interview went great. I think this is where I'm going to work."

"Good," she said. "Because this is where I'd like to live."

Later I learned that my reputation as Razor Girl had helped get me accepted into the academy.

We fell in love with Gilbert. Shannon could not get over the cows, sheep, horses, and goats alongside the roads and the open fields of alfalfa, wheat, and hay. Rural Arizona reminded me of the Canadian prairie, but with mountains. There was no graffiti or trash. It was an outdoor person's state, with tons of hiking, mountain biking, skiing, fishing, and professional sports, including baseball year-round. We started driving through neighborhoods, looking for the house we might buy someday. We rented a two-bedroom apartment on Lindsay Road, just south of Baseline Road, and found renters for Shannon's Long Beach condo. Shannon requested a transfer from her job as a computer service technician with Amcor Sunclipse in California to Tempe.

On August 1, 2007, we moved into our apartment. Because Shannon's transfer would not come through until January, she stayed with my mom from Sundays through Tuesdays, working twelve-hour days at Amcor. We drew even closer in Gilbert, because it was just us. Every weekend we biked along the canals, threw the Frisbee at Freestone Park, walked at the botanical gardens, and fished on Canyon Lake—and when we went to the grocery store, there were no lines at the checkout.

Earlier that summer, Shannon got a glimpse of my baseball life when I was invited to Midway Stadium in St. Paul for the tenth anniversary of my pitching debut with the Saints. That's when I met for the first time the Saints' vice president of community partnerships and customer service, Annie Huidekoper. (Annie had been gone from the club for a few years when I arrived in 1997). Annie invited me to throw out the first pitch for a game and set up a radio interview. She was the hard-working go-to person at the Saints, devoted to the club and the fans and the whole St. Paul baseball experience. I knew that she had lived out of the closet for years, but it didn't occur to me to speak with her, a brand-new acquaintance, about my struggle with my sexual orientation. Annie put it this way: "When I [first met Ila], we didn't talk much, but my gaydar did come up, and I clearly sensed she might be gay. But I just figured, let it be. Maybe she hasn't figured all that out yet."

My hunch was that as soon as Annie met Shannon, she'd figure out we were a couple. Connie Rudolph later told me that Annie wanted her to encourage me to come out, but Connie told her to keep it quiet. Annie respected that. We did not get to see Mike Veeck but joined Connie and her family at their home for a barbecue. After years of holding back and hiding my girlfriends, it was a relief to be open about my life with Shannon.

The Christmas season of 2007 was the happiest I'd known. Shannon and I celebrated Christmas Eve at Mom's house with my brothers and sister. I had never celebrated Christmas together with my girlfriend and my family. With Dad out of the house, the atmosphere at our house was relaxed.

On Christmas Day, Shannon and I drove to her parents' home in Indian Wells, where I met her father for the first time. We chatted about golf. They had always wanted Shannon to take up the game, and were delighted that she requested a set of clubs for Christmas. Then we were off to Gilbert. We had put up and decorated a live evergreen tree. Shannon's gift to me was a red beach cruiser bicycle. Christmas night we watched *A Christmas Story* and *Christmas Vacation*, before falling asleep next to each other.

Shannon's birthday was January 4, ten days before I was to start at the Gilbert Fire Department. To celebrate we vacationed for a few days in the red-rock country of Sedona before returning to visit the Arizona Science Center for her birthday, where we spent time at the Titanic exhibit. I felt like we had it all. I was starting a good job in a growing community, and my family and friends accepted Shannon as the love of my life.

9

LOSS

GILBERT, ARIZONA. After our magical Christmas of 2007 and a toast to our future, Shannon decided to drive to California for a few days while I studied to renew my emergency medical technician certification. I remember squeezing her tight, tears in my eyes, and saying, "Please don't go."

This holiday season had been the best ever; I didn't want to let go of it, or her.

On the night of January 6, Shannon calls to say she is on her way home. I tell her that eight o'clock is too late to be on the road.

"No," she says. "You know I love to drive, and I want to be with you—I'm already in Palm Springs."

We talk for about thirty minutes—seems like we never run out of conversation. At 11:15 p.m. she calls again from Quartzsite, Arizona, where she has stopped for gas. She is running late because it is raining.

"Please," I beg. "Just stay there and come in the morning."

Quartzsite, a few miles past the California border, is the last leg of the route along Interstate 10 from Los Angeles to Phoenix. Here the land begins to rise into sandy hills dotted with saguaro cactus—a sure sign that you are in Arizona. During the winter months Quartzsite becomes the temporary home for thousands of "snowbirds" who camp in their RVs. Shannon was not interested in stopping there.

"I love you with everything I have," she says. "I want to get to you tonight."

"Okay, I'm going to shower," I reply. "Soon as I get out I'll call to make sure you stay awake."

"Okay, I love you."

A few minutes later I call back. No answer. Shannon always answers her cell phone. I call again, over and over. No response. Worried, I phone some hospitals in the area, but there are no reports of a major wreck. Thinking she might have been in a minor accident, I get into my car and head west on the I-10. I keep calling. No answer. Sometime after midnight I call Mom and ask her to pray. I bargain with God.

MILE MARKER 27.2, THE I-10 FREEWAY. As I approach Quartzsite, the freeway is shut down. The smell of fire and burned rubber is in the air. I park on the side of the road and sprint across the median, avoiding the highway patrol officers who are securing an accident site. Then I see Shannon's white Lexus SUV, the entire top half gone. I fall to my knees and vomit.

Right then a highway patrol officer gets to me. "Who are you?" he says.

"I'm Shannon's fiancée."

He says, "Well, technically we can't tell you anything until we reach her next of kin. Would that be her parents?"

I look at the officer. "I'm the only one that knows where her parents are, so you better tell me what the heck happened, so I can explain it to them, not you."

He looks away, then back at me. "Ma'am, Shannon has been in an accident. She was killed on impact."

I go numb before slipping on the stony face I had built up during childhood. Show No Emotion. I look toward her car. No matter how bad it is, I need to say good-bye. But the officers won't let me see her.

Then I spot her shoe—I had just bought her a pair of Sketchers—lying on the highway and pick it up. This is my fault, because Shannon was hurrying home to me. My cries sound primal in the cold, rainy night—where the hell was God's hand in this!—I was too angry to ask how could he let this happen.

It happened at I-10's mile marker 27.2, just past Gold Nugget Road. Four miles east, the highway 60 overpass has a sharp curve that enters the I-10 going east. If you are, say, driving drunk and speeding, it would be easy to miss the sign pointing you toward Phoenix and simply careen straight ahead onto the exit from the I-10. In such a condition on a rainy night, it would be easy to miss the two unlighted red signs that read: "WRONG WAY." That is what a man named Lewis Young, with a blood alcohol level of .244 percent, had done in his lifted F250 truck. Shannon was passing a big rig when she would have seen his headlights. Both cars had been going eighty miles per hour when they collided. Ten minutes after Shannon said, "I love you," she was gone.

My cell phone has gone dead, so on the way back to Phoenix I stop at a pay phone to call Mom. She promises to come stay with me as soon as she can afford to travel. Then I call Shannon's parents. After they arrive we identify the wreck that had been her Lexus. Back at our apartment, they take nearly everything of hers, but I keep her bike, her clothes, and two pieces of furniture. It breaks my heart to see how little they know of their daughter's life. They know that she was in the process of transferring to Arizona but not that we were living together. They do not know that the reason Shannon wanted golf clubs for Christmas was because I had been teaching her to play. They want to choose an urn for her ashes and ask me what her favorite color was (lime green). For the funeral they want to play her favorite song; do I know what it was? (Abba's "Dancing Queen.")

Shannon's funeral took place in Cerritos, California, on Saturday, January 12. I got up and said a few words, though most people there didn't know of our relationship. But as I looked out at the faces in the seats, I saw old friends from the Santa Ana College Fire Academy, and the Long Beach and Fullerton Fire Departments, including my former girlfriend, Karen. My family was there, too, except for Dad, who said he could not handle it. Somehow I found the words I wanted to say and was able to speak them with a smile. Shannon would have liked that.

After the funeral, I stopped at the Home Depot and bought an orange bucket, a bag of concrete, two gallons of water, white paint, and a couple of two-by-fours. I painted the pieces of wood and nailed them together in the shape of a cross. On the cross I wrote "Shannon, 1/4/74–1/6/08. . . . We love you." I mixed the concrete in the bucket and plunged the cross into it. On the drive back to Phoenix, I stopped at mile marker 27.2 and set the cross in the sand. As cars and trucks raced by, I wept. The area was my personal vision of hell. On the median's embankment were the burn marks of the F250; in the dirt by the road's shoulder were not only the picture of Jesus that Shannon kept on her dash but also her other shoe, with glass in it. Then I found my leather ring, which she wore whenever we were apart. We had talked about trading it in for a "real" ring. Now all I wanted was that leather one.

The next morning I got up and played "Dancing Queen" before reporting to the Gilbert Fire Department Academy. I went to the training captains and explained that I had just lost my fiancée in a head-on collision. I dared not mention her gender. Arizona is not an antidiscrimination state, and I could be let go for no cause.

"I don't know if I'll make it, but I'm going to try," I said. "I want the job."

The men were kind. "Anything we can do to help."

The guilt I felt for taking Shannon out to Arizona crashed over me in waves. I would have welcomed death if it had come my way. I began to see that I was breakable and that I needed people. It turned out to be mostly women, who I had always had trouble drawing near, who were there for me. Connie Rudolph came. My defenses down, I told her that Shannon was much more than the dear friend I had introduced her as in St. Paul. It took a while to spit out the words that I was gay. The news did not seem to bother Connie at all. She stayed with me for several days, and just as she had years earlier, during my days with the Saints, got me out of myself in the best way possible—into nature, namely the Phoenix Mountains. Hiking the rocky trails past sagebrush, saguaro, pincushion, and jumping cholla cactuses while turkey vultures and hawks soared overhead was the spiritual tonic that Connie knew I needed.

Debbie Martin, one of my instructors at Santa Ana College, was another woman who stood by me. Years ago she had lost her daughter on a slippery mountain road in Big Bear, California, when their car went over a cliff. Debbie's listening ear and understanding of loss helped get me through.

Growing up, I had seen Mom as weak for not protecting us from Dad. Now I saw her strength. When she arrived in town, she took one look at my face and my messed-up apartment, and asked, "What can I do to help?"

She cleaned the house. She did the laundry. She never told me to stop crying. One afternoon Mom said, "Sit down on the couch, Ila, and tell me about Shannon. Tell me some stories I don't know."

As we reminisced about the silly things we had gone through, I started laughing. Then it went to tears, and then I was asleep. I slept for several hours, and when I awoke, I saw Mom, weeping.

"We all loved her, Ila," she said. "I loved her, too. You know, I think she telephoned me more than you."

"I want to die," I told her, "but I'm not going to do it. I just need some help to stay alive."

Mom is the reason I survived. Most of all she listened. Buried under the guilt I felt at Shannon's death was the guilt I carried about my grandmother's drowning. Now Mom and I talked about guilt and forgiveness and those early memories. Mom knew things that I either did not know or had forgotten. Mom's parents had been unhappy about her marrying out of the Roman Catholic faith. They didn't attend the wedding and didn't even see me until I was three months old. That visit, though, began to heal the rift. Mom always thought that Grandma was good for my Dad. He had been raised in an abusive home, and Grandma was able to bring him out of himself. Grandma had grown up scared of the water—her older brother and sister used to tease her about it. So when Mom and Dad bought their house with a pool, she was determined to learn to swim. She did not want me, her first grandchild, to know she was afraid of the water. She had spent the entire summer of 1979 just learning to get her face in the water. By the end of that year, she was doing laps, though Mom said she couldn't really swim very well.

It helped to have meaningful work, where my anger at losing Shannon fueled the energy I needed to make the grade. Each day I put myself on the line like it would be my last day on the job—nothing held in reserve. At graduation, my peers voted me the Recruit of the Academy, and the department gave me the Academic Scholar award. The occasion on May 14 was a blur as Debbie Martin pinned the badge on me at graduation. I was now a probationary member of the Gilbert Fire Department. There was so much to like about this department. For one, it had ex–professional athletes: former major leaguers like Clay Bellinger and Andy Larkin, former minor leaguer Eric Christopherson, and former professional football player Andy Bowers. I got to work alongside them and other great guys, great in the sense of being loyal to their wives, doing the right thing, spending time with their kids, giving back.

My first rotation at the Gilbert Fire Department was at Station 1, Engine 251. I could not have found a better place. I liked our department's service ethic. If that meant changing a tire for someone in 113-degree heat, we did it. If someone fell and got hurt while trimming a tree or cleaning a pool, we would finish the job for them. It was all about serving others—and I was proud to be part of the department. In a devotional I found these lines, by the blind Scottish preacher George Matheson, which sum up the philosophy I wanted to live by: "When all our hopes are gone / It is best our hands keep toiling on / For others' sake: / For strength to bear is found in duty done; / And he is best indeed who learns to make / The joy of others cure his own heartache."

My captain, Joe Sperke, a smart-ass with a keen wit, caught me one day grabbing my food out of the fridge and taking it to the bay to eat alone.

"What are you doing out here?" he demanded.

I told him I was hungry but still cleaning stuff and looking things over.

He said, "I don't know what you are used to coming from California, but get inside here, sit down, eat, chill, and hang out with us."

Most of the department at Gilbert was equally friendly and pulled their share. On our days off the guys invited me to go bicycling or hiking with them. Twenty of us hiked the Grand Canyon—my first time there. I began to feel part of the family. As in baseball, pranks are played all the time in the fire service. This one guy could not stand to have food thrown at him, so what did we do? Took handfuls of powdered doughnuts, snuck up to his room where he was sleeping, and hurled dozens of donuts at him. Another guy's helmet and car keys were put in a Jell-O mold. You always had people dunking water on your head or squirting you. I participated—I threw a stink bomb into the restroom and held the door shut for as long as I could. Someone put live chickens in the chief's office, really funny until the birds lost control of their bowels. Soot smeared around the helmets and headsets that leaves a mark on your head; oranges stuffed in your shoes so they squished when you put them on. It was a great release to just laugh.

Looking back, one of my great regrets is that I didn't have more of this sort of camaraderie in the baseball teams I played on. I had it early on in junior high girls' basketball but not so much in baseball. Oh, I had a close connection with guys like Dave Glick but never the whole team. I think if I'd had that in baseball, it would've helped me tolerate a lot of what I went through. Too bad I wasn't in the place I was now. I've learned to kid around. Example: when one of my crewmates teased me about my celebrity. "Oh, look," he said, "We have a famous person right here who has her own entry in Wikipedia. . . . When the book comes out, we have to tell people how she made this mistake and that mistake."

I just laughed and said, "Yeah, and don't forget to tell how I slipped on a crate and shot up in the air five feet and landed on my back."

Was there hidden animosity in those remarks? Maybe, but I've learned that laughing at yourself helps diffuse the attitudes of people who may feel threatened by you. Living out of the closet taught me that. Just wish I'd learned it sooner.

My first day on Engine 251 we got a code (no pulse, no breath). A driver in a black SUV had run a red light and smashed into a small car. At the scene, I saw that the front of this little car was gone. I checked the man inside for a pulse: nothing. I put on the monitor and printed out an electrocardiogram strip, which showed a flat line, or asystole. I noticed his wedding band and sent up a silent prayer for his family. Something told me right then, *Ila you are where you are supposed to be.* I could see the captain watching me, likely wondering how I was going to handle this. *Wow,* I thought, *Shannon had been even more messed up.* I had been upset that she pretty much disintegrated upon impact, but now I found peace in knowing she had died immediately. As I left the accident scene, I continued to pray for the man's family, knowing what they were about to go through. After the call, our engineer asked, "Everyone cool?"

All of us said, "Yep."

Yes, I was cool with whatever came my way. As firefighters we see a lot of bad stuff, and some people may think us cold because we don't usually react emotionally. Through baseball I had developed a high threshold for pain. That had prepared me to cope with losing Shannon. Now I had more empathy. I wanted to make Shannon proud. During my years in baseball it had been all about me. When Shannon showed me what unconditional love was, it changed my heart. Because of her, I began to move from being critical—as athletes we are judged every second—to seeing the good in others, and in myself.

Despite the ache that wouldn't leave, I kept trying to dedicate whatever resources I had to serve my family, my friends, and society. I decided to become a paramedic. I wanted to be the one on call when people experienced the worst day of their lives. For eighteen months, I worked my regular firefighting shifts while attending school for my paramedic certification. I had plenty of support from my co-workers, who gave me time to study or take a quick nap during the day. Why I was not taken, and Shannon was, I will never know, but I am so damn thankful for the three years God gave us. I used to wonder why I went through so much in baseball. Now it clicked. The game had prepared me to go through the toughest loss of my life.

EPILOGUE

AUGUST 28, 2014, ST. PAUL, MINNESOTA. Tonight the Saints play their last game ever at Midway Stadium. Next season the club is moving to a trendy new ballpark in the Lowertown area of St. Paul. I was to throw batting practice and play catch with the Saints co-owner, Bill Murray, before being introduced to the crowd, but plane and weather delays rained out the plan. The game is about to begin as the taxi drops me off at the ballpark, right in front of the mural of Twig and me. My heart rises— I'm home. I drop my bags in Connie Rudolph's office—she flashes me a thumbs up—continue through the front office and under the stadium behind home plate, where the field equipment is kept and where Mike's pig hangs out. This year's ball pig is named Stephen Colboar, after the comedian Stephen Colbert.

I enter the field. The game is a sell-out, with people sitting on the outfield warning track. Besides Connie, the Saints' longtime groundskeeper who was honored at last night's game, they're all here—Mike Veeck and Bill Murray, and Annie Huidekoper, now the Saints' vice president. Dave Stevens, the guy with no legs who was with the club the year before I came, is coaching first base. It's a true Mike Veeck homecoming. As I start to jog over to the area behind home plate, a guy grabs my arm, "Ila!"

I look up but don't recognize the face. "Ila," he repeats, "I'm really happy to see you. You've always been a pro in my book."

Then I realize it's Marty Scott, my old manager. He has lost a lot of weight and looks fantastic. Marty now works as vice president of player development for the Florida Marlins. He says that he is proud of me, and that feels good. We talk about my time with the Saints and his work with the Marlins, and exchange phone numbers.

Annie comes over to say that Bill Murray wants to say hello. I make my way to where Bill is talking to Minnesota's junior U.S. senator, Al Franken. Bill turns, gives me a big smile, and says, "Hello, Ila, good to see you again. Glad you made it."

He introduces me to Senator Franken and explains to him about my career. We talk baseball and about my work as a firefighter. I always found Bill easy to talk with. After ten minutes or so, I ask if I can take a "selfie" with him, and he says, "Sure."

I spot Mike Veeck and catch up with him. His son, William "Night Train" Veeck, works in group sales for the Chicago White Sox, the club his grandfather once owned and where Mike once worked. Rebecca, his sweet daughter who mourned my trade to Duluth, is in ill health and lives at home under her parents' care. Mike asks how this book is going and will it be a movie—questions that call up my old baseball uncertainties, given that the book proposal has yet to sell and no film producers have come calling.

Annie comes over and says, "Okay, it's your time."

Mike and I shake hands, and I thank him for all the support he gave me through the years. Annie sends me to stand on top of the third-base dugout, where I wave to the fans and sign autographs. People still remember.

"When Ila finally arrived," Annie later recalled, "I kept trying to enjoy the moment. I thanked her for coming and gave her a big hug. I finessed the schedule and brought her to the grandstand, where she had a really cool moment. She was going to speak, but the fans' cheers drowned her out. We had asked Ila for an item for the Saints' time capsule, which would be buried for fifty years at our new park in downtown St. Paul. She handed me her SSK glove from 1997. I knew it was something special, and thought, *No way is this going to be buried in the ground for fifty years. It's going into the glass case of memorabilia in our front office.*

The rain stops, and we get the ball game in. Afterward I stand at home plate with Connie, the players, Mike, and Bill while we watch the fireworks. I continue to sign autographs. It's been great to return to Midway, where so much is the same. I used to shower and change in the extra umpires room—some still call it Ila's room. I linger as long as I can, taking it all in.

Later, Annie Huidekoper asks how I am doing. It's 2014 and at last I can talk honestly about my life, myself. She tells me that before I joined the Saints in 1997, Mike Veeck had sort of pushed her out of the closet. In 1993 Annie left town to take part in the March on Washington for Lesbian, Gay, and Bi Equal Rights and Liberation. After she returned, she was in a front-office meeting when, as she recalled, "[Mike] took a deep breath and said with a big grin, 'So, Annie, how was the March on Washington?'"

I had always sensed that Mike would've been fine with my being gay. In fact, I think he probably would have found a way to lighten up my heart about the issue After all, lots of clubs sponsor bobblehead nights, but only Veeck would think to host a Larry Craig Bobblefoot Night in response to the conservative Republican Senator Craig's arrest in June 2007 for allegedly soliciting sex with an undercover policeman in a bathroom at Minneapolis–St. Paul International Airport. But of course, it was not Mike I had worried about; it was the responses from my coaches and teammates. I still wonder whether I could have lasted in baseball had I told the truth of my sexual orientation. I doubt it. But likely I would have pitched more consistently without that burden.

So I tell Annie that I am single and my life is good, but that I would like to find a lifetime partner. Annie has been with her partner for twenty-five years, and I envy her that. As we talk, I realize that throughout my life there have been women like Annie—out-of-the-closet, productive, respected women—but I had been too scared to identify with them or, heaven forbid, to reach out to them. If you're not living true to yourself, people who are can put you off. So I stayed aloof.

After the last game at Midway, Connie Rudolph and I traveled to the Wisconsin IRONMAN race in Madison. There it was: Madison, another fondly remembered place. During the race we ran right past my old apartment building on Milton Street and inside the football field at Camp Randall Stadium. Because the hotels were pricey, we camped out in Connie's motor home. My goal was to finish the IRONMAN, and I did.

After the competition was over, we camped out a couple days more and talked. I gave Connie an update on my life. Shannon's death had sent me back to living like an island, as I had done for most of my life, except during those three magical years with her. But a couple of years ago, my family told me that it was time to start getting out. After re-educating Mom again about why I would not be dating guys—she still prayed for a miracle—I went online and, for the first time, seriously surveyed the dating scene. I found a woman I liked, and we dated for a couple of years until she decided to return to her home in the Midwest. It felt so good to go out in public with my girlfriend—to be honest with the world about who I was.

I wish that being honest about these things always had a happy ending. But then I remember Mike Penner, the *Los Angeles Times* sportswriter whose work I admired during my college years. In April 2007 Penner published the most honest writing of his life in the *Times*: "Old Mike, New Christine" began like this: "I am a transsexual sportswriter. It has taken more than 40 years, a million tears, and hundreds of hours of soul-wrenching therapy for me to work up the courage to type those words."

Christine had the support of her editor, Randy Harvey; Christina Kahrl, the cofounder of Baseball Prospectus, the game's stats bible, who had successfully transitioned from male to female in 2003; and, as it turned out, a substantial number of the column's readers. But as Christine's celebrity grew so did others' expectations of her to be an activist for transgender people. In the end she was unable to maintain her identity as a woman and returned to being Mike. Along the way, he got badly lost. The day after Thanksgiving 2009, Mike Penner took his life. It made me wish I could've talked with him honestly back in college. I hope for a time when people like Mike Penner have the freedom to live as they were created, in peace.

But even a few years ago this sort of honesty had yet to seep into all parts of my life. When I began to write about falling in love for the first time for this book, I titled the section "Shane." After all, I had waited a long time to tell my story and just couldn't see my way clear to telling an inspirational story for baseball-loving girls without lying about my sexual orientation, as I had to my coaches, managers, and teammates for all those years. Coming out as gay would destroy the book's chances, I feared. I also wanted this book to be about baseball, not about being gay. So I chose a man's name, "Shane," as code for "Shannon." Then I woke up. *Screw it,* I thought. *To truly honor Shannon, you have to tell the full truth. You can't be honest about everything else and not this, since she was a huge part of your life.*

It felt so good to restore Shannon to her rightful place that I came out to the Gilbert Fire Department. The news that I was gay made barely a ripple. Were times changing or just me? Only a couple of people had a problem with it, one a man who attended the conservative Our Lady of Sorrows Roman Catholic Church in south Phoenix and came across as being all about "truth" though not so much about "grace." A year or so after I came out, one of my captains thanked me. He told me that his sixteen-year-old daughter had just told him she was gay. He said he never would have known how to handle it if I hadn't told him my story.

So maybe the inspirational book that I, masked as the all-American straight girl, had always wanted to write still can inspire, though in a different, more honest way. I can only say that this is who I am now: a Christian who loves the Lord with all her being and happens to be gay. My faith is not about religion; it's about a personal relationship with Jesus, who loves and accepts me as I am. I still don't attend church. As a Presbyterian pastor named Mark Davis said, "There's a process where people have to forgive the church before they can return to it."

I'm still working on that.

Speaking of forgiveness, in 2011 Dad and I began to repair our relationship. I told him it was time he started to repay the money he took from the SSK contract. "I don't care if its fifteen dollars a month, but it has to be something," I said. "You can't owe me a lot of money and not pay it but then go on vacations all over the world."

Dad did send money. He would occasionally send a fifty- or hundred-dollar check from his home in Napa, where he lives with his fiancée, but it was to pay off the $2,500 in student debt I still had. My $25,000 share of the SSK money has not been repaid.

Dad has always included my girlfriends in the holiday cards he sends. Maybe he has faced up to his own past and is growing more compassionate. I don't know for sure, because we don't talk about it. Through family members, I've heard that he wonders whether I would have turned out straight if he had not been so strict. Dad and I text occasionally and once a year meet up for a round of golf. I am grateful for the work ethic he instilled in me, the way he taught me to analyze situations, his encouragement to go after anything I wanted to. Never once did he shy me away from anything because I was a girl. That made it possible for me to do what I did both in baseball and in firefighting.

Mom's life has been financially hard since the divorce in 2004. She, too, has struggled with forgiveness. She lives now in the Phoenix area with Leah and her family. Mom and I often travel the I-10 freeway to visit my brother Randall and his wife Emma in Irvine, California. On the drive back, we stop at mile marker 27.2. My brother Phillip and his family now have a home in Napa, California, where he keeps Dad's old home plate and the tire swing from our house on Olive Branch Drive.

When I was young I saw baseball as a sort of endless season—easy to do in a sunny place like Southern California. I thought it would go on forever, though it never does. It's the athlete's lament. The game itself may be timeless, but the faces of the people on the field inevitably change.

Mike Moschetti, my talented Little League teammate who always loved football more than baseball, is now the head football coach at La

Mirada High School . . . Rolland Esslinger, my junior high coach, serves as the athletic director at Whittier Christian High School . . . Charlie Phillips, who gave me a college scholarship, teaches pitching and hitting at Lifeletics and works as pitching coach for a travel team called the OC Sun Devils . . . Pat Guillen, Southern California College's sports information director, is now the athletic director at the University of Hawaii. He says that he still has the ball I threw for my first pitch at Southern California College . . . Barry Moss works as a sports agent specializing in baseball operations for Group Management . . . Dave Glick works as a pitching coach in Long Beach, California . . . I'm glad that these people, who meant so much to me, have found ways to stay connected to sports and work with young athletes. I recently worked again at the World Children's Baseball Fair (WCBF) and remembered all over again how much I love teaching kids. No surprise then that in my spare time I coach young pitchers. Coincidentally they are all males—no females. I throw batting practice to some of the high school players to give them some tips on their swings and serve as catcher for the pitchers. I work on developing arm strength with the college players.

It's with the kids out there in mind that I argue that the institutions of baseball, from Little League and other youth leagues, and collegiate baseball, to Organized Baseball, must welcome more girls and women into the game. The attention paid to Little League pitcher Mo'ne Davis in 2014 was encouraging—though it's interesting that Mo'ne doesn't seem to have the deep need for baseball that I did; she says she's headed toward basketball, which offers the possibility of a college scholarship and a professional career. That's a loss for baseball, where progress for women historically has been glacially slow and too often just a footnote to the "real" game—all the women who played for an inning or a game before leaving the field of play. That continues to be the case. On May 29, 2016, the Bridgeport Bluefish of the Atlantic League invited Jennie Finch—my softball playing neighbor in La Mirada—to serve as guest manager. Jennie did well, strategizing a neat 3–1 win over the Southern Maryland Blue Crabs, but once again, it was a one-time shot, another footnote in the history of women in baseball.

If there is hope for women to make headway into Organized Baseball, it will come about because of women like Justine Siegal. I first became aware of Justine when she was playing women's baseball against my sister's team in San Diego late in the 1990s. I got to know her better in 2011 when we served as coaches for the WCBF in Taiwan. I found out she dedicated the past two decades to the cause of girls' and women's baseball. Siegal is the founder and director of Baseball for All, which strives to bridge the gap between the approximately one hundred thousand girls who play youth baseball and the one thousand girls who play at the high school level. Her nonprofit organization teaches girls to play baseball, coach, and umpire while educating the media and the public that girls indeed play this game. In September of 2015, the Oakland A's announced that they had hired Siegal as MLB's first ever female coach. (A check with the Hall of Fame Library revealed no data on any earlier women who might have done this.) So Siegal got a toehold in Organized Baseball's coaching fraternity: a two-week gig as guest instructor in the Arizona instructional league in Mesa, Arizona. While it's gratifying to see Siegal get this opportunity, like her, I want more. Girls, and the women they grow up to be, deserve the freedom to seek a continuing presence on the field. It's my hope that the story told here encourages the institutions of baseball at all levels to open the door wider to those of us who want into the game—and that more women will walk through that door. So I was glad to hear that the Sonoma Stompers signed two women, pitcher Stacy Piagno and outfielder Kelsie Whitmore, to their team in July 2016. (It was Justine Siegal who recommended Whitmore to the Stompers, having known her as a Baseball for All player and coach). The Stompers are part of the Pacific Association, an independent league. Oh that Organized Baseball would take such a step.

Yet there is still much work to be done and many minds to transform. In 2012 the priests (members of the very conservative Society of Pope Pius X) who run Our Lady of Sorrows Academy decided to forfeit a state championship baseball game rather than let the school's team compete against an opponent whose second baseman, Paige Sultzbach, was female. The school explained: "Teaching our boys to treat ladies with deference, we choose not to place them in an athletic competition where proper boundaries can only be respected with difficulty. . . . Our school aims to instill in our boys a profound respect for women and girls."

Wow! Does the school's statement mean that any woman in a powerful or nontraditional position is going to make a man treat his wife or girlfriend with less respect? Please! Not one time at Whittier Christian High School did anyone suggest that my playing negatively affected the way guys would treat women down the road. If anything, it opened their eyes to the idea that women can play, too.

I had always wondered whether the magic I had with Shannon could happen again. For the past several years, I had known a friend of a friend named Jenni Westphal. In 2014 I took a chance and asked Jenni out on a date. She said yes. I was smitten right off the bat. Jenni is athletic, smart, and beautiful, and the funniest person I have ever met. Her smile and eyes mesmerized me. Even so, we took it slow. I came to find out that while I was playing for Madison in 1998, she was finishing up her degree in wildlife ecology at the University of Wisconsin, Madison. She had played basketball there and was also a standout athlete in track and field. We even lived a block away from each other.

Jenni lived in Portland, Oregon, where she worked as a senior footwear analyst for Nike. I racked up many airline miles flying to see her. The forests and mountains of the Northwest, its changing seasons, the Pacific Ocean, the year-round outdoor sports, the wineries, its diverse culture, and its political moderation drew me. Every day I spent there felt like a vacation. I had found my kind of people, a whole lot of them. I had also found in Jenni the woman I wanted to share my life with. Despite my dream job at the Gilbert Fire Department, I decided to move to Portland to be with her.

In July 2015 the Cornelius Fire Department hired me as a firefighter and paramedic. As in Gilbert, I landed with a great department. So here I am in Oregon in a new job, far from family and friends, who I miss dearly. Sometimes it feels like I've been running all of my life—to get to first base, to pitch in the game I love, to make it as a firefighter, to find love. As Ron Shelton, who played minor league baseball before writing the baseball movie *Bull Durham*, put it, "Even when you're home, you're on the road."

I know what he means. After looking for love and baseball, though not always in that order, since I first planted my foot on Dad's home plate in our front yard, I believe I have landed safe at home. On June 4, 2016, Jenni and I married. We gathered with friends on a ridge above Cape Lookout State Park on the Oregon coast. Before Bridget Schwarting, who served as minister, and with Jenni's identical twin Janet Westphal and Olivia Dukes as witnesses, we said our marriage vows. Being outdoor enthusiasts, we didn't want a traditional wedding, so I guess you could say that we did not so much step into our new life together as hike in.

Fully committed to the most important person in my life, I have begun to rethink my old commitment to another love, baseball. A couple of years ago I played a sandlot game and hit two home runs, a triple, and a double, and turned two double plays—as a left-handed shortstop. I came off the field as excited as a kid, remembering all over again how much I love being on the diamond. My career may have ended in 2000, but I've never really let go of the game. I wanted to share that excitement with Jenni.

There's a magical place in New York's Greenwich Village called the Bergino Baseball Clubhouse, filled with baseball art, memorabilia, and gift items. It's owned by Jay Goldberg. Prominent on the wall is a large work of art—a cherry-sprigged tablecloth with a quotation on it—that was created by Jay's now-deceased business partner, Tony Palladino. It is not for sale. Years ago, as Goldberg tells it, Tony was walking down a street in New York when he passed a boy, about eight years old, with his mother. He overheard the boy say a few words that stayed in Tony's memory. "Love is the most important thing in the world, but baseball is pretty good too."

Later Tony came across an old tablecloth with cherries on it. "That's my canvas," Tony said. "And that eight-year-old's comment is my quote."

Tony and Jay had no idea who the boy was, of course, but felt he needed a name. Somehow they settled on "Gregg," which you will find in the bottom corner of Tony's art, along with Gregg's quote.

"Love is the most important thing in the world, but baseball is pretty good, too." These words of an eight-year-old pretty much sum up the message of this book. So I want to show Jenni the Bergino Baseball Clubhouse—and introduce her to other great baseball people and places in our country, like the Hall of Fame and Museum in Cooperstown, Mike Veeck and the St. Paul Saints, and a ballgame at Wrigley Field in Chicago. And I want to meet all the Greggs out there—girls and boys—and teach them about the best game ever.

Notes

2   **"There comes a time"**: Paul Wiecak, "Female Pitcher Has Simunic Steamed," *Winnipeg Free Press*, July 30, 1998, D3.

3   **"Read it," Neal said**: Neal Karlen followed me around during my weeks in St. Paul.

1. BEGINNINGS

10   **"that thing"**: Neal Karlen, *Slouching toward Fargo* (New York: Avon Books, 1999), 298. Karlen liked Ed Nottle and expressed disappointment when he called me "that *thing*." According to Karlen, the comment was made to a Sioux City radio reporter early in June 1997.

18   **"No crying," he yells**: *A League of Their Own*, directed by Penny Marshall (Parkway Productions/Columbia, 1992).

20   **"How can you let"**: From personal, telephone, and e-mail interviews with Ila Borders and her parents, Phil and Marianne Borders, between 1994 and 2015. This comment may have resonated with the family because it touched on a deep issue faced by girls who play baseball: As Jennifer Ring writes in *A Game of Their Own: Voices of Contemporary Women in Baseball* (Lincoln: University of Nebraska Press, 2015), 261: "[Ballplayers'] sense of being an outsider or 'wrong' correlates with athletic, more than sexual[,] identity: 'You're an athlete and girls aren't athletes, so which one are you?'" This is particularly true of girls who play a perceived boys' game like baseball.

25   "You don't get many 12-year-olds": Joseph D'Hippolito, "Borders Breaks Batters' Hearts," *La Mirada Lamplighter*, June 24, 1987, n.p.

25   At twelve, her fundamentals: Joe Moschetti, telephone interview, July 15, 1999.

26   Yeah, Mike Moschetti: "Mike Moschetti," Baseball Reference.com, accessed June 4, 2016, www.baseball-reference.com.

2. LIPSTICK ADOLESCENCE

30   "Being with a woman": "Quotes," Casey Stengel: The Official Site, accessed June 5, 2016, http://caseystengel.com/quotes.htm.

31   No stats exist: Jennifer Ring, *Stolen Bases* (Chicago: University of Illinois Press, 2009), 132. Ring quotes Jim Glennie, a passionate supporter of girls' baseball, as saying that it's "no tightly held secret' that girls are 'simply shoved gently toward softball after Little League and many go there simply because they have a chance to continue playing through college.'"

33   "Remember . . . Ila's 'round the back'": Susan Johnson, telephone interview and e-mail, November 11, 1999.

34   "We'll try to do things": Rolland Esslinger, telephone interview, May 19, 1999, e-mail, October 11, 1999.

35   "We still liked to sneak out": Alyse Isaac, telephone interview, undated.

36   One coach called: Rolland Esslinger, telephone interview, November 2, 2015.

37   "There were never": Rolland Esslinger, telephone interview, November 2, 2015.

42   Ila was a key: Esslinger interview, November 2, 2015.

43   Dad rationalized this: Phil Borders, telephone interviews, September 14 and October 6, 1999.

43   "I was very much opposed": Marianne Borders, telephone interview, November 10, 1999.

47   "I had to deal with": Jay Paris, "Making Her Pitch," *Orange County Register*, April 2, 1991, C7.

52   "I had to get out": Phil Borders, telephone interview, June 10, 2015.

52   "Some really encouraged her": Steve Randall, telephone interview, June 4, 1999.

52   "The hitters ask": Paris, "Making Her Pitch."

52 the "fear of striking out": John Corbett, "'Just One of the Boys,'" *Los Angeles Times*, undated.

56 "I'm going to sign": Miki Turner, "She Won't Be in a League of Her Own," *Orange County Register*, February 4, 1993, 1.

3. COLLEGE

64 "opponents are our guests": "NAIA District 3 Code of Conduct," *So Cal Baseball* program, Southern California College, 1994, 5.

69 "Hey," yells a classmate: Karen Crouse, "Borders Finishes What She Starts," *Orange County Register*, February 16, 1994, D12.

72 "Ila-mania": Martin Beck, "Borders' Blues," *Los Angeles Times*, March 28, 1995, C4.

72 "Their players were very abusive": Register staff, news service reports, "SCC's Borders Suffers First Loss," *Orange County Register*, March 4, 1994, C9.

72 "We had beaten them": Charlie Phillips, e-mail, August 6, 2015.

72 "You saw her pitch": Phil Borders, conversation with Ila Borders, 1994.

72 "Media-wise I was shocked": Charlie Phillips, e-mail, June 5, 2015.

74 "The [t]aunts are vicious": Shelley Smith, "Ila Borders," *Sports Illustrated*, March 7, 1994. http://sports illustrated.cnn.com/vault/article/magazine /MAG1004927indexhtm.

74 "Are you a lesbian?": Smith, "Ila Borders."

75 "I want people to know": Richard Dunn, "Border(s) lines," *Orange Coast Daily Pilot*, February 26, 1994, B3.

75 "A major portion of lesbian": Betty Hicks, "Lesbian Athletes," in *Sports-Dykes: Stories from On and Off the Field*, edited by Susan Fox Rogers (New York: St. Martin's Press, 1994), 71.

75 "women athletes are perpetual": Hicks, "Lesbian Athletes," 59.

75 "To most lesbian athletes": Hicks, "Lesbian Athletes," 72.

80 You can throw: Phil Borders, telephone and e-mail interviews, June 8–10, 2015.

83 "should not anticipate": Martin Beck, "SCC Uses Post Office to Fire Baseball Coach," *Los Angeles Times*, May 10, 1995.

84 "Because we care": *Youth 95*, 15, no. 2 (March–April 1995, published by Worldwide Church of God, Pasadena, CA), inside cover.

85 **"Just what is a real"**: Michael Warren, "Would the Real Christian Please Step Forward?" *Youth 95*, 3.

85 **"Will she wind up"**: Tonia Weik, *Youth 95*, 4–5.

92 **Coach Pigott didn't care**: Mike Rizzo, telephone interview, June 11, 2015.

94 **"the discussion making"**: Tim Mead, e-mail, December 8, 2013.

94 **"because it was interesting"**: Bob Fontaine, e-mail, December 8, 2013.

94 **"I've got my scouts"**: Rick Reilly, "Heaven Help Marge Schott," *Sports Illustrated*, May 20, 1996, http://sportsillustrated.cnn.com/vault/article/magazine/MAG1008139/index/index.htm.

95 **"Why not play"**: Daryn Kagan, "Woman Tries to Make the Cut in Professional Baseball," CNN Morning News, May 12, 1997, http://webmail.adelphia.net/cgi-bin/gx.cgi/AppLogie+mobmain?msgvw=INVOX MN382DE . . .

96 **I showed up for**: Barry Moss, telephone interview, May 8, 2013.

97 **"It's about the only"**: Martin Beck, "Borders Cuts Classes, Final College Start," *Los Angeles Times*, April 30, 1997, http://articles.latimes.com/1997-04-30/sports/sp-53985_1_borders-cuts.

97 **"When you arrive"**: letter from Bill Fanning to Ila Borders, May 8, 1997.

98 **"It goes so deep down"**: Neal Karlen, *Slouching toward Fargo* (New York: Avon Books, 1999), 163.

4. THE ST. PAUL SAINTS

109 **"There's a lot of guys"**: Ron Lesko, "Love for Hardball, Not Quest for History, Motivates Woman Pitcher," Associated Press Sports News, May 6, 1997, PM cycle.

112 **"The score didn't matter"**: Mike Augustin, "Borders' Act Not Bad," *St. Paul Pioneer Press*, May 20, 1997, 4D.

112 **"I don't put much"**: Augustin, "Borders' Act Not Bad," 4D.

114 **"She did a whale"**: Augustin, "Borders Takes Loss but Has Her Moments," *St. Paul Pioneer Press*, May 23, 1997, 4B.

118 **"In any other given"**: Ron Lesko, "Borders' Work Ethic, Desire Earn Her Spot," Associated Press report to the *Orange County Register*, May 29, 1997, sports sec., 1.

120   "I FUCKING MADE": Neal Karlen, *Slouching toward Fargo* (New York: Avon Books, 1999), 293.

125   "As she was getting": Mike Augustin, *Saint Paul Pioneer Press*, June 2, 1997, 3E.

126   "There is one thing": Mike Augustin, "Explorers' Nottle, Relishing Win, Steers Clear of Borders," *Saint Paul Pioneer Press*, June 11, 1997.

126   "I thought Ila showed": Terry Hersom, "Explorers Pound Saints' Pitching," *Saint Paul Pioneer Press*, June 4, 1997, n.p.

129   "She threw me": Bruce Bennett, "Dukes Defeat Saints with Pitching, Defense," June 16, 1997.

130   "When my daddy told me": Mike Augustin, "Saints Start Post-Ila Era with a Loss," *Saint Paul Pioneer Press*, June 27, 1997.

130   "I will probably be": Kevin Kotz, "'I Got Traded for a Girl,'" *Duluth News Tribune*, June 26, 1997, 1C.

5. DULUTH-SUPERIOR DUKES

131   "She is believed": "Out of the Bullpen; into the Record Books," *New York Times*, June 5, 1996.

7. ANOTHER TEAM, ANOTHER TOWN

166   "Coming up against her": Larry See, personal interview, June 8, 1999.

166   "a called third strike": See interview, June 8, 1999.

166   "It's hard to bring": See interview, June 8, 1999.

167   "Much of my work": Steve Shirley, personal interview, June 8, 1999.

170   "Too much is made of Ila": Jim Polzin, "Borders Gets New Life in Madison," *Capital Times*, June 14, 1999.

173   "I think the guys": Ron Ognar, "Borders Sparks Black Wolf, *Wisconsin State Journal*, June 28, 1999, 4D.

175   "She battled": Dennis Semrau, "Black Wolf Can't Beat the Rain," *Capital Times*, July 19, 1999.

176   "intent to exercise": Letter from Madison Black Wolf Professional Baseball to Ila Borders, October 20, 1999.

183   "Ila Borders was one": Associated Press reports, "Ila Borders Gives Herself the Hook, Retires," *Los Angeles Times*, July 1, 2000, D10.

8. OUT OF THE GAME

188   **"women have remained"**: Jean Hastings Ardell, introduction of Ila Borders, the Baseball Reliquary Shrine of the Eternals, July 20, 2003. http://www.baseballreliquary.org/awards/shrine-of-the-eternals-2003/.

188   **"that fat little bastard"**: "Artie's Baseball Challenge pt. 2," https://www.youtube.com/watch?v=iF_uNS6-n6Y.

199   **"When I [first met Ila]"**: Annie Huidekoper, telephone interview, October 28, 2014.

9. LOSS

205   **"When all our hopes"**: L. B. Cowman, *Streams in the Desert*, devotional, September 8, http://www.oneplace.com/devotionals/streams-in-the-desert-with-mrs-charles-cowman/streams-in-the-desert-sept-8-1421209.html.

EPILOGUE

210   **"When Ila finally arrived"**: Annie Huidekoper, telephone interview, October 28, 2014.

211   **"[Mike] took a deep breath"**: "Annie Huidekoper: St. Paul Saints Vice President Shares Her Story," *Lavender Media Inc.*, October 8, 2010, http://www.lavendermagazine.com/our-affairs/annie-huidekoper/.

212   **"I am a transsexual sportswriter"**: Nancy Hass, "New Mike, Old Christine," GQ, June 2010, http://www.gq.com/news-politics/mens-lives/201006/mike-penner . . .

213   **"There's a process where"**: Mark Davis, personal interview, October 5, 2015.

216   **"Teaching our boys"**: "Our Lady of Sorrows Academy Forfeits Arizona Baseball Championship over Female Player, Religious Beliefs," *Huffington Post*, May 10, 2012, http://www.huffingtonpost.com/2012/05/10/our-lady-of-sorrows-forfeits-baseball-girl_n_1507606.html.

218   **"Even when you're home"**: Ron Shelton, speaking at the Cannery Hot Stove League, Newport Beach, California, December 13, 2013.

218   **"Love is the most"**: Jay Bergino, telephone interview, March 28, 2016.